D1539071

The Flight of
Jesse Leroy Brown

By the Author

The Magnificent Mitscher
The Body Trade
Fire on the Beaches
Special Unit Senator
(The Assassination of Senator Robert Kennedy)
A Shepherd Watches, A Shepherd Sings
Jule
The Stalker
Monocolo
To Kill the Leopard

For Younger Readers

The Cay
The Maldonado Miracle
The Children's War
The Hatteras Trilogy
Walking Up a Rainbow
The Hostage
Sniper
Tuck Triumphant
The Weirdo
Maria
Timothy of the Cay
Sweet Friday Island
The Bomb
Rogue Wave

The Flight of
Jesse Leroy Brown

THEODORE TAYLOR

AVON BOOKS ◆ NEW YORK

AVON BOOKS, INC.
1350 Avenue of the Americas
New York, New York 10019

Copyright © 1998 by Theodore Taylor
Visit our website at **http://www.AvonBooks.com**
ISBN: 0-380-97689-7

Library of Congress Cataloging in Publication Data:
Taylor, Theodore, 1921–
The flight of Jesse Leroy Brown / Theodore Taylor. —1st ed.
p. cm.
Includes index.
1. Brown, Jesse Leroy. 2. United States. Navy—Aviation—Biography. 3. Fighter
pilots—United States—Biography. 4. Afro-American air pilots—Biography.
5. Korean War, 1950–1953— Personal narratives, American. I Title.
V63.B75T39   1998   98-8264
359.9'4'092—dc21   CIP

First Avon Books Printing: November 1998

FIRST EDITION

QPM   10   9   8   7   6   5   4   3   2   1

For
Daisy Pearl Brown Thorne; Pamela Brown Knight;
William, Lura and Fletcher Brown;
Jessica Leroyce Knight; Jamal Knight

It is my hope that Jesse will serve as a shining role model for all young Americans, especially young African Americans, both male and female.

—THEODORE TAYLOR
Laguna Beach, California
January 1998

Contents

PART III

PART IV

Preface

Though little is known about him, Eugene Bullard is believed to have been America's first black pilot. Rare photos display a stern, almost angry face and piercing eyes. Unable to serve his own country because of segregation and the color of his skin, Bullard flew combat missions for France during World War I and was awarded the Croix de Guerre, that nation's highest military medal.

Denied entry into the few flying schools of the early 1920s, Bessie Coleman, born in 1893 in Texas of black and American Indian parents, also went to France to learn how to fly. She said, "The air is the only place free of prejudice." In 1922 she was licensed by the Fédération Aéronautique Intérnationale, becoming the world's first black aviatrix. As a "barnstormer," putting on aerial shows with other black pilots across the country, she was killed in Florida at the age of thirty-three on April 30, 1926, diving her plane from 3,500 feet, failing to pull out.

The first black pilot's license, No. 7638, was issued in 1928 to C. Alfred Anderson. Other notable black aviation pioneers of that era were Hubert Julian, William Powell, Thomas Allen, and James Banning. These fliers were followed in the Chicago area and Los Angeles by Harold Hurd, Cornelius Coffey, Willa Brown, and Janet Waterford.

Beginning in the late twenties and extending well into the thirties, black communities turned out to watch air circuses with black pilots and parachute jumpers and wing walkers, flying off farm fields on Saturdays and Sundays, offering rides for as little as two dollars.

They were doing exactly what white pilots were doing, flying the fabric-covered open-cockpit biplanes, held together with "wire and spit," loving every minute of it, often sleeping on hay in black farmers' barns at night.

The famed Tuskegee Airmen of World War II owed their existence to such pilots as Eugene Bullard, Bessie Coleman, and C. Alfred Anderson. They chipped away at the closed doors of military aviation by proving they could fly.

As a naval reservist LTJG (lieutenant junior-grade), I'd been recalled to active duty following North Korea's invasion of South Korea in June 1950, having served in both the Merchant Marine and the Navy during World War II. I was assigned to the cruiser *Newport News* until someone in the Bureau of Naval Personnel discovered I was a newspaperman.

Soon I found myself sitting at the Navy Press Desk, Department of Defense Office of Information, servicing the Pentagon press corps. Having written for four daily newspapers, it was more my present line of work than gunnery.

I think I first read about Jesse Brown while a reporter for *The Orlando Sentinel-Star*. It was an Associated Press story and picture, out of Jacksonville, saying that he'd broken the "color barrier" to become the Navy's first Negro pilot. He was smiling broadly as the gold wings were pinned on his chest. I also recall a picture of him in *Life* magazine.

I remember the AP story saying he was from Mississippi,

a sharecropper's son. Knowing the Navy, with its tendency at the time to assign all black personnel to galleys as cooks and food servers, or to clean officers' staterooms, I wondered how he had done it; how painful his struggle must have been, one Negro swimming alone upstream in a river of white pilot-hopefuls and their often biased instructors.

Many people have been involved in the telling of Jesse's story—his widow, his brothers, his longtime friends; the pilots who trained with him and flew with him; his own many letters, his own conversations with his family, wife, friends, and fellow pilots. In the preparation of this book, I had complete access to his training and flight records; to the logs of Squadron 32 and the USS *Leyte*, from which he operated.

Above all, this is a human story, not one of whirling propellers, and the use of dialogue has been constructed from tapes, letters, and interviews with the participants. Use of the word "nigger," shocking to today's ears, was prevalent in the South and elsewhere during his life. "African American" was seldom if ever used. I have attempted to be true to the times and locales.

On duty the morning of December 5, 1950, when the first communiqué concerning Ensign Jesse Brown came from the Far East Naval Command, I quickly gathered as many details as I could and wrote the press release about what had happened at Somong-ni, certain there was a larger story to be told. For years after I began writing books, whenever I read anything about the Korean War, I thought of Jesse Brown.

The Flight of
Jesse Leroy Brown

P A R T I

Somong-ni, North Korea

December 4, 1950

On this particular Monday the weather off the northeast coast of Korea remained very much like that encountered in the North Atlantic during deepest winter: gales and intermittent snow. The afternoon sky was dark gray and the sea was gray, furrowed with curling white wave-tops. Stiff breezes crossing the deck hit faces like an icy towel.

Task Force 77, the carriers Leyte *and* Philippine Sea, *the great battleship* Missouri *and the sixteen other vessels of the Seventh Fleet were relentlessly plunging along into the wind, guiding on the cruiser* Juneau. *Only in the very worst weather were the aircraft grounded.*

For three desperate days now, priority orders had been to provide increased maximum air support day and night to the 15,000 encircled Marines fighting their way along the bloody body-strewn 15-foot-wide ice-encrusted mud road to Hungnam, the captured North Korean port. Evacuation awaited.

Ensign Jesse Leroy Brown had flown the day before in one of the Leyte's sixty-nine sorties. In addition to bombs, rockets, and machine gun fire, thirty-six napalm pods had been dropped on two parallel ridges a mile long, frying Chinese communist troops who had recently entered the war against South Korea. More than 100,000 CCP troops surrounded the Marines.

Brown's best friend on the Leyte, LTJG Lee Nelson, had flown earlier that morning across the frozen Chosin Reservoir, located not far below the Manchurian border, making attack runs against the troops that were feeding into the pincer movements along the northwest shore. He'd skimmed the windblown ice, and after his debriefing, had talked about it with Jesse at early lunch.

''It's ugly out there,'' Nelson said, meaning the weather.

''Any ack-ack [antiaircraft fire]?''

''The usual around Chosin. Small arms.''

''You get any?''

''I don't think so.'' Nelson's plane hadn't been inspected as yet for bullet holes.

Doug Neill, Squadron 32's skipper, had been giving his pilots hell for going in too low. He didn't need shootdowns or maintenance problems.

Jesse said, ''Man, am I sleepy. I was up late writing to Daisy and Pam.''

Nelson laughed. ''You'll wake up once you get on deck. It's cold, Jesse. Same as yesterday.'' The pilots wore longies, cover-alls, maybe a sweater, rubber antiexposure suits, and fleece-lined boots and gloves.

Jesse finished his coffee and said, ''Gotta go.'' He seemed tense.

Jesse started up the island structure ladder for the afternoon launch and midway met Dick McKenzie, who'd just returned from a Chosin strike in his Panther jet and was on his way to the ready room for debriefing. They'd known each other since Pre-Flight

*training in Iowa. McKenzie said, "Every man a tiger, Jess." The
response was a terse "Okay, Mac."* Every man a tiger? *The
attitude when taking off was understandably different than when
returning safely.*

```
Deck log, USS Leyte: 1200 to 1400 Steaming as be-
fore. 1237 Changed speed to 20 knots. 1317
Changed speed to 15 knots. Changed course to 295.
1338 Resumed flight operations, first aircraft
launched. . . .
```

*In rapid succession, Executive Officer Dick Cevoli, flight leader
for the Armed Reconnaissance mission; Lieutenant George Hudson,
the Air Group Landing Signal Officer; Jesse and LTJG Tom Hudner took off in their Corsair fighter aircraft into the grimness over
the Sea of Japan, followed by LTJG Bill Koenig and Ensign Ralph
McQueen, a newcomer to Squadron 32. Jesse roomed with Koenig.*

*Hudson had said to Lieutenant Commander Doug Neill the day
before, "Hey, I've been on the platform long enough. It's my turn
to fly." Directing aircraft aboard, he was missing all the action.
So square-jawed "Paddles," a very experienced pilot, took Koenig's usual place as Jesse's wingman. McQueen was flying on Koenig's wing.*

*Jesse had never said very much in the ready room preflight
briefings, seldom asked questions, though he listened intently, but
this day he'd seemed unusually quiet and contemplative, Koenig
thought. Something was bothering him.*

*The six Corsairs of Iroquois Flight climbed out and headed for
the vicinity of the Chosin, a hundred miles away, 35 to 40 minutes,
and the road where weather conditions were even worse than those
around the task force. An overcast lapped at the snow-capped
mountains and the cold was well below zero around the villages
of Hagaru-ri and Yudam-ni, hateful places in Marine history, and
at another hamlet, Somong-ni, all places of death and destruction.*

*The Corsair, once known as a widow-maker, was legendary, a
hero of World War II, conqueror of the Japanese Zero in the Battle*

of Guadalcanal, later ranging the whole Pacific, its six .50 caliber machine guns able to fire 150 rounds in two seconds.

Nicknamed the "U-bird," and the "hog" because of its long snout, the Corsair's engine had eighteen cylinders and could develop 2,000 horsepower on takeoff. It had a level-flight speed of more than 400 mph, sometimes more than 500 diving. As a proven gun platform, no fighter pilot could ask for more at the time. The U-bird was a mean flying machine.

The planes dropped to about 500 feet to search for targets after they'd crossed the desolate coastline well north of Hungnam, the port of salvation for all the Americans grinding south through the communist escape route gauntlet. They were flying along the west side of the Chosin.

Jesse had first seen the great reservoir two months earlier, in October, with the sun shining down on its blue waters. Thick pine forests covered the shores in places. He'd written his wife Daisy in Mississippi, about how beautiful and tranquil it was, like no other lake he'd ever seen. The season had changed, the shimmering blue waters and the thick green pines now hidden by white blankets. Sunlight had turned to murk and fog.

In a snowswept valley near Somong-ni, a cluster of farmer's mud huts, Koenig, astern of the lead planes noticed a stream of vapor coming from Jesse's plane though he hadn't seen enemy small-arms fire so far. But they were formation flying low and slow, comparatively easy targets, now 500 to 700 feet above the terrain.

Lacking heavy antiaircraft guns, the Chinese infantrymen had their own technique of trying to deal with low-flying enemy aircraft. They'd lie in the snow in their white uniforms and point their rifles straight up, then fire simultaneously. There might be two or three hundred firing a barrage, hoping for a lucky hit.

Carrier pilots of the task force would sometimes land with holes in the fuselage, unaware that they'd ever been fired upon. Obviously, the bullets hadn't reached any vital parts, a gas or oil line.

Earlier in the day, a Marine Corsair was hit by ground fire in the vicinity and the pilot had to crash land. The aircraft exploded on impact and the pilot was killed instantly. There was a long black scar in the alabaster surface to mark the graves of both plane and pilot.

At approximately 2:40 P.M., Koenig called to Jesse, "You're dumping fuel!"

In the Corsair, when transferring gas from an external tank, the automatic shutoff valve sometimes would not close, resulting in fuel loss. It occurred to Koenig that the valve was Jesse's problem.

But as all aircraft pulled up to go over a ridge, Jesse replied calmly, "This is Iroquois 1-3, I'm losing fuel pressure. I have to put it down." This was not a valve problem. One of those unlucky rifle bullets had hit a gas or oil line. He was ten to fifteen miles behind enemy lines.

Koenig, astern of Jesse, called into his mike, "Mayday, Mayday . . ."

By this time, Jesse had dropped his flaps, his belly tank and rockets, and prepared, as best he could, for the wheels-up crash. The Corsairs, with that long nose, had a reputation of breaking up on rough landings. The cockpit, with its center panel and console, all sorts of mechanical snares, could become a deadly metal octopus in a few blinks of an eye.

Tom Hudner, flying on Jesse's wing, said, "Okay, Jesse, I'll walk you through your check-off list." Rather than him trying to concentrate while facing the crash-landing, Hudner told him, "Lock your harness, open your canopy and lock it," and other procedures that were taught to both of them as long ago as Pensacola. The harness was especially important so Jesse wouldn't bash his face into the gunsight when he hit; the open Plexiglas bubble canopy would allow him precious seconds to get out in case of fire.

Hudner didn't take much time to look around for a clear spot because the mountainous territory they were flying over was mostly wooded but it was apparent Jesse spotted a snowy clearing about a quarter mile in diameter almost on the side of the mountain, in an upgrade of about 20 degrees.

Jesse was too busy to reply but Hudner saw him slide the canopy back. He hoped that Jesse had locked it. There was a crank to open it or close it, and a small latch at the rear to lock it. It was always supposed to be locked open for carrier landings or any sudden deceleration.

For the first time, Jesse had to contend with a skin of white that had no human aspect. There was no ideal spot on which to put the plane down. Foot deep snow covered the hillsides and partially hid rocks. There wasn't time to find a flat place. Training took over as he tried to glide downward at 100 knots.

He was now riding a six-ton aircraft into a bowl-like stretch. The altitude up there was at least 5,500 feet above sea level. Trees were along the ridge lines and some were down in the bowl. His position was approximately lat. 40° 36' N; long. 127° 06' E.

The plane slammed in uphill, out of control, skidding and carving a track on the snow and frozen ground; only the harness keeping Jesse's body from becoming a punching bag; that long engine and that huge four-blade propeller breaking off and careening away; the nose twisting to the right at a 35-degree angle, leaving a tangle of cables and wires and broken structural steel ahead of the cockpit. Up there was a gas tank with over 200 gallons in it.

It took a few minutes for the shock of the crash landing, the fright, the slamming physical and mental punishment, the screech of metal shearing, to wear off. Severe pain had come stabbing up from his right knee. He tried to move his legs but realized the knee was jammed by the buckled fuselage against the control panel, straddled by his feet. He was trapped, deep in enemy territory.

He tried to move the steel, almost blacking out from the pain. He realized that he could not get out of the wreckage without help. And help was not on the ground. It was overhead. Normal procedure would be to wait until the pilot cleared the cockpit, then Koenig and McQueen would bomb the wreckage.

Jesse became aware that acrid light smoke was drifting back over the cockpit from the empty engine mounting. So something was on fire up there forward of the gas tank.

Koenig saw it, too, and immediately got on the guard channel to call, "Any heavy transport in the area, come in! Come in!" A big fire extinguisher was needed. It could be dropped.

Every pilot, sooner or later, has to think about instant death but the unthinkable is death by fire. Was his lifelong love of aircraft and flying to end here, in a ball of fire, on this rock-strewn mountain slope near miserable Somong-ni?

Despite the pain, and each tiny move hurt, Jesse cranked the cockpit canopy open—it had closed from impact—and saw, more clearly, his fellow pilots circling above. He waved, as the smoke wreathed his face. I'm alive! I'm alive!

Cevoli, Hudson, Hudner, Koenig, and McQueen were sweeping around above, looking for any enemy activity on the ridge. The trees were thick up there in half a dozen spots, affording hiding places for the ChiComs. Other aircraft in the vicinity had been called in to assist in coverage.

The full destructive power—rockets, machine guns, napalm— of each plane would be expended to buy time for a Marine rescue helicopter to arrive. Down there was a Leyte *shipmate and friend. He also happened to be the Navy's first black aviator.*

Most fighter pilots talk a lot about planes and flying, using their hands as wings, seldom talking about themselves. Jesse was of that breed and no one on the carrier, including Lee Nelson, who was now asleep, knew much about him.

The altitude likely kept whatever was smoking up there ahead from bursting into flame as he waited for help.

Columbus, Ohio

September 1944

Daisy Pearl Nix, Jesse's girlfriend, went to the train station with him that early evening and Fletcher Brown, twelve years old, showed up as well. He'd sneaked away from Kelly's Settlement and hitchhiked to Hattiesburg to see his big brother off. While Jesse was pleased, he knew Fletcher would have to return to the farm in darkness. He also knew that Papa John would not take kindly to the adventure. So Jesse sent Fletcher home.

He stood on the platform with Daisy, holding her, teasing her about hearing that Ohio girls were a lot more friendly than ones in Mississippi. A lot more sexy.

"You just keep away from them," Daisy instructed. "You write me every single night. And I don't want to know anything about those girls."

After lingering kisses, he entered the segregated "darky car," which he'd have to ride through Tennessee and Kentucky until it reached the border of Ohio. He found a seat and made a sign to Daisy through the window glass. She was wiping her eyes and mouthing, "I love you." He smiled back and told her the same.

The train left on time and rocked through the night. He'd always taken buses to go places inside Mississippi. He looked around at the black faces in the car and wondered if the white cars up ahead were different. *Do they have nicer seats? Better toilets?* This one was old and creaky. He knew there were dining cars on many trains. *Where do the Negroes eat? Do they have a separate section?* Oddly enough, he'd never asked anybody about that. *When, oh when, will segregation stop?*

He'd bought a new copy of *Popular Aviation* at the station newsstand. He hadn't read the magazine in a long time. The issue was devoted to carrier warfare. While the train pounded north, whistle and bell cleaving the night at crossings, trackside lights flashing into the cars, clacks of steel on steel, Jesse read about the pilots and planes and air battles against the Japanese in the Pacific. By 2 A.M., when he fell asleep, he'd made up his mind about what he definitely wanted to do—fly off flattops. *Have Negroes ever flown off aircraft carriers? I'd like to try.*

The train chuffed into Columbus a little before dawn. Most of the black passengers had waited until Columbus to move forward. Jesse bought a penny postcard at the station and mailed it.

Mr. Issac Heard
Stone Building, Room #566
Hampton Institute, Virginia

Dear Ike:
   I've just arrived in Columbus. But it is still dark and I don't know how things will look. Will write soon.

                      Your pal,
                      Jesse

Jesse's cousin Ike had gone to Hampton in August, pleased that Jesse had decided on an architectural career but disappointed that he wouldn't be in Virginia. He was convinced that Jesse would have a tougher time at Ohio State. He thought Hampton would have given him a track scholarship.

At dawn Jesse came out of the station with two cardboard suitcases and walked to the boarding house at 61 East Eleventh Avenue in the heart of "colored town." It was friendly territory beginning with Ma Jenkins, who owned the three-story clapboard building. Five other Negro students were living there, as well as a nurse and a secretary.

A letter from "Professor" Nathaniel Burger, Eureka's principal, awaited:

> Good luck, Jesse. Students here at Eureka High will be eagerly following your progress at OSU. Negro youth has been starved for heroes for such a long time. As the first of our graduates to enter a predominately white university, you are our hero. Our hopes and prayers are with you.

As a black man, Burger knew what problems Jesse would be facing.

Jesse read the letter twice. *Hero? Good Lord! I've got enough on my back already.*

In bed that night, listening to new sounds, smelling new smells, Jesse knew he'd made the right decision but also knew that tomorrow he'd have to confront an entirely different way of life. OSU wasn't tiny Lux, wasn't Kelly's settlement. OSU had thousands of students, 99 percent white.

Ma Jenkins had said, "Hattiesburg, Mississippi, eh?"

"Yes, ma'am."

"We had a country boy from Mount Olive two years ago and he got so homesick he headed back to Mississippi in less than two months. Don't let that happen to you. Keep your mind on your books. An' if you get a troubled mind, talk to me 'bout it.''

"Yes, ma'am."

His mind was troubled already, though he wouldn't admit it to Ma Jenkins.

"One bit o' advice. Make as many white friends as you can. You'll be livin' in Milk o' Magnesia world an' make no mistake 'bout it. Don't depend on black brothers an' sisters. There won't be many. They got their own problems."

"Yes, ma'am."

"How old are you?"

"Seventeen."

"You'll grow up here in a hurry."

Ma Jenkins was beefy and lighter in color, but she reminded Jesse a little of M'dear Miz Addie, Daisy's mother.

In three of his four classes in the College of Engineering, there were no black students, but to his surprise Jesse didn't feel any particular animosity aside from being ignored. Half a dozen white students had openly welcomed him and two white girls had even sat with him at lunch outdoors in the autumn sunshine the first day.

Finally, on the third day, one of the girls, Sarah, a junior, said, "Why are you purposely separating yourself, eating out here alone? None of my business, of course."

"Habit, I guess."

"I hope you don't think that anyone is going to get up from a table just because you sit down. It could happen, but I don't think it will. Negroes have been students here for many years. Don't make yourself special." He was trying not to—unsuccessfully.

Jesse ate in the campus union building with them the next day and one of the brothers, a boy from Indiana, joined them. Though still uncomfortable, he felt more relaxed.

But in some ways Columbus wasn't much different from Hattiesburg. None of the restaurants on High Street, next to the campus, would allow Negro diners, he wrote Daisy. The movie theaters reserved the top six rows of the balconies for brown bodies.

Though track season wouldn't begin until spring, he met the coach and was advised to start running. World War II had affected the program, but OSU would still participate in area games within bus distance. Running was always good for the soul as well as the legs. He also joined the wrestling team.

At month's end, he discovered that, after all, there was an aviation program at OSU, brought on by the war. It was under the wing of business administration, not listed in the engineering catalog. It seemed to be an orphan, operating away from the campus, allied with the government.

Jesse made an appointment with the proper counselor and soon found himself in the office of Mrs. Ruth Waterford, saying he wanted to take any and all aviation courses. Waterford appeared to be in her mid-thirties. She had a nice smile and hair of apple red. She said, "I'm sorry, Mr. Brown, but I think you should stick to your present engineering major. I don't think there'll be any positions open for you in aviation until long after the war is over."

"Why do you say that?" *Here we go again*, Jesse thought.

"Well, aviation is a comparatively new industry. Unless you want to be a mechanic. You certainly don't need university training for that type of job. I think you are fine just where you are."

"Suppose I tell you that architectural engineering is actually my second choice."

"If that's the case, you may be at the wrong university, Mr. Brown."

"Does the color of my skin have anything to do with aviation positions not being open for a long while?"

"Frankly, yes. I'm here to give you good advice."

"I'd still like to enter the program."

"There are no class openings until next year. It's very popular."

"Thank you, Mrs. Waterford."

"My pleasure, Mr. Brown. Good luck in your engineering courses."

Out in the bright sunshine he decided it was her smile he'd first like to wipe off; her attitude was next. He thought he could deal with the openly racist Holmes Club, the Hattiesburg beer joint where he'd worked as a waiter, and the owner, Mike Lowry, who said he had little use for black people, but never with the Ruth Waterfords. He decided then and there to apply for aviation. He wrote Daisy about Mrs. Waterford and the decision he'd made. She wrote back on a birthday card. He'd turned eighteen.

Little more than a month passed when Jesse knew he couldn't survive without additional money. He dropped out of track and wrestling to work part-time at Lazarus Department Store as a janitor but soon found he could make more loading boxcars for the Pennsylvania Railroad, working the 3:30 P.M. until midnight shift.

For the first time in his life he didn't spend Christmas in Hattiesburg but stayed in Columbus, even working on icy Christmas Eve as the troop-bound freight stacked up in the yards. It was a tiring job, pushing dollies laden with heavy boxes, out in the cold up the loading ramps, then stacking them inside the boxcars. Yet he was managing 3.6 on his grades. He'd study each night after he got back to the boardinghouse, often falling asleep over his books.

He did return home for a week during Easter 1945 and saw Daisy night and day.

"I'm still thinking about joining the NROTC [Naval Reserve Officer Training Corps] V-5 program," he told Daisy. "I figure once I get in there, I can find a way to qualify for aviation. I've talked to the lieutenant who runs the unit. Dawkins just laughed when I said I actually wanted to be a carrier pilot. He said almost anybody could be a pilot, but the men who flew naval aircraft were *naval aviators*. That made them special, not pilots, like the Army, but *naval aviators*. So now that's what I want to be, a naval aviator." *Is it crazy even to try?*

"Wouldn't you be just as happy being an architect? A civilian?"

"Not right now. You know that. You've known that a long time, Daisy. I'll pick up a little extra money and the Navy'll put some money into my scholarship fund. It's a good deal, I think."

V-5 wouldn't take more than three or four hours a week from study time. It was all about preparing a student to become a naval officer. There'd be a short summer cruise on a warship. On graduation, he'd get a commission as an ensign in the Naval Reserve. *Even if it doesn't lead to a cockpit, it's a good deal,* he reasoned.

Germany surrendered May 7, 1945, ending the European War. Atom bombs were dropped on Hiroshima and Nagasaki August 6 and August 9, Japan surrendering August 14. *Perhaps there'll be peace on earth. For a while anyway.*

Jesse was spending the summer at home, trying to earn enough just to stay in Columbus. He worked at a dry cleaner, picking up and delivering dry cleaning to black customers who lived in Kelly's Settlement, his home near Eatonville. The Jungle and The Bottoms, poor places, naturally, were there. Another guy had his regular Holmes Club job.

His coworker was Martin Luther Beard, who'd graduated from Eureka a year earlier than Jesse. M. L., as he preferred to be known, had grown up in The Bottoms, raised by his day-worker mother and his grandparents. M. L.'s experience with poverty was common in The Bottoms. He was attending little Tougaloo College, north of Jackson, determined to become a surgeon. He was willing to put in fifteen or more years to reach that goal. He planned to work a year or two for enough money to go back to college; work again, then classes. Tougaloo, with its black student body, was the least expensive college in Mississippi. Jesse admired his friend. *Fifteen years to become a surgeon?* Jesse felt good about surrounding himself with black men like M. L. Beard who wanted to go somewhere, who had goals and seldom complained.

Rattling around in an old truck, hoping it wouldn't break down before the day was finished, M. L. talked about his plans to become a doctor and Jesse talked about wanting to become the Navy's first black carrier pilot. They never talked about poverty.

> 61 East Eleventh Avenue
> Columbus, Ohio
> February 22, 1946
>
> Dear Ike:
>   Happy Birthday. I was very glad to get your letter. The days around here lack a touch of spring. We're still having plenty of Columbus sunshine—namely, rain and snow. I'm having my ups and downs, Ike, just hanging in. I often think of that little chick you jived that nite on 7th Street and I have to laugh. Remember? Boy, if Gwen knew that! Wow! Give Gwen my regards. Smile!
>
> Your pal,
Jesse

Jesse enjoyed writing to Daisy or family or friends and could often be found late at night bent over his desk or propped up in bed with a pen and stationery. He wrote to Ike Heard on June 30:

> I was home only about nine or ten days for Daisy's graduation and spent them all with Daisy or my family. I hope you will get the job of draftsman for that architect you named. I know it will be excellent practice

and experience. They are really proud of you at Eureka. I think most of this year's graduating class are going to college. They've been accepted at Fisk, Southern, Lincoln State, and a few more. Professor Burger is rightfully proud of them. I saw M. L. Beard briefly. He's working in town again this summer so he can go back to med school in the fall. Write the latest and soon. Smile!

> Your ace,
> Jesse

Returning to Columbus, he'd been rehired by the railroad and worked the 3:30 P.M. until midnight shift, attending courses in the mornings. He was in the locomotive repair shop, loading and unloading engine parts from boxcars, making eighty-three cents an hour. "I very seldom pick up anything weighing less than eighty pounds," he'd written to Daisy, who was waiting tables at the University of Southern Mississippi in Hattiesburg.

"Hey, wow," Jesse had said when he saw the Navy poster recruiting students for a new aviation program. Lieutenant Earl Dawkins, at his desk, had told him, "Brown, are you crazy?" Dawkins was in charge of the V-5 program. Jesse had been pestering the burly, crew-cut Dawkins for weeks.

"No, sir. I can qualify. If that poster means what it says, I can qualify."

Dawkins got up to read it. Dawkins had a perpetual five o'clock shadow and a lantern jaw.

"When did you put it up, sir?"

"Yesterday."

"I'd like to take that test, Mr. Dawkins."

"Brown, you're wasting your time and mine. You don't stand a chance in holy hell of passing it. Even if you do pass, your butt will never sit in the cockpit of a Navy plane. Believe me."

"Why not, sir?"

Dawkins was exasperated. "Tests are pieces of paper. You see these wings on my chest? They are hard to get, Brown. You get 'em flyin' aircraft. Every day people who think they want to be Navy pilots get washed out and catch a taxi to the train station, almost crying. Pre-Flight is the toughest school on earth."

"I'd like the chance to get washed out, Mr. Dawkins. Just the chance."

"There's something else, Brown."

"What, sir?"

"There has never been a black man even to enter Selective Flight Training. Never!"

"I'd like to be the first, Mr. Dawkins. I've thought a lot about it."

"Listen to me, Brown. It's been almost fifty years since Eugene Ely put a plane down on a so-called carrier. That's a lot of white pilot tradition. Proud tradition. So along you come, a Negro smart-ass. I'll tell you right now there'll be instructors who'll give you a 'down' quicker'n look at you. Enough 'downs' an' you're out the door an' back to Mississippi or wherever you choose to go. But it won't be on a carrier deck. . . ."

Jesse was silent a few seconds. "I'd like to try, sir." He preferred Dawkins to Ruth Waterford.

Dawkins finally shook his head at the stubbornness of this black boy. "I'm warnin' you, you'll be flyin' up the side of Mount Everest."

"I'd still like to try," he said.

"Okay, I'll let you know as soon as I make arrangements for you to take the test."

"Thank you, sir."

Jesse could feel the hairy lieutenant's eyes on his back as he went out the door.

"Brown, you don't qualify for another reason."

Jesse stepped back into the office. "Why not, sir?"

"You have to complete two years of college. You've only completed a year and a half."

"But it also says, Mr. Dawkins, that I can take an exam that indicates that my intelligence level is the equivalent of a two-year college man. If I have to, I'd like to take that test as well."

Running out of excuses, the lieutenant stared back. "Suit yourself."

Daisy opened Jesse's letter and read it, hoping that he wouldn't be too disappointed if he failed. She read it aloud again: " ' . . . the test is very hard, I'm told. That's all the more reason I have to take it. It's a challenge and I will always regret it if I don't. I'm not sure I told you that the lieutenant is a pilot and I think he resents the idea that a black man could become a carrier pilot. . . .' "

Addie Nix shook her head ruefully. "He's never been able to squeeze it out of his system. Why that boy wants to fly is a mystery to me."

There was another letter to Ike Heard in late July:

I'm in the Navy, as an Apprentice Seaman, USNR, V-5, on inactive duty. I had to go down to Cincinnati to take the test and for a while I thought the mental exams were going to be too much for me, but I managed to muddle thru the five hours of written tests. One interviewer asked me a lot about aircraft types and thank God I knew the answers. By evening, about half the guys were eliminated. I took the physical tests the next day. No problem. All that running and lifting boxes in the railroad yard took care of me. I'm not sure the Navy really wants me. I'm classified "desirable" rather than "outstanding or superior." I guess I'm lucky to be "desirable." However they classify me, I'll be getting $50 a month for the privilege of taking naval orientation, drilling, etc. Yes, it was terrible about the lynchings in Georgia and I suppose you know that within the past month there have also been two in Mississippi. All of that plus this recent riot in Athens, Alabama, doesn't give a guy any love for dear ole Dixie! As you say, we'll just have to give our best and trust in God for all other. . . .

Your pal,
Jesse

Jesse went home for Christmas. He was no longer loading boxcars. Between engineering studies and the V-5 requirements, there was little time for work and the Navy was now picking up the tab.

Daisy said, "Your mother worries so much about what you're going to do."

"I know. We talked for two hours last night. I told her that thousands of pilots learned to fly during the war and not many were killed in training. Instructors go up with you until the time you solo. Afterward too. She wasn't convinced."

"And your papa?"

"He said he wished he was young enough to try it."

"Daisy, honestly, I'm only afraid of failing. And, yeah, I'm already afraid of the instructors. Dawkins told me about them. I'll stick out like a single tar baby in a sea of white, wherever I go, whatever I do. At muster, at drill, in the classrooms, at mess, in the barracks."

They were at Daisy's house, at 201 Fredma Avenue, on the front porch steps in the black neighborhood. She was now eighteen, wondering whether or not she'd ever have the chance to go to college. She was envious of Jesse.

"Well, your mama won't be alone when you start to fly. I'll worry about you too. I'll think of you every day and night. I'll pray for you. I love you so much, Jesse Brown."

"I wish we could get married now. Tomorrow. I think I

could stand the pressure a lot better if I knew you were by my side."

He had to remain single or get kicked out, but was absolutely certain that Daisy was the partner he wanted for the rest of his life. She was equally committed, but marriage would have to wait until he was commissioned ensign, if he could make it, at least two years from now, perhaps longer.

"How do you plan to take care of yourself in that all-white naval aviation business?" Papa John asked.

"I think I can take it," Jesse said. "I'll say, 'Yes, sir' and 'No, sir' an' shut my ears when someone calls me 'nigger,' which I know they'll do. I got plenty of that in the Holmes Club. The instructors try to break the white boys an' they'll sure have a lot of fun with me. Every time I stand in front of the mirror now, I look myself in the eye an' say, 'Nigger, nigger, nigger.' I'll be ready for them, Papa." He'd get to the point where the word was bloodless.

Julia said, "That hurts me to hear you say that."

"Mama, I've got to psych myself up."

"Me, I'd break a jaw or try to." *That's my papa, all right.*

"You've got to take some pain to get what you want."

Lura said, "What kinda money they gonna give you?"

"A hundred thirty-two a month once I start to fly."

"Not bad if you can have some fun doin' it."

"That's what I figure," Jesse said.

"You'll be the first one of us, eh?" Fletcher said.

"From what I hear, yes. But that's not why I'm doing it, Mule. I'm doing it for me. I just want to fly. I want to land a plane on a carrier. I want the thrill of it."

Lura said, "Man, you'll get that, I'll bet. *Whoeeee.*"

"I figure that the aircraft doesn't know whether there're white hands or black hands or white feet or black feet on the controls."

"Yeah," Lura said. "Now, you gonna bust the color line on a U.S. Navy carrier. . . ."

"I'm sure going to try."

Fletcher said, "Big brother, how come you don't talk like us anymore? You talk like a white man."

He laughed. "The minute I step foot in Hattiesburg I talk just like you do."

"You don't either," said Lura.

> 61 East 11th Avenue
> Columbus, Ohio
> 12 February 1947
>
> Dear Ike:
>
> I dug your report today and was very glad to know the score. Boy, that group of chicks that finished Eureka last June and went off to college came back for the holidays "hipped to the tip." They were flyin' high.
>
> I am still in Navy V-5. This is my last quarter in school for a while. When this quarter is over, I am to go to Glenview, Illinois, for the first stage of flight training. I'll tell you about it in detail when I have more time.
>
> Must close for now. Smile!
>
> > Fraternally yours, your pal,
> > Jesse

Dawkins said, "I'll tell you what's going to happen. You'll find out in a hurry whether or not you truly want to be a pilot. You think you do, but you don't really know. Know what a Yellow Peril is?"

"Yes, sir." Stearman N2S types flown by student pilots, easily recognized by others up in the air for their bright yellow color. The color said, "Watch out!"

From what Jesse had read, the Stearman was one of the best and most forgiving airplanes ever made. Used for primary training purposes, the sturdy dual-cockpit biplane was also possibly the world's best acrobatic aircraft.

"How many days will I be at Glenview?"

"Only one if you wash out the first day. Some do. That's why they call it Selective Flight Training. You'll be watched from the moment you climb into the cockpit. Show any sign of fear or lack of flying aptness and you're gone."

"How do I get ready for it?"

"Oh, you might pray a little."

Palmer's Crossing, Mississippi

July 1936

Jesse had memories of a close and loving family and the peculiar odor of dire poverty, of mules and sharecropping, and a dirt-strip flying field and a Negro hater named Corley Yates, and a nightclub owner named Lowry, and the death of his only sister named Johnny, and so much, much more. . . .

He remembered himself as a wiry ten-year-old barefooted boy, shirtless, in worn, patched overalls, ribs showing, skin a deep cinnamon from the mixture of Choctaw, Chickasaw, and Negro blood, peeking around the corner of the large corrugated tin shed that served as the hangar for the small airfield; remembered listening to the engine of the antique red biplane as it went from a putter to a full-throated roar, his eyes colt-wide, mouth open, in anticipation of what would happen.

That's where the abiding love had begun, on that measly, dusty forty-foot-wide, 500-yard runway. That runway was his path to the sky.

The yellow windsock atop the hangar at Palmer's Crossing was full of breeze and he knew that it wouldn't be long until the plane lifted off. Cleared by mule drag in 1926, the exact year that Jesse Leroy Brown was born, he sometimes hid in the grass to be closer to whatever planes were operating, to hear the motor thunder, feel the wind the cloth-covered fuselage created, and to smell the strong exhaust. Because he went to church on Sundays, he usually visited Saturday afternoons, careful to avoid the white folks who came over for a ride or just to watch the few planes operate.

He'd been chased away at least four dozen times the past two years by Corley Yates, the redhaired, mustached, tobacco-spitting mechanic who also bossed the field. His face was pimple corrugated, brick-colored. He had a gimp right leg.

"Git outta here, yuh kinky-headed niggah boy, I tol' yuh agin an' agin," Corley would shout. Last time he had thrown a wrench at Jesse, laughing when it missed. He had big greasy hands, but Jesse wasn't afraid of him. It wasn't that he picked on Jesse Leroy Brown especially. It was more that he thought all Negroes, young and old, were a shiftless, inferior race of people. Nine had been lynched in the Hattiesburg area since 1890.

For reasons that Jesse understood—and yet didn't—black folks weren't welcome around airplanes. What was the harm in watching while the plane was pushed out of the hangar and onto the edge of the strip, where the leather-booted pilot with his brown leather helmet on, white scarf around his neck, walked around it, pushing the rudder back and forth, looking at the engine and then climbing up into the cockpit? Jesse knew all the terms from reading *Popular Aviation*.

The pilot would finally give Corley Yates a thumbs-up. Then Corley would pull down on the propeller, engine catching with a puff of blue-gray exhaust, pilot pulling the goggles down over his eyes. The propeller would blur; the engine would roar.

Then he'd watch the grand takeoff, the climb-out. It was such a show and Jesse's heart beat faster each time. *Up there. In the sky. In the clouds.* That was where he wanted to be.

It had all begun on a Sunday afternoon in 1932 when Jesse was only six and John Brown, his papa, had taken him to an air show staged at Hattiesburg. There were ten airplanes from Mississippi and Alabama doing acrobatics all over the sky. There were white wing walkers and parachute jumpers and planes doing loop-the-loops. People from all over the county took their first airplane ride that day. John Brown couldn't afford the fee. In overalls and straw hats, father and son stood far away from the white spectators.

This day he lingered too long after Corley, greasy hands on his hips, watched the plane ascend into the hot, blue, cloudless summer sky. Corley caught sight of Jesse, his mouth still open in awe, and the yelling began again as he took off, bare feet pounding the red soil. Whatever else he'd accomplished in his ten years, running was high on the list and within a few seconds he was out of Corley's reach except for the shouting. "Coon, someday ah'm gonna catch yuh an' bas' yore head in." Jesse paid no attention.

He slowed to a trot on the unpaved road and thought again about the man up there, white scarf flapping in the wind. He could look down on everyone, on everything, like birds; he could turn and dive and roll over and loop-the-loop.

Jesse often stared up at the clouds and wondered how it felt to fly in them; to go above them and look down, caught between the endless sky and the layers of cotton below.

Knowing about young Jesse's love of airplanes, his oldest brother, Marvin, a freshman at all-black Alcorn Agriculture and Mechanical College in Lorman, Mississippi, had given him a dime one weekend to go to the Saenger Theater. He sat in the Negro balcony and watched *Hell's Angels*, a moving picture about American and German fighter planes shooting each other out of the sky. Jesse couldn't sleep that night, imagining himself firing the machine guns at a German Fokker airplane of World War I. That's what he wanted to be, a fighter pilot.

Jesse remembered the "shotgun" house at 913 Dewey Street, near the True Light Baptist Church in Hattiesburg. Three "shotguns" were side-by-side and the Brown family—Papa, Mama, Marvin, William, sister Johnny, Jesse, Lura, and Fletcher—lived in the middle one for almost five years. If you opened the front door when the back door was open, you could shoot pellets through the hall into the backyard. There was no central heat, no running water, just a well; no indoor toilet; weekly baths were in a tin tub in the kitchen, suds slopping out on the wooden floor. The fireplace was long remembered. Little William fell into it and was severely burned. His face and neck were scarred for life.

The Heard family lived next door and Jesse started playing with cousin Issac Heard when he was four or five. Cowboys and Indians, hopscotch, kick-the-can—whatever games they could dream up. Though interrupted when the Browns moved to Palmer's Crossing, three miles outside Hattiesburg, the friendship with Ike Heard lasted. Ike and Jesse were to share their hurts and dreams for a long, long time.

Losing his grocery warehouse job because of the Depression, Papa John went to work at the Dixie Pine turpentine plant for fifteen cents an hour. The plant whistle awakened everyone at 6 A.M. The plant caught fire one night, spreading quickly to workers' cabins. Fletcher was pulled through a window in his crib by a huge man named Jack. The Browns fled. It was a frightening memory. Then John lost that job in another Depression layoff.

Next, in 1938, was a sharecropper farm at Lux, twelve miles out of Hattiesburg, and Jesse usually paused from fieldwork if he was out there in the rows of corn or cotton or sugarcane when a plane passed over to say, "I'm sure gonna fly one of those things." He'd been saying that since he was about eight. The family always laughed.

The Browns lived near the railroad tracks in a typical unpainted, pineboard, one-story, leaky, tin-roofed house with a small-railed front porch, a wooden swing, and three rocking chairs. Passing trains shook the flimsy structure. Behind the house were the well, outhouse, chicken, and hog pens. The crop fields, owned by a Mr. Ingram, were out back. The rows of cotton were almost a mile long. Three other Negro families shared the 900-plus acres of rich land.

Though only five feet ten, John Brown weighed in at 250 pounds and was a powerful man with huge arms and legs. Julia Lindsey Brown, rather slight, darker in color than John, was from a family of nine children. She'd taught school before marrying John in 1918. All of her brothers and sisters had been schoolteachers. Her maternal greatgrandfather was a slave master who'd taught Julia's mother to read. Julia was part Chickasaw; John was part Choctaw.

Lux was little more than a name on a dusty mailbox off Rural Route 1, the road to Seminary and Collins. It was the site of an old-fashioned general store and a one-room church sitting in the pine woods by a gravel road. Sometimes only the sound of flies buzzing and crows cawing broke the thick silence of Lux, Jesse remembered. There were no tractors, just mules to pull the plows. The whole family worked from "cain't see" before dawn to "cain't see" after sundown.

And the whole family, dedicated Baptists, went to church on Sundays. Big John was a deacon. Julia taught Sunday school and sang in the choir, as did William and Jesse. Church was a way of childhood life and a time of joy. Jesse loved to sing the spirituals. Loved to clap his hands and rock his body.

The school at Lux, a three-mile walk from where the Browns lived, was one room of about 600 feet square, tinroofed, and heated by a kerosene stove during the winter.

Flies and mosquitoes flew in the open windows during late spring and early fall. The benches began with kindergarten children and went back, one by one, to the eighth graders. The entire student body numbered about thirty. The teacher had a high school education. She'd never stepped foot on a college campus.

Julia was strict and the children couldn't go to bed until homework was done. William once accused her of being "education-crazy," prompting his papa to lecture him. John's voice was syrupy until he became angry. Then it rumbled.

Julia checked their homework as intently as she studied her Bible. A misspelled word was always circled in red, the culprit forced to correct it, then pronounce it half a dozen times. She wanted her children to use English the way it is written. "Don't ever let me hear you say 'ain't,' " she'd say. She *was* education-crazy. She said so herself. She always had been.

Jesse couldn't remember when she'd first said it, maybe when he was five or six, or even earlier: "If you don't know, just ask." She'd said "ask" was the smartest word in the English language: "Just ask." She'd said, "Never be afraid to ask questions. People won't think you're dumb, they'll be flattered. You're telling them you want to learn, Jesse."

He'd arrive home before dusk, but already the kerosene lamps would be glowing in the front room and kitchen. There was no running water or electricity; the board walls were bare. Some black families pasted newspaper print on their walls, but Julia wanted to wait until she could afford a Sears pattern.

The Browns seldom talked about being poor. There were better things to talk about, Julia said. "I don't want to hear any of you talk about being poor. We have to maintain our dignity and pride. Poor has nothing to do with those two words." Her words were etched in Jesse's memory.

The boys' bedroom at Lux had two beds. Jesse's two younger brothers, Fletcher and Lura, shared one bed. Until

Marvin went off to college, he and Jesse shared the other bed. William slept on the living room couch, fighting the spring coils.

The lamp on the table between the beds often cast a yellow glow on the tattered issue of *Popular Aviation* in Jesse's hands. The planes had changed from wooden frames, fabric-covered wings and fuselage, and single engines, like the red biplane, to thin sheet metal in the big ones like the Ford Tri-Motor.

He read the articles about airplanes over and over. Marvin, seven years older, had picked up the magazine from the seat of a Southern Railway car. Jesse couldn't believe what was happening in the skies around the world. Many nights he didn't blow out the lamp until midnight.

3

Lux, Mississippi

May 1938

Jesse was sitting on the seventh row of benches, with one row to go, in Mrs. Smith's exclusive country day school when he got a job selling the *Pittsburgh Courier*, the only Negro newspaper distributed in that part of the country. The *Courier* and the *Chicago Defender* were really the only communication from the major cities of the Negro world: Washington, New York, Chicago, New Orleans. And the *Defender* was harder to find. Few of Jesse's customers had radios. They couldn't afford electricity or weren't near the lines, but many could read.

The *Courier* sold for a nickel and he got two pennies. He had thirty customers and would walk for miles through the woods and over fields to service them. His brothers often walked with him. The papers were dumped off the bus at the general store. One reward was getting a free copy.

One day, not long after the bus driver kicked the bundle out, Jesse shouted at his brothers, "I told you, I told you! He taught himself!" There was a front-page picture of a black Pennsylvanian, C. Alfred Anderson, who'd borrowed $2,500 to buy his first airplane. Without a formal lesson, he took off from a dirt strip. Now a veteran pilot, he'd read books on aeronautics as a youth, had hung around hangars, like Jesse, and had built model airplanes.

"I knew it, I knew it," Jesse yelled. "Some of us *are* flying. . . ."

Anderson told the *Courier* writer how he'd struggled to pay for the plane and maintain it and how tough it had been to get a license from the white authorities.

"You see, it can be done," Jesse told his brothers.

Then the *Chicago Defender* ran an article about other black aviators. Marvin sent it from Lorman. Jesse saw photos of Eugene Bullard, Hubert Julian, and the late Bessie Coleman. He read about Bullard flying for the French in World War I. He looked at the biplane flown by James Bannon and Thomas Allen on their cross-country flight from Los Angeles to New York in 1932. *It can be done.*

The *Courier* ran another long article about the struggle of American black men to participate in military aviation, citing statements of General Hap Arnold, chief of the Army Air Corps, and others. The general had said, "Negro pilots cannot be used in our present Air Corps, since this would result in having Negro officers commanding white enlisted personnel."

The *Courier* said there was a general white belief that black men didn't have the "brains or fortitude or aptitude to fly military planes." Purely political, the *Courier* said.

Jesse, not believing that black men couldn't fly military planes, clipped the article out and angrily nailed it to the wooden wall by his bed.

He wrote a letter to President Roosevelt asking why Negro pilots weren't in the Air Corps, preparing for war. He received a form letter from the White House several months later. The letter said the President appreciated Jesse's point of view.

313 Pauline Avenue
The Diary of Daisy Pearl Nix
April 26, 1937

Today is my eleventh birthday and I will spend most of it with Snook Hardy. I'll soon go through the hedge to Snook's house next door. She's going to braid my hair as her gift. We do not pay much attention to birthdays in my house. I wish we did. I had a dream last night that my grandfather Nix, who died when I was five, gave me a kitty as his gift. I do not remember much about him. He had a barbershop on Pine Street in the white section and I have to laugh over stories about my grandfather Nix. He had a secret. A lot of people thought he was white. Underneath he was as black as I am. I think my grandpapa Will is going to take me to Natchez on the train for his gift. He works for the railroad. My birthday wish is that I find a good man to marry me when I grow up and take real good care of me. I may get a cake tonight. Happy birthday to me.

Jesse would not see Daisy Pearl's diary until eight years later, when he was nineteen. Touched by its innocence, he wondered if she had someone in mind when she made her birthday wish.

Marvin was now starting his senior year at Alcorn and planned to be a science teacher. "Teaching is the best of all professions," Julia said. "Flying airplanes is not, in my opinion," she told Jesse. "You could be killed flying airplanes."

Marvin was special. He'd fallen out of a wagon in his childhood, an iron-tired wheel passing over his neck. The injury caused his head to tilt over his left shoulder permanently, making him a target for cruel taunts. A gentle, thoughtful young man, the family had always protected him. Jesse thought he was the smartest one in the family.

William, with his badly scarred face and neck, was also a target of taunts.

To John and Julia, it sometimes seemed that God had selected them for more than their share of family grief. Johnny, she of the wide smile and keen sense of humor, was married this year of '39, a cause for celebration after the church wedding. Soon pregnant, with John and Julia looking forward to becoming grandparents, Johnny Brown died from complications before she could deliver the baby. The midwife said she was sorry.

Jesse deeply mourned his only sister. "Soon, One Mornin' " was sung at the funeral service.

> *Soon, one mornin', death comes a-creepin' in my room.*
> *O my Lawd, O my Lawd, what shall I do?*

In September 1939, when Jesse was thirteen, the landlord paid a visit to the kitchen to "settle" with the Browns for their annual labor, which resulted in eighteen bales of cotton, corn, potatoes, and sugarcane—they had produced 500 gallons of high-grade molasses. John was on an errand in town. Jesse and Lura listened as Mr. Ingram said, "Well, Julia, the way we figure it, you owe us fifty dollars."

Jesse had heard his papa and mama talk about it and Julia had said that they would likely receive somewhere between $900 and $1,500, enough to get out of debt.

When Julia opened her mouth to reply, she fainted, her five-foot-four body hitting the floor. Jesse rushed to her side. A year of hard work had netted them nothing.

Granville, Ingram's brother-in-law, ran the general store, which they both owned. Granville liked to sip on a Mason jar of white lightnin' most of the day. He'd kept a debit sheet on the Browns. They'd been charged double on every single item they'd bought during the year.

Jesse went with his papa to visit Granville at the store and heard the shouting, which finally stopped when Granville said he'd call the sheriff, threatening arrest.

Jesse told his brothers that he planned to wait for Granville after he closed the store that night and beat "the tar" out of him. "Don't tell Papa," he said.

When drunken Granville staggered down the two rickety steps from the store porch in the profound Lux darkness, he was hit across the chest with a two-by-four.

Late the next afternoon, John said to his family, "I heard Granville got all his ribs broke last night. I'm sure glad we were havin' supper 'bout that time."

There was no reaction from the brothers whatsoever.

1607 Corrine Street
The Diary of Daisy Pearl Nix
February 8, 1940

Yesterday was a terrible sad day for me. I was standing in front of Miss Henry's class reciting the *Gettysburg Address* when Mr. Thomas Hall, director of the Negro funeral home, opened the door and whispered to Miss Henry. My daddy had been taken to the hospital. The hearse was always used as an ambulance to transport patients who were seriously ill. Mr. Hall said I was needed at home to take care of my sisters and brother. I finished Mr. Lincoln's address and got into the front seat of the hearse and rode home, feeling helpless and frightened. As soon as school was out, Snook came over to stay with me. Mama was notified and rushed to the hospital. My daddy had a heart attack. I pray that he'll be all right.

The more Jesse read of Daisy's diaries, the more he knew she was the right girl for him.

Glenview, Illinois

March 1947

He took the train from Columbus to Chicago, then city transportation to Glenview for his Selective Flight Training.

A large blue-gray bus lettered U.S. NAVAL AIR TRAINING COMMAND was waiting at Glenview station. Playing an old game, he decided not to wait until last to board. That way, he wouldn't have to walk past everyone to get to the rear. So he boarded first and the Negro driver, a sailor, stopped him. "Hey, boy, you're on the wrong bus. We goin' to the air base. . . ."

Jesse displayed his Apprentice Seaman orders and the driver read them with disbelief, holding up a long line, squinting up at Jesse's face several times.

"They aren't counterfeit," Jesse said quietly.

The driver finally shrugged and wagged his head for Jesse to proceed to the rear of the bus. He was wearing his Ohio State track warm-up jacket.

A tall, dark-haired, red-cheeked, brown-eyed pilot candidate sat down beside him on the last row of seats. Looking over, he said, "OSU, huh?"

Jesse nodded. *If he didn't speak first,* Jesse thought, *there would have been silence all the way to the air base. Let the other guy say the first words, black or white.*

"I'm Gus Gillespie, Dartmouth," he said, extending a hand.

He shook it. "Jesse Brown."

Probably money in his family. He has that look about him. Old man a stockbroker? Isn't Dartmouth an Ivy League college? We've got about as much in common as a donkey and a Derby winner.

"So off we go to be flyboys," Gillespie said cheerfully, seeming to accept that Jesse was hoping to be a pilot.

Two other fledglings occupied the other seats without speaking.

"Try to," Jesse said, smiling back.

"I have a hunch I can fly an airplane. I like speed. I'm a good driver," Gillespie said.

Probably had one of those little British sports cars at Dartmouth. Jesse pictured Gus Gillespie driving with the top down, a pretty girl sitting beside him. Jesse nodded and kept the genuine smile on his face. He thought, *I could like Gus Gillespie, but maybe it's too soon to tell him about the dirt strip at Hattiesburg. About Corley Yates, about Lux and chickpeas, about the Holmes Club, about being called ''nigger'' all of his life.*

"Where you from, Jesse?"

"Small town in southern Mississippi, Hattiesburg."

"Winthrop, upstate New York, near the Canadian border."

Gus looked like he'd be from a town called Winthrop. Now that the bus was almost loaded, he wondered if Gus had noticed that aside from the enlisted driver, Jesse was the only Negro aboard. Then he said to himself, *Quit that.* It was like the first day at Ohio State. Gus had his own concerns and they likely had nothing to do with race.

The white Marine guard at the air station gate knew that BROWN, J. L., was not a cook or a steward and took a long time examining his ID and orders. This was a place for flying and no black man trying to be a pilot had ever set foot on the premises. The guard finally shook his head and shrugged, like the driver had done.

Jesse figured he'd had natural "humiliation" training for quite a while at the Holmes Club, and so long as it remained impersonal and no one cursed him or hit him, he could endure almost anything the Navy sent his way. *Be polite and let the words and looks sail over my head like flat rocks across the Bouie.*

He checked in and submitted his orders to the Officer-of-the-Deck's clerk. *Same old routine. Same old mind-set.* The chief petty officer frowned and stared in disbelief as he matched Jesse's orders with his skin color. "You sure you want to go through with this?" he asked. *What are you doing here, man?* was what he meant.

"I'm sure."

The date and time stamp slammed down on his orders and the CPO muttered, "Room 252, Transient Barracks."

Feeling the CPO's eyes on his back, he went out the door to find the Transient Barracks.

On the walk to the barracks, he could hear the Yellow Perils as they took off and landed. He'd seen the pictures of them, but this was his first look at the real thing. They had pneumatic-tired fixed wheels and radial engines. They looked beautiful, reminding him of the planes he'd seen as a boy.

He found Room 252 and entered it, prepared for the appraisals of whoever was there. *No one! But there's an empty bunk and an empty locker. Perhaps the others are out flying.* He checked the names on the other lockers: BAKER, BIDWELL, SAVELO. As he was unpacking, a tall blond youth—BIDWELL, F. E., according to the name tag on his shirt—walked in, mouth dropping, feet stopping as he confronted the new occupant. "Ah, you got the right room?"

"Room 252," Jesse said. "Is that a problem?"

"No, oh no." He fumbled for more words and finally said, "I'm Frank Bidwell. Welcome."

"Jesse Brown," Jesse said, extending a hand. *Two more to go*, he thought.

At evening mess in the huge hall seating more than 200, he felt eyes of those near him. They all stood back of the benches awaiting the command to sit down. Soon a Marine sergeant in immaculate khakis shouted, "A-ten-*shun!*" They all popped to. The Marine shouted again. "Be seated!"

Though the college apprentices at his table seemed to take him in stride, the Negro serving stewards took immediate offense. Here was one of them who invaded their white boy realm. Jesse found it hard to believe. Not one of them spoke to him. They even glared at him. They served him reluctantly. He looked at the other plates. His was only half-full. *What's going on?* He was shocked but decided not to complain, not make a scene at this first meal. If he could find a way, he'd take one of the stewards aside the next day and ask what the hell was going on. He was going to have enough problems with white skin.

March 17, 1947

Dearest Daisy,

It has been a long, long and uneasy day. In a few minutes, taps will sound and the lights will go off. I'm rooming, temporarily, with three other aviation candidates. They seem to be nice guys, although they were all surprised. I don't blame them. Everyone seemed to be surprised when I came into the mess hall like an earthbound crow. Even the mouths of the "brother" food handlers dropped when I showed up. I'm sure that not even the commanding officer of the base knows that Brown, J. L., is a Negro.

Today I had another complete physical and drew clothing. Day after tomorrow I'll take my first flight.

One of my roomies, Savelo, W. D., said they don't

discriminate here. He said they're just mean to everyone. Nice guy from Philadelphia.

I know I'll be lonely, but I'll think of you and feel
close to you. I don't know how long I'll be here. Some
don't make it past the third day. I'll write again as soon
as I can.

All my love,
Jesse

LTJG Roland Christensen, USNR, a clean-cut Nebraskan
of Danish descent, looked out of the instructor's ready room
window on the hangar's upper level and was surprised to
see a slim black candidate below in a flight suit and cloth
helmet, goggles up on his forehead. He seemed lost in the
milling crowd of white aviation cadets who were checking
the Morning Flight Boards to see who was with what instructor at what time. Yellow Perils were already taking to
the air.

It was a routine weeding-out day, Jesse knew. "An average of ten a day might be gone before Pre-Flight," Dawkins had said. Every pulse was racing. There would be eight
hours of instruction, then a solo flight.

Glenview was just a dry-lipped way station. Passing Glenview, up in the air, inside out, upside down, was the first
step. "If you don't like it, if you don't have the guts, go
home to Mama," Dawkins had said. "That's the way it
should be," Jesse had agreed.

Chris, as he was known to the other instructors at Glenview, hadn't heard that a Negro was scheduled for Selective
Flight Training. It was about time, he thought. In fact, he'd
never really known a black person. There were only a handful in western Nebraska, none in his hometown of Chappell
on the Panhandle. He'd been in the Navy almost six years
and couldn't recall ever seeing a black person with wings.
He hadn't thought about it, one way or another, until that
moment.

He studied the bewildered hopeful for a moment. There was always that insecure look on the faces of those who hadn't made a few flights. Chris thought this particular one, awash in a milk lake, might need a friendly hand. He called over to the bored Flight Commander, an often truculent officer who thought he should be bossing a carrier squadron. "I'd like to teach the Negro fellow if it's okay with you."

"Okay with me?" Scoggins said. "Yeah, it's okay with me. I don't think you'll get any competition for him. He's all yours, Chris. Good luck."

"What's his name?"

The commander checked the roster. "Brown, same as his skin," he said with a short laugh. Apprentices were generally assumed to be losers unless they swiftly proved otherwise. The boogie boy was a wash-out cinch. *How did he get this far?*

In a few minutes, Christensen was on the hangar deck approaching Jesse. Chris said, "Welcome to Glenview." His instructor's shirt name tag said who he was. "You'll be flying with me while you're here." They shook hands.

Jesse said, "Yes, sir," stiffening to attention. "Yes, sir" and "No, sir" would be automatic for a long time to come, he hoped. *Easy to say.*

"Relax," Christensen said. He walked over to the flight board and chalked in Jesse's name alongside his own. Four other names were already up there. "You ever flown?"

"No, sir."

Chris had made his first solo at the University of Arizona toward the end of World War II in a Waco biplane that had many of the same characteristics as the Stearman. Trained to be a combat fighter pilot, he found himself instructing cadets, a letdown. Among the Glenview professionals, Chris had the reputation of being strict about flying procedures; otherwise, he was considered easygoing.

"Let's go over to the corner," he said.

Jesse followed him, amid the glances of other baffled instructors, along with a few frowns. *A black boy here? Unheard of!*

"Where you from?" Christensen asked.

"Mississippi, sir."

"I'm from Nebraska. Your family into farming?"

"Yes, sir." Jesse didn't say what kind. *Maybe they don't have sharecropping in Nebraska.* He knew the lieutenant was trying to make him comfortable.

"We have something in common. I was born on a dryland prairie farm which my grandparents homesteaded. They lived in a sod house and plowed with oxen."

"I've never been to Nebraska, sir."

"Full of farmers. Let's go."

As they walked out toward the flight line with its rows of Yellow Perils, Christensen asked, "Why do you want to be a naval aviator?"

"It's something I've wanted to do since I was a kid?"

"Why the Navy? Why not the Army?" Every pilot knew about the Tuskegee guys.

Jesse replied simply, "I'd like to be a carrier pilot." *Just forget my color. Please. Just teach me.*

Nearing the Stearman, Christensen stopped and turned to face Jesse. "Let's talk another minute. You were told yesterday what that parachute is all about? Right?"

"Yes, sir."

"What that rigger might not have told you is that we've had people killed in these aircraft. Chutes have also saved lives, so what you're going to be sitting on is a lifesaver. Regard it that way."

The Stearman was highly maneuverable and easy to control, even at low speeds, but it wasn't an easy plane to land, Jesse had read. It carried 46 gallons of gas in the upper wing and that weight put the center of gravity behind the wheels. He knew that much about it.

"You'll see it's got narrow landing gear and can ground loop if you give it a chance," Christensen said. "You can skin a wing tip and embarrass yourself. Know it, Jesse, but don't sweat it. I haven't had a ground loop yet and I've ridden these old birds through more than five thousand landings. Yet I treat it like a pet bull. It can turn on you when you least expect it. We'll always make a three-point landing, same as on a carrier; carriage wheels and tail wheel touching the ground simultaneously."

"Yes, sir." He was trying to remember every word. *One ground loop may be forgiven. Two might send you packing* was really what the instructor was saying.

"We'll stay up a minimum of an hour and fifteen minutes every day for eight or nine days. By that time, I have to be convinced you've got what it takes."

"Yes, sir."

Jesse blew a breath out as they walked on, sweating despite the cool spring air.

The lieutenant soon climbed aboard the Stearman, slipping easily into the front cockpit. Jesse mounted the rear one. There was no radio communication between the cockpits. A gosport—a rubber speaking tube inserted into the instructor's cloth mask—connected back to the student's earphones.

"Make sure that seat belt is fastened tight," Christensen said over the gosport.

Jesse acknowledged, heart trip-hammering. He'd waited so long for this moment. Helmet on, goggles on, gloves on, an aircraft, a cockpit. He'd waited so long.

A ground crewman climbed up on the port wing and inserted a crank into the inertia starter, winding it up. The lieutenant called out, "Contact, switch on," and the crewman engaged the starter. The Lycoming engine coughed, with a backfire of blue smoke, caught, and the radial pistons began hammering steadily.

Engine puttering, propeller turning, Christensen began to taxi out to the runway. Jesse felt every bump. He looked at the few instruments on the panel. Airspeed indicator, oil pressure, altimeter, engine temperature, fuel gauge. The N2S-5 Yellow Peril was a monument to simplicity; a throwback to the dirt-strip air circus days of the twenties and thirties.

He saw the wings flap a little with the bumps and looked back at the movement of the rudder. The ailerons remained flat. *Lord God, I'm actually going to fly. The date, March 18, 1947; the time, late morning. Now! Like a bird, like a kite, like Eugene Bullard, like C. Alfred Anderson. Remember the date!*

Christensen shouted into the gosport in his flatland prairie voice, "Brown, enjoy yourself today. You'll get your chance tomorrow!"

He headed the Stearman into the wind and ran up the Lycoming until it roared, until the plane shivered with anticipation and excitement.

This is the moment, Jesse thought. *Finally! Finally! See me now, Corley Yates, you SOB.*

Christensen yelled into the gosport, "Up we go!" and the wheels began to roll forward, now and then a bump, the whole body of the plane alive. Jesse knew that the throttle was wide open.

Jesse could barely see over the nose. The tip of the wooden propeller had vanished in a blur of motion, playing tricks with his eyes. Side to side, trees and buildings and empty spaces with grass flashed by. Then the flow of air beneath the wings began to lift the Stearman and he felt the tail come up, yet the wheels had not left the earth.

Christensen shouted, "Sixty-five knots, normal climbing speed!" and they were airborne, going upward, gradually at first, then more sharply.

Jesse wanted to yell—a yell of triumph—and finally did.

"You all right?" Christensen was looking at Jesse in his rearview mirror, sharing this ultimate thrill of first flight. He remembered his own first flight.

"You betcha!" But the wild wind flow over the cockpit caught his words and threw them gloriously back into the turbulence created by this fabric-covered wonder.

He wished a photographer was straddling the short space of fuselage behind the lieutenant to take his picture at this moment, record his first flight for all to see; showing his shining brown-black face wreathed in the beige helmet, the goggles, the grin. *Oh Lordy, the big grin. What a sight for Daisy. This black boy—up, up, and away.*

Christensen banked the plane, reading off altitude: "A thousand feet . . ."

Jesse could see all of Glenview, roofs of houses and buildings. *So this is what it is like. Somehow I knew this was how it would be. Earth sweeping by and under!*

The wind had a bite. It was cold up here, though Jesse didn't really mind the icy wind flow. The wing wires were singing, though he couldn't hear them. The sun was out strong and the sky was deep blue and the Yellow Peril was turning north now, over farmland. And there was airspace forever, only disturbed by other Yellow Perils. One, off to the left, maybe a mile away, was doing acrobatics, sun bouncing off the slick, dope-coated fuselage. *What a moment!*

"We'll do a few of those within a week," Christensen shouted. He added, "Eighty knots."

Jesse knew that the top cruising speed was about 90 knots. From the calm, crisp voice on the gosport, he believed that the instructor was enjoying himself too.

"Okay, we use basic commands up here. When I say, 'I have it,' I have control. When I say, 'You have it,' you have control. When we change control, I want you to acknowledge by wiggling the stick. When I have it, I want you to follow me through on the controls so that you'll feel every maneuver, every movement. When you have it, I'll stay off the controls unless I need to come back on for safety reasons. Now, wiggle the stick if you read me . . ." Jesse wiggled it, suppressing a laugh. *Oh Lord, I'm a kid again.*

Oh Lord, I'm already in heaven.

On both sides and ahead, the sky faded into a gauzy horizon. Looking up, the distance to the roof seemed endless. Sun shimmered off Lake Michigan. The early aviators had discovered this new world, above land and sea, but hadn't been able to describe it. He'd read that in a book by Antoine de Saint-Exupéry long ago. It was true, he knew now. This was a new world, a private one, far from earth, adventuring beyond it.

As if showing a baby how to walk, Christensen began to exercise the Stearman in smooth and easy maneuvers. More banks and climbs. Jesse found his body fighting the banks, leaning to the other side, attempting to remain straight. He heard the lieutenant shout, "Go with it!" without looking back. He knew what was happening in the rear cockpit, could see in that mirror.

Jesse responded and let the plane take control of his body. Soon he was "going with it." Dawkins had said that some people were natural athletes, could play baseball, football, basketball; some were natural swimmers; then there were natural pilots, and they often turned out to be good athletes as well. *Maybe Dawkins was right.*

After an hour of flight, Jesse loving every split second of it, every minute of it, he thought that maybe he'd be a natural pilot, after all. A hawk, an osprey, a rider of the wind.

From the gosport he could hear, "We're going home."

All too soon, Jesse thought. *Much too soon.*

Chris, descending, guided the Stearman back to the Glenview main runway. "Watch the altitude. Watch and listen. I'm going to parallel the landing strip on the downwind leg." He cut the power back to idle and began a gentle left-hand turn.

"Remember, Jesse, we make our approach at sixty-five knots, power off. We make a hundred-and-eighty-degree turn, line up with the runway, and make a three-point landing. Stall speed is forty-six knots."

Jesse listened and watched the altimeter, the stick; he felt every movement. The gentle turn, the heading approaching the runway. He mentally checked off the steps:

Speed sixty-five knots, lined up. Going down, going down.
Stick coming back.
Aircraft just above the runway. Maybe fifteen feet.
Stick coming back all the way.

Then touchdown, with a very slight jolt in the three-point attitude.

Lord God! Oh Lord God.

As the lieutenant cut the engine after they'd taxied up to the flight line, Jesse shook his head at the wonder of it all; at this day that he'd always treasure if he went no farther than Glenview. *How can I be so lucky to have found the path to the sky?*

As they headed back toward the hangar, the lieutenant talked about his favorite subject. "You've got to become convinced that your airplane is designed to fly and wants to fly. Your job is to guide it into various kinds of performance and attitudes. . . ."

When they were about twenty feet from the hangar's main entrance, a head poked out of the instructor's ready room. "Looks like you developed an oil leak, Chris." Then a laugh.

Jesse felt like he'd been slapped in the face. The words didn't need interpretation. He'd never heard himself referred to as an "oil leak." He looked up and saw a half-bald head. The pilot was grinning at them.

Christensen looked up too in dismay. "Thanks, Bob," he said.

They continued on into the hangar. "You may get that kind of crap for the next year and a half. Ride with it, Jesse."

"I'll try, sir." *Ride with it or quit now. Take the insults! Get the wings!*

"See you in the morning," Chris said.

"Yes, sir." Jesse saluted him, trying to put his mind back on the flight, keep it on the flight, not on oil leaks.

He went by Gus Gillespie's room on the way back to his own. The Dartmouth student had gone out of his way to be friendly since they had met on the bus.

Jesse saw that he was packing. "What are you doing?"

Gillespie lifted his head. His eyes were red-rimmed. "I threw up all over the cockpit. I took Dramamine right after breakfast and thought I'd be okay. We started doing banks and turns and I held it as long as I could. The instructor was watching me in that damn mirror."

"You mean you don't have a second chance?"

"No. The instructor brought the plane back down just after I vomited and sent me to see the flight surgeon. He asked if I ever got seasick. I admitted I did. He said air sickness was compounded by fear of flying and that's all she wrote. I argued, but he said it was for my own good. How'd your day go?"

Jesse didn't quite know what to say to the Dartmouth guy. "I managed okay."

He wrote Daisy a long letter that night, attempting to describe the first flight and all that he felt about it. He knew he wasn't doing it justice. It would take a poet. He didn't mention the bald-headed instructor or the "oil leak." He told her about Gus Gillespie with sadness but was all too aware that it happened daily.

5

Glenview Naval Air Station

March 21, 1947

The fourth day had begun with half an hour of infantry drill, a repeat of the day before, a repeat of those NROTC afternoons three times a week at Columbus. Midmorning found Jesse on the flight line, waiting for the lieutenant to return from a scheduled hop. The buzzing of the Yellow Perils was constant. They provided entertainment.

There was one more missing face. SAVELO, W. D. of Philadelphia had washed out on his first time up. He'd decided he didn't want to be a pilot after all. By nightfall, DELAPP, K. had replaced Savelo. Jesse had been told that roommates would come and go over the next months, that it would be a merry-go-round. The services were unique in that respect.

Baker and Bidwell were still left. He'd barely talked to them. They weren't unfriendly. They'd just paired off and the time at Glenview would be short, anyway. He'd keep occupied and cordial. If he found a friend, great. If not, okay too.

After the flight the day before, he'd gone to the gym to

shoot some baskets and had gotten into a pickup game when a player hurt his ankle and dropped out. At Eureka High he'd played guard and had spent time, when he could, on the OSU court. Not as a member of the team; he just played to have fun.

After Jesse scored eight points, an officer had come over. "You look pretty good. Want to join the station team?"

"I won't be here that long, sir."

"I realize that. You guys come and go every week. We still field a basketball team."

"Okay with me, sir."

Now Christensen's Yellow Peril 206 touched down on the runway and Jesse watched as it moved quickly to its parking spot. There was constant traffic, with aircraft landing every minute or so and taking off at almost the same rate.

After the prop stopped whirling and the engine died with a chug, the lieutenant and his student climbed out. "You did fine, Hoover," Christensen said. "Tomorrow I want to see you get out of a stall."

Hoover, whoever he was, looked relieved. He broke into a smile and saluted. So tomorrow he'd have to get out of a stall. That was okay with an instructor sitting in front of you. Stalls were sometimes fatal. Jesse wondered how many flights Hoover had made.

Christensen called over, "We need some gas. It'll be a few minutes."

"Yes, sir."

Jesse clearly remembered reading about stalls. One book had said:

> To practice a stall, pull the nose high, the airspeed drops and keep the stick back and wait for the shudder, the nose falls, and you recover speed. But . . . if the aircraft falls in a spin, you will be in trouble if you don't recover. Don't stall at low altitude.

While the plane was being refueled, Jesse stood beside the lieutenant, who marveled, "You know they made more than ten thousand of these things in Wichita during the war. A lot of them have already been sold off as surplus. With new 450-HP engines in them, they're great crop dusters. You won't find a sweeter airplane than the Stearman."

Sweeter? Jesse didn't think he'd ever hear a plane called "sweet." *Yet maybe that's what pilots are all about. They have love affairs with their sweethearts and their wives and they have love affairs with their aircraft. And it follows that they also have terrible experiences with some planes and are killed by them. That's flying,* Jesse thought.

The ground crew refueler soon said, "All done," and the tank truck pulled away to load another Yellow Peril.

Teacher and student waddled toward the airplane, parachutes banging their behinds, and climbed in, Christensen first.

The routine began again: *Crank into the inertia starter, the smoky cough, the engine roar, the jouncing taxiing to the runway; then the sprint down it, the liftoff; then FLIGHT, as magical as on hawk's wings.*

Christensen guided upward to 5,000 feet. Jesse watched the altimeter closely, trying to read all the instruments, trying to figure out what they were saying.

There were white puffballs of clouds now unlike that blue Delft bowl of the day before. *Perhaps no two days up here are exactly alike.* Jesse looked around. He'd never thought too much about the weather in Mississippi. There'd been the damp heat of summer and thunderstorms racing out of blue-black clouds, earthshaking rumbles and swords of lightning; hail that machine-gunned the sharecroppers' tin roofs. The weather was another thing about this business of flying.

The gosport came to life. "Okay, we'll do some simple things now, Jesse. I told you yesterday how the movement of the ailerons is controlled by side pressure on the stick. It causes the airplane to roll or bank in the direction of the pressure applied. Pressure to the right causes the right wing to go down and brings the left wing up. . . ."

He talked Jesse through the movement of the elevators and pressure on the rudder pedal, causing the airplane to swing or yaw about its vertical axis in the direction of the pressure. "Your hand and your feet control this aircraft; your brain controls your hand and your feet. Got it?"

Jesse nodded and answered, forgetting that the gosport was one-way communicator—teacher to student.

"Now, I'm going to bring the nose up. Slow down and put us into a stall."

The engine changed rhythm suddenly. The sound of the wind rushing across the open cockpit changed to that of a calm breeze, then faded away, and the Yellow Peril, without wing-lift, began to fall like a bird that had been shot. Then it began to spin.

Jesse felt a moment of panic.

The nose was falling swiftly to earth.

Jesse gritted his teeth and held on.

Christensen's calm Nebraska voice came over the gosport. "Now, we're going to recover. Stabilize first." The engine roared again and the Yellow Peril and the horizon, which was at a crazy angle, just a few seconds earlier, soon became stable and level.

Christensen repeated the stall procedure three times and each time it became less frightening.

"You see why we do this at five thousand feet."

Jesse nodded emphatically.

After the last time, the lieutenant leveled off at 3,000 feet and said, "Okay, your aircraft, Jesse." The speed needle stood at 66 knots.

He didn't think those words would come so soon. He wasn't prepared for them on this, his second flight.

"You have it," the hollow gosport voice said.

Jesse wiggled the stick to acknowledge.

The gosport voice said, "Increase your speed, Jesse."

His left hand pushed the throttle. The Lycoming answered with a happy roar.

Jesse's feet experimented with the rudder and Stearman No. 261 yawed to port, then to starboard.

The gosport said, "Gently, Jesse, gently."

Jesse was amazed at how little pressure was needed to turn the plane.

Christensen said, "Go gently, Jesse." The calmness of his voice helped slow the heartbeat.

He hadn't moved the stick. The aircraft was flying itself, as if it was on an unseen highway in the sky.

Christensen said, "Fly it, Jesse. . . ."

He moved the stick gently forward and the nose dropped. He edged it back and the machine rose. To the left, gently again, and the left wing settled. Center and he was level. To the right, and the right wing settled.

Good Lord Almighty, I'm FLYING. Look up here at me. Up here, Daisy and Mama and Papa and Marvin and William and Lura and Fletcher and Ike Heard and Martin Luther Beard and Professor Burger. And Johnny—yes, poor dead Johnny. I'm FLYING!

"You're doing fine," Christensen said.

Yes, I am. I'm doing fine!

On Saturday, March 22, Jesse boarded an R4D, the Navy's designation for the famed DC-3, twin-engined workhorse of civilian aviation, for a flight to Pensacola, Florida.

As the latest addition to Glenview's basketball team, he would play guard against the Pensacola Naval Air Station quintet.

In addition to the fun of racing up and down the hardwood court, he'd have the chance to fly in something quite different from the Yellow Perils, his first time in a large aircraft. He told Christensen that he was excited about both the ride and the game.

Pensacola was the cradle of naval aviation. The first Navy fliers in the pioneer days of World War I had trained over the Gulf of Mexico. The Navy and Marine aces of World War II, roaring into the air off the *Yorktown, Lexington, Hornet,* and other historic flattops, had streaked down the runways of Saufley, Corry, Whiting, and Barin fields. Pensacola *was* naval aviation.

The team was a mixture of would-be pilots and permanent Glenview station personnel. Jesse enjoyed talking to his seatmate over the noise of the Pratt & Whitney engines. The service R4Ds, except those awarded to admirals, were not soundproofed. The flight from Illinois took more than five hours.

Approaching the air station over the sunny bay, Jesse caught a glimpse of the old buildings and rows of beautiful houses where senior officers lived. His seatmate said that Pensacola, once a naval shipyard, had cannon and powder magazines that dated to the Civil War. The transport landed at Chevalier Field at Mainside Administration.

A tractor-drawn "cattle car," the most ignoble four-wheeled type of transportation on earth, seen at military bases around the world, took the team to the Pensacola gym. Game time was six o'clock and muscles, grown stiff on the flight, needed to be stretched. It was now four-thirty.

Jesse peeled out of his dungarees and put on the Glenview basketball uniform in the dressing room. He began to warm up out on the court and noticed that his coach, a senior lieutenant named Horton, was arguing with another officer on the left sideline near the visitor bench. Horton was waving his hand and shaking his head.

After Jesse had done a round of shooting baskets, Horton called him over. "Jesse, I'm sorry, but you can't play tonight."

"Why not?" Sweat was pouring down his face.

"Because you're a Negro." Horton seemed wildly angry.

"That's the only reason?" Jesse asked with disbelief.

"Yes, goddamn it. Florida is segregated and I was told you shouldn't have been allowed in the dressing room. My fault, Jesse. I didn't tell them in advance. It just didn't occur to me. I'm from Chicago. You can't even be on the bench. You can sit in the colored bleachers."

Jesse stood in silence for a moment. "But, Mr. Horton, this isn't a civilian place. This is a military base! Doesn't that make it different?"

"It should, but in this case it doesn't. I can't appeal to the commanding officer. He's away for the weekend. The bastard exec made the decision. It's an order. You were spotted when you got off the cattle car."

"Okay."

Horton said, "I'm sorry, and I'm ashamed."

Jesse nodded and headed for the dressing room. A teammate came in.

"What are you doing?"

Jesse said, "I've got a stomach ache."

"Too bad."

Yes, it is. Too bad for everyone. He didn't go to the colored bleachers. He had tennis shoes and his basketball shirt and trunks. He found the track and ran until his throat burnt and his guts felt knife-cut.

Yellow Peril 216 was churning along at 5,000 feet and Lieutenant Christensen spoke into the gosport: "Jesse, make sure your seat belt is fastened as tight as it'll go."

Jesse checked it. It was already as tight as it would go. Below was Lake Michigan.

"We're going to do a slow roll. Follow me on the controls; watch the horizon."

Again there was sudden apprehension. Before they took off, the lieutenant had said, "We'll do a few acrobatics today. You may never use them in combat. The idea is to build your confidence, make you trust the aircraft and yourself. You can't do it in level flight. . . ."

He followed the stick movement and felt the plane rolling over, as if it were on a skewer. The horizon turned upside down, along with Jesse's stomach, fear making his hands grasp the seat. He felt the seat and shoulder straps restrain his body. Then 216 completed the roll and Jesse felt his muscles relax. He was still part of the aircraft.

"Again," said Christensen and this time Jesse felt a little more at ease.

They made a few clearing turns to check on other aircraft, then Christensen said, "All right, we'll do a loop. Follow me again on the controls and watch for the horizon when we're on top."

Jesse had seen the rolls and loops over that dirt airfield back in Hattiesburg as a boy, gulping and wide-eyed, but seeing them and doing them were two different things. For a few seconds, he wondered if he really wanted to be a pilot.

The gosport said, "We'll nose her over, give it more power, and build up speed. We need a hundred and ten knots to do a loop. We'll try for a perfect circle. If we do it right, we may feel our slipstream at the bottom of it. . . ."

The nose went over, and the Lycoming picked up decibels.

"In a good loop, you stay pretty much in your seat. If we flatten out or hang up a little on top, you'll hang on your seat belt. . . ."

Suddenly Jesse was upside down, hearing the Lycoming roaring, surprised that gravity didn't pull his body out of the seat; he felt only a slight rushing in his head. He was on a roller coaster at 4,000 feet. He acknowledged his fright as they went down again and leveled off.

He saw Christensen monitoring his face. He tried to smile but couldn't.

"Once more. When we get to the top of the loop, I want you to put both hands up in the air. Don't hold on to anything. Trust your seat belt."

Jesse nodded, holding his breath again. Was this necessary?

"Here we go. Keep your eyes open."

At the top of the loop, upside down again, head pointed to the waters of Lake Michigan, Jesse raised his arms and laughed, even though his heart was pounding.

They did four more loops that late morning, Jesse's belly hanging on the safety belt, and then Christensen said, "Okay, Jesse, I've shown you how. You do it."

Jesse looked into the mirror. The lieutenant's hazel eyes were nailing him. He hadn't expected it to happen so soon.

He nodded and eased the stick forward, opened the throttle, picking up airspeed; then, trying to duplicate Christensen's loops, he pulled back on the stick and up they went, looping. Jesse pulled the plane on through and let out a yell.

Christensen gave him a thumbs-up and said into the gosport, "Not bad. Do it again."

Soon the Yellow Peril was headed back to the air station with Jesse at the controls.

One day the rain slanted down and hit the windshield, skimming over his head. One day he flew in clouds, guiding around them. Every day was better; every day was sweeter.

For the next seven flights, Jesse made all the takeoffs and landings. They weren't at all perfect, but even experienced pilots sometimes had problems with the three-pointers if there was a crosswind. Jesse didn't ground loop but could feel the slight lean and yaw that might lead to an embarrassing "downer" if he was slow to correct.

Throughout all the flying, the lieutenant had kept score in the front cockpit, filling out a form that would become part of Jesse Leroy Brown's flight records. They covered every conceivable aspect from cockpit check to emergencies in flight. On the ninth day, Christensen noted:

> This student works very hard. Is interested and asks questions. He uses his head, thinks, makes corrections. Flies and holds attitudes good. Student is ready for solo.

Except for initial takeoffs and final landings at the air station, all traffic patterns and landings were practiced at Arlington Racetrack, outside of Chicago. The horse track had been leased to the Navy during the war for primary flight training. The large grassy surface in the center of the track was more forgiving than asphalt or concrete.

On Tuesday, April 1, 1947, Jesse entered the traffic pattern at Arlington, made what he considered two good landings, and then the gosport voice said, "Taxi back upwind to the big tree at the far end of the field." He hadn't been told he'd solo this day.

As they sat with the engine idling and the prop turning slowly, Christensen turned and said, "Well, I think we've done everything required of us."

He got out of the cockpit and stood on the wing. "Take-offs, landings, stalls, spins, rectangular patterns, emergency forced landings. Now, I'm going to sit down in the grass over here and relax while you go fly around the field a couple of times. Then make three landings and come pick me up. You ready?"

"Yes, sir." Jesse grinned his thanks and waited until the lieutenant stood clear. He opened the throttle and the plane gathered speed, lifted up into the air, and made two tight circles. He could see Christensen down on the grass.

Solo. Every beginning pilot's first goal is to be totally in command of the aircraft, the front seat *empty*. No one to tell him what to do or how to do it. Confidence built with every minute that passed. He'd be totally responsible for the aircraft. He could fly it; he could land it. He could make two inches on that flight up the side of Mount Everest, as Lieutenant Dawkins had so uniquely put it.

He "shot" the three landings without a problem and after the last one picked up the lieutenant and flew the plane back to the air station, parking it handily.

Walking away from the flight line, Christensen said, "I'm proud of you, Jesse, for a lot of reasons. I honestly think you'll be a fine naval aviator." Jesse could see that he meant it sincerely.

Jesse didn't quite know how to express his gratitude to this calm and gentle white man from Nebraska. He'd heard some bad things about instructors, from Dawkins and others, but Christensen had encouraged him from the start. He had been patient; he'd taught him well.

They departed with a handshake. "I'm going to keep in touch with you," Jesse said. The lieutenant said, "I hope so."

But it wasn't over. The Navy had a way of making sure that candidates like Brown, J. L., were for real and deserved to go on to Pre-Flight. Sometimes instructors became too friendly with students, cut corners a bit to see them advance. So, for the final solo, a "check" pilot, a total stranger, rode the front cockpit and observed from the ground. His name was Breen, the first of many check pilots. He noted in his report:

```
Good basic airwork. Soloed very well. Completed
two safe solo landings.
```

Hot dog! Jesse used Western Union to tell Daisy he'd finished at Glenview, that he was headed for Iowa. The dream he'd had since he'd been ten, since the days at Lux School, was about to become a reality.

6

Kelly's Settlement, Mississippi

September 1940

While still living in Lux, Jesse had enrolled in Bay Springs High School, closer to Hattiesburg, to finish up his secondary education. There was no school bus to take him back and forth to Bay Springs. Walking or hitchhiking daily didn't seem to be a good option, so Julia made arrangements with a family to board Jesse four days a week in exchange for work after school.

Jesse didn't like Bay Springs from the moment he entered, but he did like the cinder track and ran five or six miles daily. The school was one of the poorest in the state and the teachers struggled to give the Negro students even a basic education.

The Browns soon moved on to Kelly's Settlement, part of the white folks' Eatonville, and a nicer farmhouse, though still without electricity or running water. Eatonville was essentially a brick school for whites and a general store; still sharecropper country, still piney woods country, still redneck. Kelly's Settlement, "cullud town," was a little larger than Lux, but some of the white landowners were remarkably like the Ingrams.

Without a car, transportation was always a problem, but the Browns usually found neighbors who'd take them to the Sunday services at Shady Grove Baptist Church. God remained their strength and hope. Sometimes any or all of the Browns could be found walking from Kelly's Settlement to Hattiesburg. Sometimes they rode a wagon. In the summer heat, Julia would hide beneath her umbrella. Generally, some driver—black or white—would pick her up.

The Browns never looked for trouble at Kelly's Settlement but seldom ran away from it when it came. Jesse didn't. The dollops of warrior blood, via the reservations at Meridian, surged on occasion.

Fletcher, whom Jesse had aptly nicknamed "Mule," was out in their pasture on a Saturday afternoon when Jack Bailey, a strapping white in his early twenties, rode up on his horse and yelled, "Hey, boy, open that gate." He wanted to take a shortcut.

"Boy," to black ears was always a fuse, of course. Slavery had done that.

Fletcher yelled back defiantly, "Boy, Papa doesn't want this gate opened."

Bailey said, "Nigger boy, I'm comin' in there to whup your ass." He opened the gate and entered.

Fletcher picked up an oak limb and stood his ground but called for Jesse, who was up by the house.

Jesse came on the run, saw his younger, much smaller brother with the limb, backing away from the six-foot Bailey.

A bruising head-on tackle and then Jack Bailey got battered around his face. He was left on the ground, stunned and bleeding from the teenager's attack.

Jesse stood watch silently until the humiliated Bailey left the pasture and got back on his horse.

Any attack on a white person was almost certain to get a

reaction and before sundown Bailey's father drove his pickup through the road gate. The embarrassed son had stayed home.

Papa John was ready for him. He was sitting in one of the two front porch rockers. He had a .38-caliber pistol in his hip pocket. A .10-gauge double-barreled shotgun was on his lap; a Winchester .74 rifle rested in the doorway. With a straw hat on his large head, overall straps over his bare shoulders, his biceps bulging, John Brown was a formidable sight.

Julia, Jesse, Lura, and Fletcher stood near John.

As Bailey Sr. approached, John spoke first, dangerously calm. "Mr. Bailey, what happened this afternoon was unfortunate. But no one was hurt bad. I think we ought to leave it like that."

Mr. Bailey eyed the guns and John for a moment, then said, "I think you're right, John." He drove away. Jesse well remembered that afternoon.

For the next two nights, John and the neighboring farmers took turns patrolling the houses. If the Browns had owned the house, it might have been torched. Jesse remembered walking with his papa, who carried the .10-gauge.

Only cricket chirps caused a disturbance.

Services were over at Shady Grove Baptist on this December Sunday and the Browns, always in their best clothes, John in coat and tie, were on the stoop talking with Reverend Woullard, a baldheaded bull of a country preacher, when a neighbor kid came running up. "War is on!" he blurted out, gasping. He'd run several miles. "Japanese aircraft have attacked Pearl Harbor . . . bombing the Navy base there . . . ships sunk. . . ." He panted it out.

Jesse said, "What are you talkin' about?"

"I swear it . . . we got a war on . . . you go home and listen. . . ." Joe Riddick was shaking with excitement. His chest was heaving. By now, the Browns had a Philco radio powered by a car battery. Battery time was precious.

Reverend Woullard said, "Where is Pearl Harbor?" Many Americans were asking the same question.

Julia said worriedly, "It's in the Hawaiian Islands. . . ." They went home.

She had five boys to think about. Marvin was classified 4-F because of his tilted head and would not go into service. John had served in an all-black cavalry battalion in World War I, training to go overseas when the fighting ended more than twenty years earlier.

Life changed for the Browns that late morning, as well as most other Americans. War against Germany, Italy, and Japan was soon declared.

A few days later, coming across a wintry cornfield, unloaded shotguns safely over their shoulders, Jesse, his friend Easter Slawe, and Lura each had a pair of rabbits for their efforts. Around much of Mississippi, hunting was for food, not sport. Dogs trotted with them.

"I just don't talk about it anymore. All I said the other night at supper was that President Roosevelt has ordered the Army Air Force to accept some of us for pilot training and it started a ruckus. Mama, as usual."

Easter said, "Think they'll do it? Put those fancy wings on us black boys so we can strut aroun'? 'Off we go into the wild, blue yonder.' Man, will we get girls!"

"You know how it happened?"

Easter shook his head. Jesse had gone to school with Easter at Bay Springs.

"The President's wife was at Tuskegee and C. Alfred Anderson took her up for forty minutes. She said she'd heard that colored people couldn't fly airplanes. When she got back to the White House, she told the President that he should start a flying school for us at Tuskegee, and that's what he did. The story was in the *Courier*."

John allowed the family ten minutes of battery time every other night to listen to NBC or CBS. He got the battery charged at the nearby black-run filling station. Jesse kept up with the war as best he could.

He seldom hitchhiked to the old tin hangar anymore but hadn't lost his interest in aviation. With all that was happening—four-engine planes being built, huge bombers— he'd postpone those plans until after the war was over. Even Corley Yates had left town to go work as a mechanic on an Army Air Force base in Alabama. Now and then, he thought about Corley.

Hattiesburg, Mississippi

October 1942

Childhood had passed. Just turned sixteen, Jesse was smoothly muscled and had become a good athlete. He'd transferred from subpar Bay Springs to Eureka High School, in Hattiesburg itself, hoping for a better education. Jesse was living with his oldest brother Marvin at his aunt's house, 816 Whitney Street. Marvin taught science at the school.

He was reunited with cousin Ike Heard, his childhood playmate on decrepit Dewey Street. The "shotgun" houses came alive, though they hadn't seen each other in ten years. Immediately, starting the eleventh grade together, they were close friends again.

At 140 pounds, Jesse was a speedy halfback on the Eureka football team, played basketball, and was even better at track and field as a runner and long jumper. He found he had a talent for math, though he didn't know why. It seemed to come naturally. He was the top math student in his junior class. Already, he'd gone beyond his mama's level. He was taking French.

The high school campus was mostly red clay with a few straggly clumps of grass, often muddy when it rained and dusty in dry spells. It was a typical Mississippi Negro school of that day: used books brought over from the white schools; used football and basketball uniforms brought over from the white schools; used band instruments. Used everything.

Julia had said, "We have to make do with what we have. We can't change the color of our skin. We can only hope for better days."

When? Jesse thought.

Jesse had known about separate toilets, separate drinking fountains, the back of buses since he was three or four. He'd always bitterly resented the walks to the back of the bus. They seemed like a hot mile.

The problem was that better days in Mississippi weren't in sight. And it was certainly true what Mama had said, there was no way to change the color of his skin. Leaving was the only option. Sure, the Browns had heard about the North and about how colored folks were treated up there, but none of them, except Julia, had ever seriously considered leaving the piney woods. Julia was ready to go "because of education opportunities."

In time, Jesse knew he would go; he was absolutely certain of it. He didn't plan to work in a local warehouse like his papa had done or a lumber mill for white bosses. In time—and it might be a long time—he'd fly a DC-3 passenger plane. If he couldn't fly for a white-run airline, he'd find a way to buy a plane and fly black people around the South with his own airline. The hell with the color line.

He said that to Ike Heard and Ike said, shaking his head, "Jesse, you are a lunatic. Black folks aren't gonna fly aroun' in airplanes. They're too scared an' takin' the bus is all they can afford. . . ."

"I'm thinking 'bout tomorrow, Ike."

Ike lived on Atlanta Street, where Jesse was born, two streets over from Jesse's aunt. Jesse often came by Ike's house and he saw him in school. Ike kept talking about architecture. He was planning to apply to Hampton Institute in Virginia. He said, "We'd make a great team." But Jesse had been thinking about flying for so long that he couldn't envision any other career.

Sometimes Jesse would stop "Professor" Nathaniel Burger, the principal, in the hallway to ask about an advanced problem. The tall, thin graying man with the pencil mustache also taught geometry and always wore a tailored suit and tie to set an example. Occasionally, Jesse went to Burger's home at night if there was something he couldn't solve. It was true what his mama had said: "Just ask."

He tried to keep abreast of what was happening at Tuskegee. All primary training over there was being done by Negro pilots, but the flying instructors were white, according to the *Courier*. Tuskegee Airmen, now numbering more than 400, helped one another, boosted each other against a usually white enemy, he read. Negro officers could not stay at nearby Maxwell Air Corps Base, couldn't enter the officer's dining room or club. Most white pilots did not want them as wingmen; didn't trust them, they said. Jesse shook his head reading the *Courier*.

Overseas, black pilots of Squadron 99 were soon to shoot down Nazi planes at a rate equal to those of white groups.

"I don't understand," he said to Ike. "We keep hearing about the white heroes, but only the *Courier* and the *Defender* pay any attention to our people."

One day in late spring, 1943, Jesse went to Professor Burger's office to talk about college, saying he'd been thinking of Ohio State, a long way from the piney woods. He'd maintained an A average since transferring from Bay Springs. He could thank his mama for that.

"Why Ohio State?" Burger asked. Boys from Eureka, if they wanted to go to college, usually picked Alcorn or Tuskegee or Hampton or Howard. If Jesse wanted to be educated in Ohio, all-black Wilberforce was in Columbus.

"Another Jesse went there."

"He's your hero?"

"One of them."

Owens had attended OSU and had won the 100- and 200-meter dashes, as well as the long jump, in the historic 1936 Olympics, held in Berlin.

"I think I might get a track and field scholarship. At least, I'll try for one." Jesse was the best Negro track and field performer in the state that year, competing with other black runners and jumpers.

"I know a little about Owens," Burger said. "There were no athletic scholarships at Ohio State then. He had to wait tables and serve white students, work in the library. He ran an elevator five to midnight seven days a week. Are you prepared for that? Who are your other heroes?"

"Joe Louis." The heavyweight boxing champion of the world.

Burger nodded. Louis was the first Negro to win the Associated Press Athlete of the Year Award in 1935 and Owens followed in 1936. "Who else, Jesse?"

"Charles Lindbergh and Eugene Bullard, the first Negro pilot."

"Well, you've got some good heroes and Ohio State is a fine university, but I think you might be shooting too high. What about Alcorn or Tuskegee?"

"I want to go to a white university. I want to see if I can compete with them on the track and in the classrooms."

Burger was proud of Jesse and all the boys in this class. He called them his "pride and joy." Almost all of them wanted to go to college. Ike Heard had told Burger he wanted to be an architect. Martin Luther Beard had told him he wanted to be a medical doctor. There were others shooting for the top. Now Jesse Brown wanted to take on Ohio State.

"You talk this over with your mother?"

"Yes, I did. She thinks like you do, but I don't want to go to a Negro college. I'd breeze through."

"I doubt you'd breeze through. But if you can get into Ohio State, that's fine. What do you want to do? I've never asked you."

"I want to be a commercial pilot, but they don't have a flying school. So I think I'll try architectural engineering." Ike had finally talked him into it.

"An architect, eh?"

"An architectural engineer," Jesse corrected. "There's a difference, I've heard. I'll deal in materials for skyscrapers. The architects ask the engineers about tensile strength of metals and girders and materials like that—at least, that's what I'm told."

Burger, impressed, said, "I'll try to help you get into Ohio State."

Several days later, Burger stopped Jesse in the hallway to say, "There were only seven Negroes to receive diplomas from Ohio State last year." It sounded like a warning.

After graduating from Alcorn State Burger had taken his master's degree in education from Cornell University, one of the few blacks on campus. He'd suffered.

Spring had come to southern Mississippi with warmth and moist April greenery. Jesse's class of 1944 was about to graduate the eight boys and twenty-four girls and in a few months he'd be registering for the draft. Though the Allies seemed to be winning, fighting was still fierce in Europe and the Pacific islands. Julia Brown's nightly and Sunday prayers beseeched God to end the gunfire. An uncle was flying a P-38 with the Tuskegee Airmen.

It was nearing time for the Eureka senior prom and he stood in a group that included Ike Heard. They were near the school shop building, not far away from half a dozen girls who always gathered there for the lunch break.

Jesse had been watching one of them, Daisy Pearl Nix, a pretty, slender sophomore, with large expressive eyes. He'd watched her for almost two years. There was something about her that had attracted him at first sight. Having never had a girlfriend, not even dated, maybe it was time to start.

Finally, just before the bell rang, he walked over. "I'm Jesse Brown. . . ."

Daisy, surprised that he'd approached her, said, "I know who you are." The athlete, the whiz kid; he was talked about a lot on campus, a plum to be picked.

Snook Hardy overheard the invitation and Daisy soon began giving Snook a play-by-play of the budding romance.

Daisy, also known as "Tootie," went home and told her mother she'd been invited by Jesse Brown to go to the prom. Her late father had given her the nickname of "Tootie" and everyone thought it fit her perfectly. She was lively, full of sparks and laughter, full of music.

Addie Nix was known in the neighborhood as "M'dear Miz Addie" and was also known as an up-front, no-nonsense, straighttalking, churchgoing lady. Mrs. Addie was a maid for different white families in Hattiesburg. She didn't take nonsense from them either. Oldest of seven children, life had never been easy for Addie Nix. She'd given birth to Daisy at the age of fourteen.

After Brad Nix died, when Daisy was thirteen, leaving twenty-eight-year-old Addie with the five children, she took in ironing at home in addition to working as a domestic. There was no welfare in Mississippi and M'dear Miz Addie was too proud to accept handouts. Daisy often went along to help her mother while a grandmother baby-sat the smaller children.

"Who is Jesse Brown?" Addie asked, already suspicious.

Daisy said he was a nice boy, track star, a good scholar, went to church at Shady Grove; family lived in Kelly's Settlement; he was now working nights as a waiter at the white-owned Holmes Club, saving money to go to college. The Holmes Club, with a rowdy reputation for beer-drinking, was a haunt for GIs from Camp Shelby and Mike Lowry, its owner, was said to be involved in bootlegging.

Addie said, "No!" Flat and firm, Daisy later told Jesse. No nightclub beer-drinking boys around her daughter.

Daisy pleaded Jesse's case but got nowhere, and went two doors away to Miss Lucy May's house, asking for help. Lucy May had been a beautician in Chicago. She was worldly and refereed other disputes in the neighborhood.

She accompanied Daisy Pearl back home and began sweet-talking Mrs. Addie, saying she'd fix Daisy's hair and that she had a dress that Daisy could wear with a little alteration. "All Daisy Pearl will have to buy are shoes and a bag."

"You don't even know this boy."

"I know about him."

"Please let her go," said Lucy May.

Addie turned to her daughter. "You tell Jesse Brown I want to talk to him. Then I'll make up my mind."

The next day, relating what had happened, Daisy said to Jesse, "You have to get permission from my mama."

Jesse hesitated, then said, "I'll come up Sunday afternoon." The Holmes Club was shuttered on Sundays, due to the "blue law," an institution in the deep South.

He lived across town and about four o'clock got off the bus at the bottom of the hill. The Nix house was at 105 May Street. After a difficult period of answering questions, including beer drinking, Jesse was told that Daisy Pearl had to be home by midnight, "safe and sound." He knew what she meant.

Jesse quickly agreed and quickly departed, but in the remaining weeks before the prom he talked with Daisy at every opportunity, falling in love with her. He told her he wanted to be a pilot and she was impressed. She didn't know any other boys who knew what they wanted to be.

They took long walks and made dates to see movies with another couple, then had ice cream on the way home. There really wasn't any place in Hattiesburg for young Negro couples except church socials. No one in their circle had a car.

There was a choice of walking or riding the back of the bus. They preferred to walk.

Jesse and Daisy dated whenever they could, wrote letters to each other. Neither had access to a phone.

Three mornings before the prom, a letter from Columbus, Ohio, in hand, Jesse searched the Eureka hallways for Daisy and found her going into English I. He yelled, "I got in! I got in. . . ." and swung her off her feet.

"Got in where?"

"Ohio State!"

Eyes glistening, she said, "Oh, Jesse. . . ."

Putting her down, he dodged through the pack of students, heading for the office of Professor Burger.

Jesse hadn't traveled very much. He had only been to Jackson, Laurel, Biloxi, and a few other places inside Mississippi. Staring down at the Ohio State form telling him to report on campus September 27, 1944, he had a sudden hollow feeling. He wasn't too concerned about the academics. The teachers at Eureka had done a good job, went out of their way to help him, and he wasn't afraid of not making the OSU track team. As usual, it was the age-old black-white conflict that made him suddenly apprehensive. He hadn't thought about it all that much.

He could apply for a dormitory room or live off-campus. The form didn't ask about race. Jesse looked at the two small choice boxes. *Two in a room? Suppose the other guy is white and from Georgia? Live off-campus? Find a rooming house?*

He took the form to Professor Burger at his home. "It's up to you, Jesse. The university is probably 98 percent or more white. You can't run from it. You're going to stand out like a stick of licorice on a vanilla cake."

"I don't plan to run from it. It's just that . . ." He'd never had to make a decision like this. *Put myself in a room with a white man? Sleep in there?*

Burger said, "You don't want to be embarrassed, right?"

Jesse nodded. "I heard a story about one of us who went

to Penn State and roomed by himself in a dorm. It wasn't because he wanted to be by himself. He went back to Alcorn."

"Okay, I have a friend in Columbus." He made a call to Ma Jenkins.

The last time they talked Burger said, "Jesse, I truly admire your courage. If you don't know it already, Ohio State has a bad reputation for racial attitudes and policies. Try to stand up for yourself."

Jesse said he would.

"Another thing," Burger said. "If you fail, always know that there are other places and people to help get you there. But it's not how or why you fail, it's how you handle it. You only fail if you do not learn from it." Burger had been saying that to his students for years at assemblies. Jesse had heard it before. *All true*, he thought.

On prom night Daisy wore a pale blue dress that had a fitted bodice and flared skirt, with minor alterations by Miss Lucy May. Her shoes and bag were silver. Her hair, by Miss Lucy May, was in an upsweep. Her corsage was made of pink carnations.

When Jesse came to pick her up in a car that Ike Heard had borrowed, her beaming sisters and Addie Nix were in the front room. Daisy stepped out of her room and Jesse said, "You're beautiful."

Addie promptly said, "Yes, she is."

Jesse, who looked pretty good himself in a white tux jacket, black pants, black shoes, and a black bow tie, returned her home just before midnight after telling himself he was going to marry Daisy Pearl Nix someday.

The Holmes Club was smoky and noisy and by late night the stench of beer was so strong that Jesse almost gagged on it. When Mike Lowry had hired him to wait tables late the previous year, he'd said, "Let's get somethin' straight, a lot of these soldier boys are from the South an' if you don't like bein' called a nigger, this ain't no place for you to work. A nigger is what you are. But you get your wattah hot an' your dander up an' I'll fire you quick as look at you. Okay?"

That word burned his ears and soured his guts. It had burned his ears and soured his guts long before Corley Yates. Jesse stared at Lowry, pulled in a breath, and said, "Okay, as long as they don't put their hands on me."

"I can't guarantee that, Jesse. You spill some beer on a drunk GI an' I can guarantee what'll happen."

A fight, of course.

"Let's jus' hope they won't be more'n words, okay?"

"Okay."

"You know a riot can get goin' in a place like this almost ovah nothin', these beered-up soldiers a long way from home an', packed in here like river herrin', can go off their rockers. . . ."

Jesse nodded that he understood.

"Anybody throws a punch at you, you duck and leave that table. I got three big 4-F farmboys as bouncers an' they do the fightin' here, understand?"

"Yes, sir."

"You got a good recommendation from that nigger pharmacist Hammond Smith where you worked last summer. He said you were a good boy."

"I'll thank him," Jesse said.

"I'm startin' you at six dollars a night plus your tips, if you get any. Be here at five, an' quittin' time is midnight, more or less. . . ."

Jesse said, "Thank you, Mr. Lowry," and went outside into the gray fall afternoon. He made it to the back of the building, then threw up. *Nigger.*

After four years of saving for college, wearing the same clothes, only splurging for a picture show now and then, he had a little over $600 in the Trustmark Bank account. He had no choice but to live with the gut-wrenching word.

The first night the leader of the jazz band, which was

composed entirely of elderly black musicians, said, "You jus' be polite an' keep your cool an' you'll be fine here. . . ."

As the GIs staggered around between the tables, spilling beer was a given, but only twice in almost a year was a punch thrown at him. He ducked it and retreated, letting the white farmboys take on their own kind. He tried to ignore the nigger boy name-calling.

Jesse told Ike Heard, who was working in a cotton broker's office that summer, consigned to the back room, not allowed to show his face up front, "I'm in training for ·Ohio State."

Ike knew what was happening at the Holmes Club and how Jesse was handling it, closing his ears night after night while being called "Nigger, nigger, nigger. . . ."

The night before Jesse was to leave for Columbus Mike Lowry stopped the music and stood up on a chair to announce he was going to pass the hat for Jesse Leroy Brown, a local boy who was going to enter Ohio State tomorrow. Stunned, richer by more than $700, Jesse went out into the night, fighting tears. Most of the contributors were white soldiers, many of them not making $25 a month. The main contributor was Mike Lowry himself.

Ottumwa, Iowa

April 10, 1947

John Brannon was startled when the Negro came through the door of Room 224, Barracks 10, bags in hand, introducing himself as Jesse Brown. The black man seemed friendly enough, he thought. Like Christensen, Brannon had never really been around Negroes and his honest preference would have been a white roommate. They exchanged small talk and Brannon decided he'd make the best of the situation.

Jesse thought that maybe the Navy should post an announcement: "Hey, there's a black man coming your way. He won't bite."

John Brannon was a compact Tennessean, fighter-pilot-size, most fighter pilots being medium- or small-sized. Long legs didn't tuck easily into fighter cockpits. He had a slow tinder-dry voice. He didn't ask Jesse how he'd arrived at Pre-Flight School at Ottumwa. In fact, he had no idea that Jesse was the first of his race to aim at Navy wings.

Jesse took the empty bunk and empty locker and began life in Iowa.

There were second looks. Of course. If your face was brown or black and you were isolated alongside almost 300 white faces, you'd naturally get a second look. It was no different than Glenview.

Christensen had said he'd probably be running into one or another of the trainees for as long as he was in the Navy. They'd sweat together, fly together, perhaps go to war together. Perhaps even die together.

He was already long awake in his top bunk when reveille sounded, followed by the strident barracks hallway loudspeaker ordering fall-in for muster: "Ten minutes to hit the toilets, the *heads*, get dressed, run down the stairs, assemble for calisthenics."

Aside from a few groans and moans, the scramble to and from the head was mostly silent and the bodies bounded down and out, tucking shirttails. Ever thus for pilot candidates beginning the second day at Ottumwa, intimidated by the bugle, the loudspeaker, unseen hard-eye pressure. "Get your asses into high gear. *Now!*" Brown, Brannon, Barker, and Anderson were already in high gear.

The chief petty officer, an enlisted man, awaited in the chilly quadrangle for the new class. "On the double, line up in ranks of three. Straight lines, you idiots," he yelled, loving it. In a brown winter jacket and razor-edged pants, fore-and-after khaki "doughboy" hat tugged over a graying blocky head, the chief looked like a World War II veteran out of central casting.

"C'mon, c'mon," the CPO yelled. "Second line, back up about three feet. Third, the same. You people deaf? I said straight lines. . . ." *Intimidate these collegiate mamas' boys!* His oblong shirt ID badge said: CHIEF AVIATION ORDNANCEMAN C. F. SHAW, USN.

The preliminaries of V-5 and Glenview were over at this very moment, Jesse knew. The drive to defeat 297 current candidates was under way, punish them until their bodies cried out, squeeze their brain cells, break their spirits. There was little time for discrimination.

Finally Shaw yelled, "A-ten-shun. Hope you goats know what that means. In case you don't, it means stand still and stiffen, eyes straight ahead, mouth closed, and stay that way until I'm through. . . .''

Jesse felt Shaw's blue eyes more than saw them. Jesse stood fifth man to the right, first line in his platoon, and the chief was midway of the line, perhaps thirty feet out. *I'm the only ebony face amid sixty-odd white ones.* Jesse's heart beat faster. The blue eyes seemed to be lingering. *Is he about to say: "Well, well, what do we have here?" Surprise, surprise, a spade!*

Then the eyes went away, thankfully.

Finally the CPO intoned, "I'm Chief Shaw, in charge of your well-being or lack of it. I don't know what kind of shape you're in, but I plan to find out over the next sixteen weeks. Before I'm through with you, every muscle you own will cry *QUIT*. I won't let you get out of Pre-Flight unless you show me your guts. You're going to be marching all the way. To mess, to classes, to church. You'll march till you drop.''

No one dared even to blink.

Jesse, again glad that he'd run almost every day in Columbus, that he'd worked the freight yards, wasn't worried about Shaw's physical threats. Five feet ten, he weighed 147 pounds, a rail of muscle, his stomach board-flat.

Shaw stepped aside and let an airman second take them through half an hour of push-ups, squats, and jump-ups. Shaw walked away, having accomplished his scare tactics.

After chow-down in the mess hall, with the black and Filipino kitchen help again looking at Jesse with a mixture of wonder and suspicion, even disdain, the college boys were mustered, this time before a commander with at least three inches of "fruit salad," World War II combat ribbons, below his wings. Different in style and tone than Chief Shaw, he was about the same in content.

"Good morning, gentlemen. Welcome to Ottumwa. The Naval or Marine aviator is more than the pilot of an aircraft. He must also possess the mental equipment and the moral stability that distinguishes the responsible officer from the average civilian pilot. We are trained for war. We are trained to kill. . . ."

Jesse was a long way from Lux cotton rows and he knew it, listening to the standard speech.

"Quality will always be a first requisite so long as the task of the man who flies over water is as exacting as it always will be. Quality is the essential factor in the man who is catapulted off a carrier at night, is directed into contact with an enemy snooper, who stalks his prey until the kill, is vectored back to his carrier, and alights on a flight deck with only truck lights, some radio coaching, and the luminous wands of a Landing Signal Officer to guide him."

Jesse was a long way from Kelly's Settlement and he knew it, looking at this combat hero.

"It takes quality to push an airplane over at twelve thousand feet and dive it straight down against flak. Even if combat were lacking, the ordinary job of navigating an airplane over unmarked reaches of ocean is work for a man with brains as well as brawn. The man who wears the wings of gold will always have a claim to quality."

Jesse was a long way from the beer stench of the Holmes Club, suddenly feeling exalted.

"We're here to teach you all the things we think you should know. We'll be seeing if you can take it. Now's the time to find that out—not when you're up in the air with the lives of your fellow aviators depending on you."

He paused a long moment to let the words sink in, then said quietly, "Good luck, gentlemen."

Jesse was jolted by the abrupt bawl of the rating: "A-ten-*shun*. A-bout *face*. Foh-ward." He was still absorbing the senior pilot's words.

A few minutes later the base commander, a highly decorated captain, refused to officiate at Jesse's swearing-in, stepping aside to let his executive officer do the honors. Bleak-faced, he looked the other way as the black man raised his right hand. Jesse tried to ignore the insult but couldn't. His eyes registered both anger and pain. *Welcome to Ottumwa*, Jesse thought.

Until the year before, there'd been a mixture of Aviation Cadets and commissioned officers going through flight training, but now the new category of Aviation Midshipmen had been added to the mix. There was a Catch-22 to the Holloway Plan, named after an admiral. The new law required an AvMid'n to serve two years before commissioning as an ensign, even though he wore wings and could fight and die in wars. Pay, rank, and prestige suffered. Yet there was no shortage of applicants. Winning gold wings was grasping the Holy Grail of naval aviation. Death was not required.

They went off at a trot to draw uniforms, khaki for normal wear, blues for dress. Academy-style uniforms. Indoctrination classes after a thirty-minute meal, then close-order drill again.

Just before dismissal, the airman second called Jesse over. "Chief Shaw wants to see you in the office. . . ."

Oh God! What about?

He practically ran to the unit office, took off his hat, and entered. Shaw was at a desk, checking papers.

"Sir," he said.

Shaw looked up. "Drop the 'sir.' Didn't you learn ratings in ROTC? I'm a noncommissioned officer."

"Yes, sir. Yes."

"Brown, I want to tell you that you're not going to get any special treatment here—from me or anyone else. I've been in the Navy eighteen years and have served with Negro men from the start, good and bad, ship and shore. Up to the war, they served mainly in the steward's department, as you might know. Now they're in every department. I don't know how you managed to get here and don't give a damn, though I am surprised. Far as I'm concerned, performance is the only thing that counts whether your skin is black, white, or polka-dot. My job is to test you to the limit. Understand?"

"Yes, Chief Shaw, I understand. I don't want special treatment of any kind. I'm not used to it."

"Good."

Relieved, Jesse went to his room. Yet he still felt like he was walking on quicksand. He wasn't alone in that feeling, he knew, and it had nothing to do with race. Ottumwa would start the Mount Everest climb.

Jesse looked at himself in the mirror, now clad in khakis, with a black tie, one small gold anchor on his left shirt collar tab. A brown-skinned son of Hattiesburg, Mississippi, had made it up the first rung of one of the most exclusive all-white clubs in America. He couldn't wait to send a photograph home: *Look at Jesse Leroy now!*

Ottumwa Naval Air Station, sixty-four buildings not far from the Des Moines River, had opened in the spring of 1943 to train naval aviators. It was mostly a sea of gumbo mud then. Thousands of would-be pilots took their first rides over the cornfields.

To Jesse, it seemed more a college campus than a naval air station. A few weeks after Hiroshima and Nagasaki flight operations had ceased and the Stearmans and their support aircraft were flown off to Corpus Christi, Texas. Not a single plane was left behind. It was all books, lectures, and classrooms.

Often, only the morning and evening raising and lowering ceremonies for the flag served as a reminder that this was an active military base. Yet it was unique in many ways. The Drill Hall, which was huge, with an arch roof over space enough for seven basketball courts, was used for marching in the severe winters. It had also served as a spare hangar. The swimming pool, which Jesse already feared, was said to be one of the two largest in the world, an indoor lake. He'd stared at it the first evening with a feeling of dread. Getting into it was inevitable.

Cold rain pelted down outside. Spring was always late in Iowa.

"Okay, gentlemen, we're going to play some games this morning," said the middle-aged CPO, a squat, swarthy, hairy man with a New England-sounding nasal accent. His nameplate said SANTINI.

"I can tell how well you'll pilot an aircraft just by the way you play these games. I can also tell you why you shouldn't try to sit in a cockpit," Santini said. The room was filled with pinball-type machines, drawing boards, and odd-looking contraptions likely designed by psychologists.

Lose to a pinball machine? Lose to a drawing board? This is a diabolical room, Jesse thought. He would relay this thought to Daisy later.

A few minutes later he tilted a table to run a steel ball through a maze. Santini watched closely, clipboard and pen in hand. There was a stick and rudder machine where you had to match light patterns on a screen. Then you had to move a pencil on drawing paper that had parallel curving lines. That one was judged by speed and the ability to stay within the lines.

An apparatus had a seat and rudder pedals to tilt a six-foot board shaped like an archery bow. A steel ball bearing coursed a groove on top of the board and the test was to determine how long the player could balance the ball on the center of the board. The time was recorded. Pass or fail. There were other miserable games.

On finishing an hour later, he asked Santini, "How did I do?"

Santini answered matter-of-factly, "We'll let you know. Dismissed."

Jesse wondered if all instructors at Ottumwa were like Shaw and this one, getting kicks out of seeing students squirm, keeping silent, letting the machines play the evil games. *Santini didn't say a single word after his opening speech. He's seeking failure. He probably thrives on it. That's what they are all about,* Jesse decided.

Dawkins had been right once again. They'd all do their damndest to send you home. He'd stepped up to another level at Ottumwa and there may not be any Chris Christensens around. He'd take it hour-by-hour and hope that the "oil leak" mentality instructors would be few and far between.

He already recognized that Pre-Flight living was as orderly and disciplined as the inner workings of a fine watch. Hour-by-hour, minute-by-minute, drill-by-drill, inspection-by-inspection; bugle call-by-bugle call. Precise places for every item in his locker. It was all summed up by the fact that his toothbrush had to be exactly one-quarter inch from the cabinet walls. Not a half-inch, not an eighth, *a quarter-inch.* There was a rule and regulation to be confronted dawn to dark, and beyond. And what did it all have to do with flying an aircraft? Well, he figured to sit in that cockpit and fly the aircraft the way it should be flown, peace or war, required the highest degree of order and discipline.

In that cockpit on an inky night, he'd have to reach for a lever instantly, and he'd have to know exactly where that lever was, sight unseen, like the toothbrush. Life would be in fractions of inches. He figured that's what Pre-Flight was all about.

> Daisy, you truly wouldn't believe this place. Tennis courts, badminton courts, a football field, two baseball diamonds, two basketball courts in a big gym, a cinder track for running. I'll make a lot of use of the latter. Four hours of classes, four of physical training.
>
> Naval Academy rules apply. When the instructor enters the classroom, the first midshipman who spots him yells, "A-ten-*shun*," and everybody jumps up. When the instructor asks you a question, you shout, "Sir,"

then give the answer. When you pass an officer in a corridor, you back up against the bulkhead (the wall) and stand at attention. I guess it all makes sense. Smile!

We march or trot everywhere. I pity my white classmates who didn't grow up walking five miles to school. You walk off demerits with a rifle, heel to toe.

I'm sure we'll lose a number of "goats," as Chief Shaw properly classifies us, simply due to lack of physical coordination. More will probably quit before we ever reach Pensacola. We won't even touch a plane for months and by that time a lot of faces will be gone. Not mine, I hope, I hope.

I think of you constantly.

> All my love,
> Jesse

He always got up at five o'clock, half an hour before reveille, to shower and shave quickly, then he'd clean the room and make his own bunk while his mates were still in theirs. It was pure habit, dating back to childhood when the family would be out in fields at work before sunup. He followed the routine because he didn't want to share demerits if there was a surprise inspection. Nonetheless, the easygoing Brannon was a little nonplussed by all the rooster call activity. He preferred to sleep until the last moment.

Dear Mr. Christensen:

Just a note to let you know how things are going. Classes started the Monday following my arrival. We were sworn in as midshipmen the next day.

I'm trying to get adapted to this place and I think I'm going to have quite a bit of trouble passing my swimming tests, but I've got to do it, somehow.

De Lapp is not here. He checked out, got out of the program, or so I was told. Five or six leave every day. It is unnerving.

I shall keep in touch with you. I'll write when I get the chance. I shall always appreciate—and never forget—the start and help you gave me at Glenview. My deepest regards and best wishes are yours, always.

Very sincerely,
Jesse L. Brown

Looking at his roommates, listening to them, imagining how they'd lived, he couldn't help but think of his own past life, comparing the sharecropped farmhouses in Lux and Kelly's Settlement. All the while growing up in those hot and cold pineboard structures, he hadn't really realized the constant smell of hardscrabble poverty. Marvin, escaping to college, had talked about it away from his papa and his mama and his brothers. Marvin had said, "Leave when you can. Leave that smell." Do my roommates know what a "slop jar" is? Jesse thought. A "slop jar" was a big crockery jar used by the Browns on cold winter nights to urinate and defecate in to avoid walking to the outhouse in bare feet.

He'd had a new life in Columbus and was having one here and if all his dreams of flying were shattered, if he was sent out through the main gate, it would still have been worthwhile. He was living in the white man's world, perhaps an unwanted intruder, but he was taking from it, learning from it, each day. Even if asked, it would be a long time before he talked about the sharecropper world.

Dearest Daisy,

I'm sending you pictures of yours truly in my new uniform. I'm also sending them to my family. Please be sure to show them to Professor Burger. If he wants one to put on the bulletin board outside his office, I'll have it made. Tell him I'm doing fine, so far.

Out of our original group from Glenview, three are already gone. Somehow it seems a little cruel to kick out people, but Clark, the older, quiet, new roommate, who served four years on a carrier as an engine me-chanic, said something like, "Hey, you might end up as a pilot on a multiengine bomber. You want the guy sitting next to you to be A-100 percent. And if you're a fighter pilot, you want the guy flying wing on you to be just as good or better than you are. There's a reason for tough standards."

He's right, of course, but I hope I won't be in mul-tiengines. I'm putting in for single-engine fighter air-craft. And I hear that the Navy is getting jets in a few years. No props, just a big whoosh from an engine that doesn't have too many parts, compressed hot air doing the job. Think of it.

I had a dream about us last night. We'd just been married and were coming down the aisle, you in a beautiful dress and me in my white uniform, with gold wings on my left chest. We were the most handsome couple that ever walked that aisle. Outside, we went under a V of swords.

I wish you were here tonight in my arms. Of course, not in this barracks room, but here in Iowa. I miss and need you so much. I think of you every day and every night and know you'll be beside me in thought.

All my love,
Jesse

Ottumwa

April 18, 1947

The interior of the cavernous pool building was dank and smelled of chlorine. In the pool were twenty-odd midshipmen making efforts to pass what were probably the stiffest swimming requirements in the military. Sounds of splashing and voices from the white bodies echoed hollowly. Half a dozen enlisted instructors walked along the tile edges. Many past graduates remembered the "pool" as being wet torture.

Jesse had admitted he didn't know how to swim very well. Truthfully, not at all.

The chief instructor said, "I can't believe that. You grow up in a desert, nigger?"

"No, sir. Mississippi."

"Brown, you know what this is all about? It's about saving your own life. It's about *survival!* You get shot down over water, ride the aircraft in; you parachute over water and hope you don't get tangled up in the shrouds; you blow up your vest and float until a boat or a seaplane picks you up, if you're lucky. But you may have to swim. You may have a crewman fifty yards away who is injured and needs help. How the hell do you get to him? *You swim!* That's what you do. *You swim.''*

Tight-lipped, dripping, he was standing by the edge of the pool, embarrassed, facing the exasperated instructor. The afternoon wasn't going well. He'd jumped in and flailed, holding his head out of the water.

"Okay, I'm going to put my own brand of life jacket on you and into the water you go. To swim, you flail your arms and kick your feet. Can you do that, Brown? Show me!''

"I'll try, sir.''

The instructor was wearing trunks, so Jesse didn't know what his name or rating was. Probably another CPO. He looked to be in his mid-thirties. Blond-haired, he had a supple swimmer's body and a perpetual disgusted look on his face, seamed from the sun.

Strapping what appeared to be a tennis ball can on Jesse's back, he rattled on. "I can't believe you. Wasn't there a river near where you lived?''

"Yes, sir. The Bouie.''

"Didn't you ever get into it?''

"Yes, sir.''

"Stop the 'sir' stuff, for Chrissakes. Jump into the pool—away from the side.''

Jesse took a deep breath and leaped, going straight to the bottom, the silly tin can providing no buoyancy, as the CPO had expected. He floundered and bubbled out of his nose.

There were at least twenty-five other midshipmen in the pool. Some were watching. One of them was John Brannon, who later said to Jesse, "I think that tin can was psychological.''

The CPO watched him, then said to two enlisted men, "Go get him.'' Jesse was blowing water, coughing, eyes wide with panic.

A moment later Jesse listened as the nameless CPO said, "Hicks, I don't have time to bother with this goofus. Put remedial swimming on his record and teach him how. That's if you want to. I don't personally care. I just as soon kick his black ass outta here." He moved away.

Hicks said, "Come on with me. Let's go to the shallow end."

Jesse, standing there like a wet brown seal, completely humiliated, wondered why the CPO hadn't done that in the first place.

Not on any of those pieces of paper he'd filled out was the question: CAN YOU SWIM? Those in charge must have assumed that anyone seeking to be a naval aviator could swim. Navy aircraft didn't often fly over the mountains and deserts. They flew over water.

No black person could swim in the Hattiesburg Civic Pool. But there was always the Bouie and Lux Creek, where he'd splashed around up to his waist. His brothers, lke Heard, and Martin Luther Beard all swam, but it just didn't seem important to Jesse to learn. Besides, he was always too busy trying to earn money. There was no excuse that he could think of.

Hicks, who wasn't much older than Jesse, said, "Okay, get back in the water, hold your breath, and duck your head under."

Jesse could hear the deserved vexation in Hicks's voice. He felt like a toddler.

> Dear Daisy:
>
>   I'm having no trouble with the classes—principles of flight and aerology this week—but swimming is something else. Now in a pool for the first time in my life, a big pool, I'm classified as a beginner, a child. I have to do a backstroke, side stroke, breast stroke, and butterfly. You'd think it wouldn't make any difference what stroke I used, but I might have a leg injury or both arms hurt, so they figure I need all the ways to swim. Or maybe I have to tow a guy.
>
>   Printed up on the pool test board is: 50 YARD SWIM,

FLOAT 5 MINS.; SWIM 80 YARDS, USING FOUR STROKES; SWIM 200 YARDS, FOUR STROKES; CARRY TIRED SWIMMER, 50 YARDS; SWIM UNDERWATER 100 FEET; SWIM ONE HALF-MILE FULLY CLOTHED; SWIM ONE MILE AND TOW OR PUSH A TIRED SWIMMER 220 YARDS; SWIM A MILE, ANY STROKE. SWIM IN FLAMING WATER. Why underwater? The enemy may be shooting at me from above.

I'm not sure I can make it. I'm an athlete, but I'm a runner, not a swimmer, and those two things require different muscles. I get in bed aching all over. Some, not all, of the white boys are good at it. Come to think of it, I've never heard of a great Negro swimmer. Maybe it's something we don't do well. Track, field, boxing, basketball, we've got our great champions, but not swimming. And I'm sure struggling.

I understand why the tests are so rigid. We're going to be flying over water and some of us will ditch at one time or another.

If I get by all the tests, I face riding the Dilbert Dunker. That's a synthetic trainer designed to approximate the most feared of all forced landings on the sea—a plane crashing into the water nose-down and then flipping over on its back. Dilbert is a cartoon character who can't do anything right. I feel like Dilbert. Say a prayer for me.

All my love,
Jesse

The days passed at the dreaded pool. Brannon and Anderson had conquered it.

Hicks said, "Brown, I've got to admit you're a fast learner, but come over here in your spare time and practice. You're never gonna be a good swimmer, but you can make it if you really try."

"I never thought I could do the mile."

"But you did."

"I doubt that Chief Phillips even wants me to pass."

"He doesn't. He's a UDT man, in case you haven't heard. He simply thinks that all humans should be frogs and doesn't forgive anyone who doesn't take to water like a spaniel."

By now, Jesse had heard all about Phillips making reconnaissance swims into enemy positions in the South Pacific, highly decorated for underwater demolition.

Hicks added, "He hates it here, like everyone else, considers it below him, and wants to get either to Little Creek or Coronado where there is ocean water. That's why he's tough on every midshipman, you included. Nothing personal."

> Dear Mr. Christensen:
>
> It was a real pleasure to read your letter. Congratulations to you for a nice baby daughter. I'm sure she must be cute.
>
> After the first two weeks of swimming, I guess I'm none the worse off. I've passed all except two of the tests. Those are: (1) swim 200 yards, 50 yards each stroke, and (2) the rescue carry, then I have parachute and the Dilbert Dunker. But I'll pass them somehow, although I'll have to do a lot of work on my side, breast, and crawl strokes.
>
> Well, I suppose that about covers everything up to now.
>
> > Best wishes,
> > Jesse

He watched as a midshipman who lived in Barracks 10 failed the underwater swim of 100 feet. He appeared to do about 30 feet before surfacing. His next try resulted in perhaps 20 feet; the third one was less. He was out of breath.

"He's gone," Hicks observed. "He just can't hold his breath that long."

"Why can't he come back tomorrow?" He'd been rooting for the failures.

"He was here yesterday. Couldn't do it then. Can't do it today. He wouldn't make it tomorrow. He's gone."

There was a look of despair on the swimmer's face as he argued with Chief Phillips, who suddenly walked away, shaking his head. The swimmer ran to catch up with him.

"Doesn't this get to you?"

Hicks said, "I guess I've seen more than a hundred guys lose it here in the pool. Phillips told me it's for their sake. They'll live longer selling insurance. That's the way you've got to look at it. Okay, go up the ladder."

Another enlisted instructor was waiting at the top for Jesse to perform the parachute drop. He'd seen it done a number of times. The parachute harness was located on the platform which was about twenty feet above the side of the pool, attached to a track which extended, on a slight downgrade to the middle of the water.

Strapped into the harness, he took a deep breath and stepped off the platform and slid out to the end of the track, where he was automatically released, plunging under. He worked his way out of the harness underwater, and then came to the top, pulling off his shoes. Next he peeled out of the flight suit, treading water and tying off the legs, scooping up air with them for buoyancy, like water wings. Then he slowly set out for the mile swim, hating every stroke of it.

Dearest Daisy:

In addition to your wonderful letters, lately I've heard from Mama, my brothers, Professor Burger, Ike Heard, and M. L. Beard, all in response to the news of my actual flying at Glenview. Mail call means so much to me.

I've got a bad cold from climbing in and out of that miserable pool. Sick Bay gave me some pills and I'll survive. I thought about asking the UDT man to skip a couple of days. But he'd know I was mainly trying to dodge it.

Say hello to everyone for me. Tell them I'm doing fine, but keep the letters coming. I admit I'm lonely here and that probably won't change wherever I go.

All my love,
Jesse

The pool finale was the infamous Dilbert Dunker to simulate an open ocean crash. The actual cockpit of a metal SNJ trainer, the Dunker was positioned on steel tracks that were angled up at 45 degrees.

Jesse had watched other tight-lipped cadets being strapped in. Two instructors were always treading near the impact point. The blunt end of the cockpit would hit the water, turn over, and sink to the bottom.

Now it was his turn and he sat there sucking deep breaths.

He heard, "Let 'er rip . . ." and it all happened within seconds. The Dunker sped down the tracks, turned over, and settled to the bottom on its side, Jesse frantically tugging at the harness, breaking it loose, and swimming up to the surface.

Hicks shouted over, "Brown, you can say goodbye to the pool."

Thank God, Jesse thought, *another ten feet up the side of Mount Everest.*

Barracks room shadowy, all four in their bunks. King who'd replaced Barker said to no one in particular, "You know, I didn't realize until today that we're all competing with each other unconsciously. We've been doing it since the first day on the drill field. How sharp is your push-up?"

Jesse remained silent. *True enough, though.* King had run behind him over the obstacle course. It was a brutal run, usually producing bruises and shin scrapes, blue lumps of one kind or another. Jesse had done it easily, track and field style. King had problems at the wall.

The course was a mile in length and included ropes to climb, logs that had to be straddled over water, logs to be crawled under, a ten-foot-high wall, and other difficult barriers. Some runners lost it on the smooth side of the wall, failing to vault high enough, sliding down it face-first, unable to grasp the top and vault over to land on their feet and run for the next obstacle. Too many tries and they headed home. The old story.

After three attempts, King had finally made it, he said.

"They do their damndest to make you go home, knowing all the time that you'll do your damndest to beat the guy next to you. They win both ways. Pretty smart, huh?"

Yes, it is, Jesse thought. And in his particular case there was that added incentive to compete physically and mentally, one that he'd never discuss unless the listener had dark skin. He didn't want to be the first of his race to try this white meat grinder at Ottumwa and lose.

He remained silent.

Ottumwa

Late May, 1947

The old aircraft Assembly and Repair building had been converted into a gym with a trampoline for tumbling and a standard-sized ring for boxing and wrestling; mats for hand-to-hand combat. Early in World War II, reports had come in from the Pacific that the physically fit aviator was less likely to be shot down; if he was shot down, his chances for survival on a life raft or in the jungle were greatly improved.

Wartime training didn't allow the luxury of staging fights and wrestling matches or hand-to-hand combat for student pilots. Peacetime did. No one got tossed out because of losing a fight or getting pinned on the wrestling mat or dumped upside down in hand-to-hand. It was the continuance of competition that counted, the sainted test of will. Could you take a punch?

Master Sergeant Haines casually looked over the group and his eyes finally settled on Jesse. "You look like you're in better shape than most, so we'll begin with you. . . ."

All eyes were on him, as usual.

"Okay, who wants to climb into the ring with Brown, J. L.?"

There was silence. No hands went up.

Jesse felt embarrassed. *Are they afraid of me? Or, God forbid, do they not want to come in contact with my skin?* He waited.

Finally a Tennessee mountaineer voice near the end of the line said, "I'll do it." Jesse thought he recognized the voice and craned his head around.

John Brannon was grinning and nodding, pointing to his chest.

"Okay, a couple of guys volunteer as cornermen. Give 'em water at the end of each round. Gentlemen, the idea here is to beat the hell out of your opponent. Just like the guys do in Madison Square Garden."

While his gloves were being laced on, Jesse had mixed feelings about fighting Brannon. *I'd really rather fight someone I don't know. I hope John isn't doing it because of our friendship.*

Jesse had had his share of fistfights, but he'd never boxed anyone. Perhaps Brannon had boxed; perhaps he was even good at it. As they got into the ring, Haines acting as the referee, Brannon said, "Jesse, let's go all out."

Jesse replied, "You've done this before?"

"A few times."

The bell rang and the second that Brannon crossed to the middle of the ring Jesse discovered he moved with a fighter's grace and speed, jabbing twice before Jesse even got his hands up; he bobbed and feinted.

Jesse got hit half a dozen times in lightning succession until he began to block the punches with the big gloves. The blows stung but didn't hurt all that much.

"C'mon, man, fight," Brannon urged.

Jesse had been reluctant. He was in much better shape.

Jesse finally swung and landed.

For the next nine minutes, Jesse didn't box. He just slugged wildly. A looping overhand right in the third round stunned Brannon, dropping him to his knees.

At the final bell, when they hugged each other, Jesse panted, "Man, you can *box*."

Master Sergeant Haines said to the group, "That's a draw. I need two more in the ring."

After chow, Jesse and Brannon sat outside the barracks in the twilight. Jesse, looking over, said, "Thanks for today. I was in a bad spot for a few minutes. I thought I'd just have to stand there until Haines picked someone to fight me. And the guy would have to do it. That was embarrassing, John."

"I volunteered because I thought you'd give me more trouble than anyone else. And you did. If we'd had on eight-ounce gloves, you would have knocked me out with that one punch. But you can't box worth a damn."

"Wrestling comes up at the end of the week," Jesse said. "That's more skin contact. We'll be mixing sweat."

"For God's sake, come off it. Somehow or other you've got to put that out of your mind. You're getting your head all screwed up over this skin thing. I understand why you're sensitive, but most of us white guys are rooting for you. Just tell Haines to pick someone. Don't let him put you through that volunteer crap. That makes you special."

On Friday Jesse said to Haines, "Sergeant, please don't ask anyone to volunteer. Just assign me a wrestling partner."

Haines frowned and shrugged. "No problem, Brown."

Jesse pinned his opponent in less than thirty seconds, falling back on techniques learned at Ohio State.

His athletic ability was never questioned, except for swimming.

Less than six weeks into Pre-Flight, there were rumors that the naval station might be shut down and then, mid-May, in bold black headlines, the *Ottumwa Daily Courier* said: NAVY ORDERS AIR BASE CLOSED.

There'd been military budget cuts in Washington. The news sent shock waves through the midshipmen barracks, as well as officer quarters and the town. Would the program end? Would the cadets be sent home?

A jittery two days later, after the community and the district representative had pleaded to Washington to save the base, the commanding officer tentatively announced that the Pre-Flight contingent would be flown to Pensacola sometime in June to continue training.

The somber mood around the base and in town wasn't helped by rain that fell steadily across South Dakota, Minnesota, and Iowa in the week leading up to May 31. The Des Moines River was watched every spring when the rains began. Now it was a foot over flood stage.

Close-order marching, which Jesse now believed he could do in his sleep, was confined to the Drill Hall. Everyone ran from one instructional building to another while gutters spilled over and the former cornfields turned to green mush.

The downpour over the flood plain increased and within another week the river crested at twenty-one feet, flooding most of the town as well as part of the naval station. The same thing had happened in May 1944. This new flood sealed the fate of the air base.

A month later four-engined planes began transporting the surviving Pre-Flight students and seventy ground school instructors to Pensacola. Truck caravans took instructional equipment and books.

PART II

Somong-ni, North Korea

December 4, 1950

Trapped in the open cockpit of the crashed Corsair, the bitter cold and chill factor already beginning to numb him, Jesse could only think of survival. Though he was a professional and had logged hundreds of hours in the air by now, there'd been no specific training at Pensacola or elsewhere about how to cope with this predicament. So many things might happen flying aircraft that no instructor or training manual or pilot bull session could ever cover all of them.

Without power there was no longer any use for the radio communications system in his helmet and he'd taken it off, not thinking it would protect his ears. He'd lost his gloves while attempting to unbuckle his parachute, two buckles in the groin area on each leg; one across his chest. The gloves had gone under the seat and down into the floor beneath it. The only way to retrieve fallen articles in flight was to invert the airplane and have them fall back. Even on the ground, retrieval was difficult.

The right knee was held viselike by the warped control panel. He had one option: attempt to reach up and grab the top of the strong hooplike structural aluminum canopy frame and pull himself out in a chinning motion, enduring the pain.

Suddenly the deep silence of the slope was shattered with the familiar roar of a single Corsair as it made a low pass overhead. Jesse caught a glimpse of the tail section but had no idea who the pilot was. The roar and sight were heartening.

Pensacola, Florida

August 1947

Jesse watched out of the window as the R5D rumbled low across the Gulf of Mexico lining up to land at Pensacola's Chevalier Field at Mainside Administration. His thoughts were of the overnight visit in March and the Glenview basketball team; the exec's decision to keep him off the floor. *Is the exec still here?*

Not too far from the Alabama line, the air station faced Pensacola Bay, with Bayou Grande behind it to the north. Whoever selected the site back in 1824 would have never believed that flying machines would operate from its sands. Except for occasional hurricanes, Pensacola was weather-wise perfect. Aside from summer heat and wilted uniforms, some dog flies and mosquitoes, cooling rain, airmen hopefuls were in paradise. They were surrounded by water. There were inviting clouds to dodge.

The ancient buildings came into sight again. Fleet Admiral Halsey and other carrier admirals of World War II had trained here. It was the Westminster Abbey of naval avia-

tion, with its sandy beach and moss-stained walls, palm
trees and live oaks draped with Spanish moss. But Jesse had
an uneasy feeling about it, much more than he'd had entering Glenview or Ottumwa. *This is Old Dixie. Black man,
beware!*

Unless conditions had changed in two months, he wasn't
likely to be asked to join the station basketball team for
home games in the fall, and he'd decline if they only played
him at bases or colleges up North.

Class 8-X-47 had approximately eight weeks of Pre-Flight
unfinished after the close-down of Ottumwa. The same routine of half a day in classrooms and the other half to physical
training would happen here, he'd been told. *Now that swimming is no longer on my agenda, I've gone over the physical hump*,
he thought.

The transport eased down on the runway and the door
opened. Tropical heat flowed in. A hurricane, with winds
up to 110 miles an hour, had passed over the base only
thirty hours before and the damage was visible. The humidity reminded him of home, which was 100 miles away.
In fact, he'd written Daisy that the plane would fly over
Hattiesburg enroute to the air bases. Perhaps it did, but it
was above cloud cover.

Two cattle cars took the Ottumwa contingents to the brick
barracks where room assignments were posted on the first
floor: FUTRELL, O., BROWN, J. L., KEEFER, J. P., and O'REILLY, C.

Jack Keefer said he'd been held back from Class 6–47 after
breaking his leg on the obstacle course. At six feet two, he
was almost too tall to occupy a fighter cockpit. Californian
O'Reilly was out of USC. Oel Futrell had played with Negro
kids in Choudrant, Louisiana, where he was born. These
strangers all seemed to have no problem with a chocolate-
hued candidate from Mississippi. *Great. That's the way it
should be*, Jesse thought.

But, like Brannon and his roommates at Ottumwa, they
were surprised at his early-morning routine. Again silently
out of his bunk well before the loudspeaker bugle call,

neatly and fully dressed while the others yawned. "Habit," he explained. *Lux.* "Don't let it bother you." *"Cain't see" before dawn to "cain't see" after sundown.*

At assembly on the Grinder, Chief Shaw, also lately of Ottumwa, yelled, "Work uniform this morning. After chow, you're going to the officers' golf course. That hurricane knocked down a bunch of trees. We've got to saw 'em an' get 'em outta here. . . ."

Keefer, standing next to Jesse, moaned loudly.

Shaw bellowed, "Who was that?"

Keefer confessed.

"Get his name," Shaw said to the rating. "Ten demerits!"

Carrying a rifle, he'd walk them off on the Grinder. Nothing had changed with Shaw.

Keefer muttered to Jesse, "I didn't come here to saw trees for the damn braid."

Jesse took an immediate and joyful liking to Jack Keefer. Dark-haired and good-looking, he was Virginia born and bred, a junior at the university, usually smiling and outgoing. During the first hour, Jesse asked him why he wanted to be a naval aviator. Keefer replied with a grin, "Shoot some Russkies down, of course. Be just my luck to miss a war. Maybe I'm already too late."

Keefer has the right attitude, Jesse thought.

The daily routine wasn't much different than Ottumwa and Jesse, knowing his family was following every move, sent a schedule back to Daisy and the Browns: reveille at 0600, taps at 2200, hurry all the time except Saturdays and Sundays. He scribbled a note on the bottom:

> Notice they give us twelve minutes for breakfast, six men to a table. More than they did in Iowa, the stewards again seem to resent me. Crazy, isn't it? My own race. When you want more food after wolfing down the first serving, you hold your plate up. They ignored me completely the first two days. On the third day, I

held my plate up and let it drop. It crashed, and one came running. Oddly enough, the black civilian workers always smile and wave at me. They know what's going on via their grapevine.

There are about 600 of us going through all the phases from indoctrination and Pre-Flight to solo, instrument, night flying, acrobatics, formation, carrier qualifications. Sometimes I feel the weight of 599. I look in the mirror in the morning and feel that weight.

Jesse recognized that the pressure was finally getting to him, really chewing away at him, often without his realizing. Continued glances, occasional silences when he was thrown into a group of whites, even the way some of the instructors said, "Brown!" *Is this the same way they would say it if I was a white "Brown"? Or am I seeing things and hearing things that don't exist?*

Futrell mentioned that Jesse seldom joined in conversations in the room. When he did talk, it was mainly to Keefer. Eventually, Charlie O'Reilly said, "Why don't you mix in with the guys? None of my business, but sometimes you seem aloof."

Jesse said, "I don't mean to be," and let it go at that. How to explain the canyon, the gulf, the wide river that separated them? He knew that he was sometimes seen as standoffish, going his own way. Sometimes that was the only way. It had been the same in Columbus. He didn't want to force his body into white society. One black man surrounded by hundreds of white men in a special circumstance. The military only amplified the circumstance. He just hoped the midshipmen around him would understand that he didn't like to be aloof or standoffish, but there was a canyon and a river and they would always be there. Pensacola was widening the gulf, but he had the feeling that once he got into flying it would all change.

*   *   *

Jesse and Keefer sat in the shade of the hangar. It was another 100-degree day in north Florida.

Jesse said, "You sure disappear whenever we get a pass." They had Saturday afternoons free and after church on Sundays until 7 P.M.

Keefer finally turned his head and looked straight at Jesse, for a moment considering what he was about to say. "For God's sake, don't tell anyone but I'm married. My wife's here."

Jesse was stunned. From the first day he'd read anything about the program in Dawkins's office, student marriage was an automatic farewell. Wives, it was said, took away total concentration from the task of becoming officers and naval aviators.

"Don't look so shocked. I'm probably not alone," Keefer said.

"Where is she?"

"Here," Keefer repeated. "She has a room and works in a drugstore. When anyone sees us together, I say she's my girlfriend."

"Aren't you taking a big chance?"

"We love each other, Jesse. Why should we be apart? We're just trying to make sure she doesn't get pregnant."

Jesse immediately thought of Daisy. "How long have you been married?"

"Two days before we left Charlottesville to come here."

"And you signed the paper saying that you weren't married?"

"That's right. And if I'm discovered I'll say, 'Thanks for the fun' and go back to Charlottesville and we'll finish up school. She's majoring in art. Very pretty lady, Jesse. Very nice lady."

"I'd like to meet her sometime."

"I can arrange that."

Dearest Daisy:
    I've told you about Jack Keefer, I consider him my

best and most loyal friend. Yesterday he told me a secret. He's married. His wife lives in a rooming house
and works at a local drugstore. He's gambling that the
Navy won't discover her. He loves her very much and
wants to spend the rest of his life with her. 'Why wait?'
he said. Keefer told me that the Navy has investigators
who try to find out which midshipmen are married.

I'm so tempted. Jack Keefer couldn't love his wife
more than I love you. And I don't think Jack needs her
as much as I need you.

Jesse soon met Joan Keefer at dinner in a small Cuban
cafe on Fernando Street. He found Joan to be all that Jack
had promised. A deeply tanned, pretty blonde, with brown
eyes and a nice smile, she talked easily and asked questions
about his family, about Daisy.

Jesse was even more envious of the handsome Keefers
before the evening was over. He didn't learn until later that
she'd personally checked out the cafe to make certain
there'd be no problem with color. The owner was a shade
darker than Jesse.

Two days later Jesse was walking down a corridor in a
classroom building when an instructor passed him and said
distinctly, "Go home, nigger boy!" There it was—finally. He
had known that it was coming, but he still wasn't prepared
for it. Not from the mouth of an instructor.

He froze. Suddenly he wanted to run after him, beat him,
stomp him. He'd never seen the instructor before. He hadn't
even noticed his rank, but he looked to be World War II.
He wore wings. In the fleeting glance, he was slim and
wearing khaki shorts and a short-sleeved khaki shirt, regulation tropic. He had on wire-rimmed aviator's shaded
glasses and moved with long-legged authority.

The words followed Jesse around all day and he knew
he'd toss all night long, hearing them, trying to remove
them from his mind.

He didn't know how to deal with it. He could go to the

battalion commander and tell him about it. He could go over his head and ask for a meeting with the base commander, report the incident. But he hadn't seen the officer's name tag. If he found out the name and caused the instructor to go on the base commander's mat, it would make matters worse. He had a lot of flying to do before leaving Pensacola and knew that the instructors stuck together. They were in control and could write goodbye "downs" by the handful.

In the future, if he was unlucky enough to draw the man in the hall, he'd deal with it then. Just how, he didn't know.

He decided to say nothing. It wasn't something he'd like to discuss with his roommates, even Keefer. Nor with Daisy or his family or Ike Heard or M. L. Beard. They'd been through it before and had heard the same words in different ways. Perhaps write to Christensen, now far removed from the Navy. He'd ask his advice.

Three days later Jack Keefer walked into the room. The other occupants were in class or otherwise busy. About to take his shoes off, he was ready to "hit the rack" for a quick nap before evening chow when he noticed a white card on the pillow hump of Jesse's bunk above him. The letters on it, in red, spelled out: NIGGER, GO HOME!

Shocked, he stared at it. The message was sickening. So far as he knew, none of the midshipmen were racist, but there were more than 500 spread out in the Pensacola complex and maybe a few had some deep-seated hatreds that weren't evident to others.

Access to the barracks and to individual rooms was open around the clock. There were no locks. The rooms could be inspected day or night. Theft was not even considered, though there might have been a few instances over the years. Anyone, midshipman or officer, could have entered the room, dropped the card, and slipped away without being seen.

The bunk itself had not been tampered with. The corners were regulation and the spread was so taut that a quarter would have bounced on it. Jesse would never pull a demerit for sloppy bedmaking.

Jack thought about taking the card away and tearing it to bits, but whoever did it might have other things in mind. *Though it will hurt, Jesse should know,* he finally decided. *Perhaps the base commander should be told.* He used his right thumb and forefinger nails to grasp an edge and turn it face-in. If O'Reilly or Futrell arrived, they couldn't see what had been printed. Hopefully, he could take Jesse aside and tell him about the card; let him make the decision about telling the brass.

Jesse came in first. Jack rolled off his bunk and said, "Take that card off your pillow, don't read it, and come outside with me. Take it by a corner."

Jesse, frowning, said, "What's wrong with you? What's this all about?"

"Just do as I tell you."

Jesse turned the card over and murmured, "Oh no."

"Come on out!"

He followed Keefer out and down the steps and away from the barracks. They walked silently for a few hundred yards, then Jack said, "I saw it on your bunk after I got out of class and went to the room. You have any idea who might have done it?"

Jesse sighed, but didn't answer, looking over toward the sparkling bay.

Jack said, "It's hard for me to believe that any of the guys did it."

At length Jesse said, "I don't think they did."

Jack stopped walking. "What are you saying?"

Jesse took another pause. "An instructor?"

"Jesus Christ!" Jack's mouth hung open. "Good God!"

Then he was silent for a while and they resumed walking.

"Three days ago an instructor passed me in the hall, and just as he went by he said, 'Go home, nigger boy.' "

Jesse described him as much as he could, admitting he hadn't seen the name tag.

"Have you seen him since?"

"No."

There were almost 200 instructors on the base, many nonflying, and they were scattered over the instruction buildings and airfields.

"I did see wings on his chest."

They were near part of an ancient brick wall and Keefer veered off to sit down. Jesse followed him.

"I'd think about going to the old man, tell him what happened in the hallway, show him the card. They've got photos of all the instructors. Pick out the one in the hallway. . . ."

Jesse stopped him. "Without any proof he put the card on my bunk? I'd be dead! All his buddies would gang up. . . ."

"But you think he did it?"

"I don't know, Jack. But I can't connect anyone else."

"If naval intelligence could fingerprint the card?"

"Jack, hey, think what you're talking about. I'm not about to cut my own throat. Naval intelligence involved? I've been called a nigger hundreds of times. It's just that this place and this time is different, altogether different. If someone had seen him put the card there and would say so, okay. I'd stick it to that SOB big-time. I said long ago, before I left OSU, that I'd take the words, but I wouldn't let anyone play me. . . ."

Jack thought a moment. "Guess you're right, Jesse."

He took the card, ripped it, and tossed it into a trash barrel that they passed on the way to the barracks.

Jack had the last words. "Of course, if it was me, I'd catch him in a dark alley and beat the piss out of him."

Jesse mustered up a laugh. *Pure big Jack Keefer.* Yet the-man-in-the-corridor remained worrisome.

Under a blue sky and in high heat, having completed the training syllabus, scoring A in the middle 20 percent, Jesse Leroy Brown graduated from the Pre-Flight School. Of the sixty-six original members of Class 8-X-47, thirty-six had survived.

As the regiment marched by, dipping colors, Jesse wished that everyone in Hattiesburg was present on the parade grounds near Mainside. He'd made it through what many midshipmen believed was the toughest part of becoming a naval aviator. The failure rate in Pre-Flight remained higher than in any other phase, including flying.

As soon as "dismissed" was shouted, Jesse ran for the barracks. Granted two weeks' leave, bag already packed, he was headed for Hattiesburg. He placed the graduation certificate in the bag and was out the door.

By now, M'dear Miz Addie had a telephone for the first time in her life, but long-distance calls, triple the cost of locals, were banned. Daisy and Jesse had communicated daily by mail. The Browns, still in their Kelly's Settlement house, still without electricity, did not have or even think about the Bell System.

Jesse had written Daisy that he'd be taking leave as soon after graduation as possible. He'd hitchhiked or ridden the bus the times he'd been home. White drivers seldom picked him up on the roadside, so he depended on black drivers for free transportation. But this day was special and he decided to go ride the back of the bus cheerfully.

He took city transportation into Pensacola and within an hour was on his way to Hattiesburg, changing in Gulfport to get on Route 49 north. As the bus swept past Saucier, Wiggins, and Maxie, all redneck towns, he felt both relief and joy. Relief that he'd hurdled Pre-Flight, joy to be returning home. There were Negroes, of course, in the last four seats and the wide one at the very back.

Others got on or off at the stops, taking note of a brother in what appeared to be a Navy officer's uniform, a cause for curiosity. Jesse answered questions all the way from Gulfport to Hattiesburg, his ego stroked with every mile. It was good to be back among the black faces, no matter the seating and what it represented.

Arriving in Hattiesburg, Jesse took the city bus to Daisy's house and was soon telling Daisy and M'dear Miz Addie how it felt to be standing there with thirty-five other graduates, in his whites, accepting the certificate, the handshake of the station commanding officer, knowing he was different and in a strange way, relishing it. He could see the eyes of parents and girlfriends who attended. *Yes, it's me, Jesse Brown, on my way to gold wings, I hope.*

The next day after church, he went home to Kelly's Settlement and repeated the ceremony for his mama, papa, and younger brothers. Dinner was the usual fried chicken and mashed potatoes and greens, blueberry pie. It was good to be home.

"Next step is basic flight training. I'll be flying an SNJ, an all-metal two-seater monoplane. It's got a Pratt & Whitney nine-cylinder engine in it and can go two hundred and eight miles an hour. With a closed cockpit, the Texan is like a combat plane and can mount a machine gun as well as practice bombs. . . ."

Daisy sat there in the kitchen with the small hushed audience, listening to what she'd already heard the day before. *What does anyone know about Pratt & Whitney engines?* Daisy thought. *All Jesse wants to talk about is flying, just flying. No one's asking any questions. They're overwhelmed by what Jesse already knows, who he is.*

"You know what I'm going to like about the SNJ? The wheels come right up. The Stearman has fixed wheels, so it's not a true bird. The SNJ, pulling up its link to ground, is a true bird. . . ." Papa John's mouth stayed half-open, listening to his third son. Julia was trying to follow it all.

"It has a variable pitch propeller and sounds like a fighter when it takes off." He imitated the sound.

Daisy couldn't help but laugh. *Oh, Jesse, he's flyin' so high.*

On Monday, he left his uniform at Daisy's house and went to work at Hattiesburg Hardware, doing anything the boss asked. He needed money to augment the $82 a month the Navy was paying him.

The night before he returned to Pensacola he said to Daisy, "You know I've been talking a lot here, playing the big hero. You'd think I was already an ace. But the truth is I'm more worried than ever about what's ahead. They don't need all the pilots they're getting and the word is out to make it even tougher than Pre-Flight. I may be a complete and total washout."

"Don't talk like that and don't think like that," Daisy said. "That's not like you."

"I'm just being truthful."

He said, "Daisy, I need you there, need you by my side."

"I want to be, but you've already told me we can't get married until you're commissioned."

"I told you about Jack Keefer's wife. I've heard about others."

Daisy shook her head. "If we're caught . . ."

"I get kicked out."

"And waste all that time you've put into it?"

"If I wash out, I'll waste it, anyway."

"Oh, Jesse, why is everything so difficult?"

"That's the way it is."

She said, "Think about it. Let's don't do anything until you really think about it."

He'd thought about it enough. "Okay, I wasn't going to tell you, but I will. About a month ago, a flight instructor passed me in a hallway when I was changing classes. He said, 'Go home, nigger boy!' Although Dawkins warned me, I never thought I'd hear that from an instructor. Then I got a card that said the same thing."

"Will you have to fly with him?"

"Maybe. And there might be others who think that way but just haven't said anything."

"Have you talked about it with your roommates? With Jack Keefer?"

"Yeah, just with him. I think most of the guys are pulling for me. One night I went over to the theater to see a sorry B movie and sat with the other guys in the midshipman section and an SP ordered me to move to the colored section. Instead I went back to the barracks to study. The next day Keefer polled the class and wrote a letter to the base commander saying that Class 8-X-47 would boycott the movies in the future unless I was allowed to sit in the white section. Other classes heard about it and joined the protest. . . ."

"So what happened?"

"Two days later the theater segregation ended for me, but only for me. Enlisted segregation continued and I felt embarrassed, so I began to time myself to go there after the lights were down."

He really didn't want to talk to Daisy about the loneliness. But that was a part of it, the biggest part. He was, in fact, alone most of the time, in class, in the barracks room, even on the drill field. He was alone in his head, if nowhere else. *How can she help?* Jesse thought.

On weekends the other midshipmen walked around the base with their parents or parent, with their girlfriends or civilian friends. They had bonds and links. He had stayed away from social events at the cadet club: the dances. He'd walked and he'd read and he'd run and run and run. He'd shot baskets and now that he knew how to swim he went to the pool or down to the beach.

The loneliness was overwhelming, but he didn't talk to Daisy about it.

Lieutenant Tipton

October 1947

Aviation Cadet Regt.
Class 8-X-47 P-M
NATB, Pensacola, Fla.
21 September 1947

Dear Mr. Christensen:

It was really a great pleasure to hear from you. I've been trying to imagine you as a baby-sitter, but I imagine that your new daughter Nancy makes it a lot of fun. I should like a picture of her very much.

I am about five weeks out of Pre-Flight now. We started our basic flight routine last Monday and were supposed to have been assigned to a squadron tomorrow to start flying this week. Of course, this latest hurricane broke up everything, so now we don't exactly know what the score is. We will start out with the SNJ at Corry Field.

I hope you'll soon get set up in your new business and hope it will be a success.

I think of you quite often and often express the hope that I'll get another instructor who will be half as good and kind as you were. When I start flying, I shall try very hard to remember what you taught me and go on from there. It will mean a lot to me, in more ways than one, if I can make it thru.

I will close now and I wish for you the best of everything.

Sincerely,
Jesse

In the classroom for basic flight indoctrination, Jesse saw the long-legged, sandy-haired senior lieutenant who'd passed him in the passageway, whispering, "Go home, nigger boy."

Seated beside Jack Keefer, he asked, "Is he a flight instructor too?"

"They often do both classroom and flight. Why?"

"That's him."

"Uh-oh."

The lieutenant, eyes lingering on Jesse, said, "The washout rate on the SNJ is about the same as the Stearman, but don't let that fool you." His name tag said TIPTON. "It's a more complex plane, as you should know, with retractable gear. . . ."

He sounds Alabama to me, Jesse thought.

"If the wheels aren't locked down, you crash," Tipton said, continuing to stare at Jesse.

"The hydraulics are actuated by the Power Push handle. . . ."

Jesse finally looked away.

"If you have to go full rudder to correct for a drift on touchdown, you don't want the tail wheel to be two-blocked in the same direction or you'll be guaranteed a wild and woolly ground loop. . . ."

Tipton's eyes stayed on Jesse.

A few days later Keefer said, "I found out about Tipton. The guy's a hero. Got the Navy Cross for knocking down four Japanese aircraft at the Marianas turkey shoot. Flew off Pete Mitscher's *Lexington*. How do you figure him?"

"I don't," Jesse said. "But anyone can hate. We've got a senator in Mississippi who's probably a lot worse than Tipton."

Jesse signed a document in late September:

```
I have read and understood all course rules,
flight instructions, Squadron Orders, and the
Crash Control Bill.
```

Then he passed the blindfold SNJ cockpit instrument checkout, locating every one of them.

Two days later, back in a flight suit, an inflatable Mae West life jacket, provided with a parachute pack, he bumped slowly along toward Corry Field in a cattle car with other apprehensive students. Though they were no longer roommates, John Brannon stood a few feet away. They talked about "hanging in."

It was Day 1 of basic flight training, a day when most student mouths tended to be dry and most hearts, including his own, beat a little faster. Academics nearly over, the same hard rules applied more than ever—make too many mistakes, goodbye.

Stage A would consist of twenty flights, eighteen of them usually with the same instructor; the final solo, of course, would be with a different check pilot.

The World War II hangar, with big chalkboards labeled MORNING WING and AFTERNOON WING, was about 100 yards from the SNJ flight line. Students milled around the boards to find their names matched with instructors and the period in which they'd fly. The routine was not unlike that of Glenview.

He located his name and that of the pilot who would take him aloft and acquaint him with the aircraft. No more gosport. This time there'd be two-way radio communication and Lieutenant William Zastri, USNR, could explain the machine and what to do with it once the wheels were tucked up.

The instruction briefing officer laid it out: "Anyone who gets a 'down' has to fly two 'ups' on the same test or appear before the Summary Flight Board, facing your instructor, the check pilot, chief instructor, and the squadron commander. If the Board decides your record is still promising, that you just need a little extra coaching, you'll be given a few days' grace—if you request it. If the Board decides to send you higher up to a senior officer panel, you are usually doomed. You obviously lack the ability to become a naval aviator. . . ."

Jesse had never heard such threatening words, spoken in such a cold, methodical way. If they were meant to threaten every student in the hangar, even the cockiest ones, they did the job. Jesse glanced around at Keefer, at Brannon, at O'Reilly. They all wore a look of alarm, a plank-walk look.

Jesse had seen a blank instructor's form, smuggled into the barracks and passed around like contraband. It listed the various maneuvers and alongside them a square in which to check the percentage score. Two down-checks in the bottom category of 20 percent of the students and you likely head for the Southern Railway or Greyhound.

From screwing up the simple cockpit check-off to taxiing out and takeoff to cross-wind landings, with sixteen maneuvers in between, there wasn't a single easy procedure in the whole lot.

Takeoff: Tab, throttle, heading, nose, pull-off, swerve.

Jesse had taken the form into the midnight can and sat on the stool for more than an hour, studying it.

> *Student's Reaction Toward Flight*: Spin, stall, landing, emergency, formation, nervous, sick, tense, confused, afraid.

Any and all, Jesse thought.

Afternoon, October 1, 1947, Flight No. A-1, Squadron VT-1A. He climbed into the forward cockpit of SNJ 316. Lieutenant Zastri climbed in behind him. The sky over Pensacola was mostly blue, with a few drifting white puffballs; wind westerly at 19 knots. *Nice day for flying.*

Jesse knew by now that instructors would remain basically strangers, teaching an hour or more each day over several months. They'd meet in the hangar or on the flight line, get airborne, land, and go their separate ways. Some would be friendly, like Christensen. Others would keep a distance, being both teacher and judge.

Zastri was not unlike the other instructors, a cut above the ordinary human being, Jesse decided. He was rather handsome, with black hair along the sides of his fore-and-after. Warm brown eyes. Looked like he might have been a good halfback at some college. He appeared to be about thirty. His name sounded Pennsylvania or New Jersey, but his voice sounded Southern.

Zastri said, "We're going to do some level flight, no funny stuff. Just get you familiarized with this aircraft. Demo is what we call it. You've flown before?"

"Yes, sir. At Glenview. A Stearman."

"Sweet old plane. Well, we'll get up there and I'll let you take the controls. May even take a nap myself."

Oh yeah, Jesse thought. He felt as if he were being set up for a quick fall.

His SNJ was fifth in line for takeoff and soon the tower said, "Cleared for takeoff, 316," and Zastri two-blocked the throttle and they rushed down the runway and into the air.

Jesse hadn't flown since Glenview, six months earlier, and compared to the SNJ, with its canopy and retractable wheels, the kindly Stearman was horse-and-buggy. Listening to Zastri, who seemed to be a pleasant fellow, chatter about the aircraft and its tendencies, Jesse still felt uneasy.

Perhaps all students felt uneasy in their first A flight, trying to remember everything that had been told to them in Pre-Flight; trying to watch all the instruments; the movement of the stick, the rudder pedals.

Fear of flying was not involved here. Fear of "pranging," fear of making mistakes during this demo session was riding in the cockpit with him. Sweat was the common denominator of all student pilots at Pensacola.

Zastri's voice came through the earphones. "I'm leveling off now. What does your altimeter say?"

"Sixty-five hundred feet, sir."

"Okay. I want you to do some turns for me . . . right and left. Ease her around. . . ."

"Yes, sir."

Jesse turned the 316 to the right, slow and easy.

Silence behind.

Then he turned it left.

No words from behind.

To the right again. *I must be doing okay,* he thought, *or the lieutenant would be telling me otherwise. Come on, man, say something.*

Now, to the left.

Silence.

This had to be the easiest flying on earth, going right and left across the blue sky, yet Jesse felt tremendous pressure from Zastri. Flying should be fun and yet this simple maneuver was hell. It didn't involve steep turns or spirals or stalls or acrobatics, but it was still hell.

Forty-five minutes later, on the way back to Pensacola, the lieutenant said, "On the report, I'm going to write: 'Student has tendency to slip turns. In level flight, he tries to turn the nose of the aircraft by use of rudder alone.' " *Dumb mistakes*, Jesse thought. Two check-offs.

Silence again, then Zastri said, "Now, let me show you. . . ."

As soon as Jesse jumped out of the cattle car, he went to the squadron office and requested a weekend pass.

On Saturday Daisy was across the street at a neighbor's house, sitting by the front window, when she saw Jesse, in uniform, walk up to her front door and knock.

She ran out, calling his name. He turned on the porch and met her, saying, "Put on your best dress, honey. We're getting married today."

Daisy was stunned. "We can't do that, Jesse. You'll be kicked out."

"We have to do it. I'll take the chance. I won't last down there unless you're by my side."

"Have you thought about it, Jesse? Have you really thought about it?"

"Day and night." *Yesterday, in particular.*

"How can we be together?"

"I'll find a way. Jack and Joan Keefer are together. Now, go pick out a dress and let's get the license. City Hall should be open all day."

Daisy was still stunned. "How did you get here?"

"First bus out of Pensacola. How I got here doesn't matter. We have to hurry. Let's go inside."

"Jesse, are you sure we're doing the right thing? You told me it was against regulations."

"I know. They have to be disregarded sometimes. In battle, air, sea, or land. Things don't always go the way they're planned. . . ."

"How am I going to help you if I'm here in Hattiesburg and you're in Pensacola?"

"I said I'd find a way."

Daisy shook her head but said, "All right."

M'dear Miz Addie and Daisy's sisters and brother weren't

really surprised. Marriage had been talked about for months. And Jesse showing up unexpectedly was nothing new.

"Let's go get that license," Jesse said.

Addie said, "I can vouch for Daisy. What about your parents?"

Under Mississippi law, both the bride and groom had to be twenty-one for legal marriage. Daisy was nineteen; Jesse was twenty.

"There's not time to go out and get them," Jesse said. They were twenty miles away. He didn't have enough money for their taxi fare.

"I can have someone say he's your father," Addie Nix said. "He works for J. C. Penney."

"We need a car," Jesse said.

"How about Robert?" Daisy said.

Robert Steed was a mutual friend.

"I'll call him."

Robert not only agreed to provide wheels but said he'd arrange the ceremony. He was a church deacon.

In midafternoon Jesse and Daisy exchanged vows in the parsonage of the St. James Methodist Church, Robert Steed as witness. Snook Hardy learned about it from a letter. She was attending college in Baton Rouge.

After a triumphant meal prepared by Addie Nix, they spent their wedding night in Daisy's room. After paying for the license and giving the pastor five dollars for his services, Jesse had three dollars and change left in his pocket. Finances were not a concern that day.

Soon, many people in the black community knew that Jesse Brown and Daisy Pearl Nix had married. They weren't about to tell the Navy.

Pensacola

October 1947

Oct. 8
Does not use enough right rudder in climbs. Could
not line up with runway for takeoff. Instructor
had to take over to do so.

Oct. 9
Overcontrols on takeoffs.
Forgets to apply right rudder in a climb.

Oct. 9
1. Brief summary of the immediate difficulty: 50%
Borderline Grades in Reaction Toward Flight.
2. In view of the present difficulty, and a review
of the student's past performance record, it is
my opinion that he does not warrant board action
at this time.

It was all impersonal, unfeeling, as it should be. Jesse felt as if he were a number, not a person.

He was in trouble already and knew it was his fault. Four flights into basic and he was making the same errors each time. Zastri was patient enough, seemed eager to have his student fly the airplane the right way, but wasn't about to be less than truthful on the daily report. *Race is not playing a part*, Jesse thought. *It's my brain, my hands, my feet.*

```
Oct. 10
Veers off heading 30 degrees in stall recover-
ies.

Oct. 13
Makes large corrections in nose attitude during
steep turns—chasing the altimeter.
```

It's sloppy flying, Jesse admitted to himself. He was beginning to panic at night thinking about climbing into the SNJ for the next day's flight.

Dearest Daisy:

Oh, how I miss you. Here we are, husband and wife, 100 miles from each other, and we might as well be 900 miles away. I think of you constantly, maybe too much. At least once a day I think about taking off this uniform and coming home to you. If we could only see each other now and then.

Am I doing well? No! I make mistakes every day that I fly and wonder if I'm improving at all. It all started so easy at Glenview with Lieutenant Christensen and the Stearman. It fooled me. Leaving there, I thought I could be the premiere bird. I don't think that anymore.

I realize I was more worried about being black in a sea of white than I was about flying an aircraft. Every flight I take I discover that my main enemy at this point isn't human; isn't white. It has an engine and wings and rudder pedals and a control stick. It is neutral and waits out there every day for me to handle it properly.

```
Oct. 14
Does not keep plane trimmed up in climbing turn
stall entry.
```

```
Oct. 15
Does not apply enough left rudder in approach
turn.
Comes in wing low in straightaway to landing.
```

```
Oct. 16
Still overcontrols badly on takeoffs.
```

"I'm losing it," Jesse said to Jack Keefer. "I don't know why. Maybe I'm not cut out to be a pilot." His face was creased with worry; eyes red-rimmed from lack of sleep.

"You're probably not doing any worse than the rest of us. Is Zastri giving you a hard time?"

"I don't think so. He seems friendly enough. . . ."

"But you know some of them can seem Mr. Nice Guy and still drum you out of here."

Jesse nodded. "I'm flying with another guy tomorrow. I don't know why. That really worries me. Why would they change instructors? My nerves are a mess."

"I've heard they do it all the time. Zastri may be at fault. Personality clash. He might not like the way you part your hair."

Jesse laughed softly. "I don't have that much to part."

"What did he say?"

"Just that another pilot would be riding the backseat tomorrow. I threw up last night."

"Maybe they want to compare notes. Those guys talk to each other in the ready rooms. Keep doin' your best, Jesse."

"That may be the problem. My best is not good enough, damn it."

```
Oct. 17
Made good takeoff from Corry but shoved forward
on the stick when picking up wheels. Couldn't
hold 95 knot climb-out. Doesn't use trim tabs
enough. All turns at altitude were good and held
altitude good. Tried to enter field downwind.
Forgot to lower flaps. Instructor had previously
set 600 ft. as downwind leg, so first approaches
were low from 500-ft. pattern. Has trouble hold-
ing nose straight in takeoff run. Can't seem to
hold 80 knot climb out of field.

                          J. Chenoweth, Lt. USN
```

Jesse read it and said, "Oh Lord."

On Sunday he went to services at John the Baptist on North Tenth Avenue, the oldest Negro church in Pensacola. He went to join his kind and pray and listen and sing. The congregation looked at him with awe and the preacher made mention of his presence. He was the first midshipman to ever enter John the Baptist.

He felt at home, remembering where he came from.

When you go to the white folks' church,
You won't never see a smile;
But when you go to the colored church,
You can hear them laugh for a mile.

He enjoyed the singing as always, the old songs, the hand clapping, the feet tapping. He was smiling now, and his palms were slapping. He was looking from shining black face to shining black face, and he was singing.

I'm gonna ride on the whistlin' chariot
Some of these days;
I'm gonna walk and talk with angels,
Some of these days;

I'm gonna tell my Jesus, "Howdy,"
Some of these days.

He listened to the shouts of the preacher and the shouts of "Amen" and "Preach it, brother" and "That's right," from the deacons and the congregation, remembering the churches of boyhood; the choirs, the glee, the rhythms.

When I get to heaven, I'm gonna take my stand,
Gonna wrestle with my Lord like a natural man.
When I get to heaven, gonna be at ease,
Me an' my God gonna do as we please.

Jesse walked out into the autumn sunlight after the almost three-hour service, feeling uplifted. He stayed around outside the church while the members chatted with each other and with him, every now and then looking over at the preacher who was surrounded with ladies in hats and men in coats and ties.

Finally the crowd began to thin and Jesse waited until the last talker was walking away. He moved quickly to the preacher and shook his hand, saying, "Preacher, I need your help."

The plump minister said without pause, "You got it, Officer."

"I'm not an officer yet, but I hope to be one."

"How can I help you?"

"I've got a bride back in Hattiesburg and need her by my side. What I'm doing now has never been done by one of our race. I'm in training here and trying to become the Navy's first black aviator and there is a regulation that says I cannot be married. It says I'll be kicked out of this program if I am married. At the same time, I think I might fail if my Daisy isn't here to hold my hand, to talk to me, to tell me that she loves me. . . ."

"I see. But what can I do about your circumstance?"

"You can tell me if you know of someone in the congregation who might rent us a room where she can stay. It will have to be someone I can trust, someone who will understand our problem, my problem. . . ."

The preacher nodded and thought for a moment. "There's a lady named Mrs. Clayton, Lucille Clayton, who lives not far from here. She's a widow and has two or three bedrooms in her house. She might consider doing what you ask, renting you a room for your bride. She's a fine lady, Pensacola's leading Negro socialite, and often does work for the church. Come on inside and I'll give you her address."

Jesse left John the Baptist and found the residence of Mrs. Lucille Clayton at the corner of Cervantes and DeVille. Introducing himself, he asked if he might talk to her for a little while. He said the preacher had said she might be able to help him.

Sitting in her parlor, sipping iced tea, he told her about Daisy and about the Navy; about breaking a rule. "I have to be honest with you," he said.

"Will I get into trouble if they find out?" Mrs. Clayton asked.

"No, I will. They'll end my training, my chance to fly off carriers. I can't pay you very much. I make eighty-two dollars a month."

She sat rocking for a little while, then said, "I'll do it for ten dollars a month if she'll help me with social events. How old is she?"

She was a small white-haired woman, with a narrow face and a warm smile. She wore gold-rimmed glasses and Jesse could see that the house was well kept, filled with antiques. She reminded him a little of his mother.

"Turning twenty."

"How old are you?"

"Just twenty-one."

"I've thought about taking in boarders, but I've never done it. My husband paid this house off before he died and I get by with insurance checks and Social Security. I am lonely sometimes. Maybe your Daisy will make my life a little brighter."

Jesse said, "I'm sure she will" and departed the Clayton house.

He called Daisy from a pay booth and told her to pack her bags and to arrive the following Saturday.

```
Oct. 20
Does not use trim tabs when changing aircraft at-
titude, resulting in airspeed and attitude var-
iations.


Oct. 21
Takeoff overcontrolled.
Attitude and airspeed variable on downwind leg.
On 180° power approach started approach from po-
sition about 110° rather than the 180° abeam po-
sition.


Oct. 22
In spin entry became confused and applied for-
ward stick—in entry did not move stick ahead of
neutral in recovery.
```

The aircraft spun like a wind-caught leaf and Jesse had a sick feeling in his stomach, not so much from the sudden maneuver but from the knowledge that once again he'd made a mistake with the stick. He knew better. He knew how, yet. . . .

This was not fun and games. *Stay in a spin and you get killed.*

After a rocky landing, walking away from the flight line, Jesse asked Zastri, "Do I have a chance?"

"I'm trying to teach you, Brown. That's what I'm doing. I've given you exactly one check, only one, in the top 20 percent and that was for that takeoff yesterday. You did it correctly. You're doing less than average, in my opinion, but I still think you have the potential. Prove me right,

Brown. I haven't given up on you." He paused and added, "Yet."

"Thank you, sir."

Zastri stopped and displayed the day's negative score sheet. "We'll try again tomorrow."

Jesse thanked him and they went their separate ways, Jesse to the barracks and the lieutenant to the instructor's ready room in the hangar.

O'Reilly and Keefer were in from their hops. O'Reilly asked, "How'd it go?"

Keefer had his eyes closed, trying to take a nap.

Jesse said, "Bad," and sat down on the edge of his bunk.

"Me too," O'Reilly said. "I got burned on climb and glide turns. I slipped and skidded all over the damn sky."

Keefer kept his eyes closed but said, "We've been flying three weeks and these guys seem to want 100 percent. That's not realistic."

O'Reilly said, "They've been ordered to weed us out."

Jesse said, in dismay, "I think I'm a prime candidate for the weed-out."

Keefer raised his head. "For God's sake, Jesse, we all are. It's been that way since Selective. You hear about that guy in Class 7 who got bounced for not wearing his goggles on takeoff?"

O'Reilly said, "I've heard that was a bunch o' crap. I've heard he got bounced because he called his instructor an SOB, which was probably true. They've been telling stories about this place since 1919."

Jesse said, "All I know is that I've got to recover from a spin tomorrow the way the book says to recover." He rolled over, tossing his legs up on the bunk and cupping his hands behind his head. "It's my tough luck if I don't do it the right way."

O'Reilly said, "Fellows, we've all got a bad case of check-itis. It comes with jitters and loss of sleep and constipation, all of which ends if you get kicked out."

Jesse joined with a hollow laugh. "So we've got something to look forward to."

```
Oct. 24
Poor planning in his altitude emergency attempt
to land downwind.
Coordination in climbing and gliding turns
poor.
Crosswind landing he has tendency to land with
nose veered off to one side of landing.
```

At this rate, once again, Jesse wasn't sure he'd ever make it.

Mrs. Clayton's

Late October, 1947

Jesse met Daisy on the 10:40 A.M. Greyhound, which had traveled via Biloxi and Mobile. In the back of the bus, she'd talked with a middle-aged woman who'd gotten on in Biloxi after visiting her mother. The woman's husband was a chief cook at Pensacola and they lived off-base in "cullud town." Well-dressed, she was well spoken.

The woman had said, "It's a lot better now than it was before the war. Back then, the station issued a welcome letter to the officers' wives reporting aboard for the first time. Among other things, the letter said, 'When hiring Negro cleaning and kitchen help, watch out for theft. . . .' "

Jesse had gotten weekend leave and after they held each other a long time in the bus dock, he retrieved her cardboard suitcase.

She was wearing a felt hat, green dress, and a light cotton coat. She had a purse and in a cloth bag were birthday gifts from Jesse's family, relayed by Daisy to save on parcel post.

Jesse said, "I have enough money for a taxi. There's no direct bus service."

"If it's not too far to Mrs. Clayton's and that suitcase isn't too heavy, let's walk. I'd rather have you buy us a good meal."

"No distance at all," Jesse said. It was about five miles to Mrs. Clayton's. The weather was overcast, chill but no rain.

As they began to walk, Daisy asked, "Have you paid her?"

"I will today."

Jesse realized that he'd forgotten to ask Mrs. Clayton about meals. *Maybe Daisy can cook her own. Ten dollars a month probably doesn't cover meals.*

"We'll get along," she said.

"We have to." If he was anything but a midshipman living off-base and had dependents, he'd get a food allowance. Eighty-two dollars every thirty days didn't cover secret wives. There were no rings on her fingers.

In the morning Mrs. Clayton asked, "How does it feel to be a pilot's wife?"

"It's very scary and he's not even a pilot yet."

"Is he flying today?"

"Just before he left me last night, he said he was scheduled to fly today. I worry about that."

They'd sat on the couch in Mrs. Clayton's front room holding hands before he'd returned to the base about eight o'clock, saying he had to do some "headwork," meaning manual study.

"I've prayed for him every single night since he joined the Navy and now that I'm his wife I'll pray harder and longer."

"The main thing is that you're together. That should be comforting to you both."

Daisy nodded. "We'll spend Saturdays and Sundays together. We'd like to start going to John the Baptist."

Mrs. Clayton reflected a moment, then said, "I think you and I'll get along just fine." Then she smiled. "Now, Daisy, if you'll do the breakfast dishes, I'll do my socializing for this morning." She rose up and went to the phone.

Daisy's room was as clean and neat as the rest of the house. Off to one side of the double bed was a thick oak dresser; on the opposite side was a writing desk and chair. On the desk were pictures of two teenage girls. They matched the many photos in the front room, including teenage grandchildren. Mrs. Clayton had said the room was occupied by the daughters when they were young. There were many antiques.

One photo in the front room, in particular, had caught Daisy's eye—a smiling young man in a white sailor's uniform. Mrs. Clayton had seen her looking at him. "That's Roger, my only son. I had him when I was forty. He was killed in the Battle of the Coral Sea on the *Lexington*. He was your age, only nineteen. I've never quite recovered from that telegram."

Jesse had said he wanted four children, two boys and two girls. Daisy hoped she could give them to him. They both came from large families; they were both healthy, so the possibility of four children was there. She believed she was qualified to be a good mother.

```
Doesn't look around enough in the air.
Failed to correct for drift on final landing and
landed wheels first at base.
```

Jesse suddenly realized just how much the lieutenant was monitoring him from the rear cockpit, even to the movements of his head. He'd been more concerned with the instruments than with what was flying around him, if anything. Well, it was easy enough to start looking over and up and down.

Another pair of stupid mistakes, however. They were eating him alive and at what point would Zastri say to the chief instructor, "The hell with him. He's not learning."

But the next day, the presence and magic of Daisy Nix

Brown seemed to work. Or perhaps it was the prayer. Maybe self-confidence at last. Maybe none of those. Maybe he was just learning. Lieutenant Zastri made a single notation:

    Satisfactory progress.

And on Wednesday he wrote:

    Satisfactory hop.

There wasn't one mark in the bottom 20 percent. He stamped SAFE FOR SOLO. Jesse was overwhelmed.

He spent a nickel to call Daisy. "I may be out of the woods, thank God." He told her what had happened. No mistakes either flight. "Now, if I can just keep it up."

"No reason not to," she said, sharing his relief.

"I don't know. Every day seems different. The aircraft is always the same, but I'm not. I can't tell you what it is. Every time I taxi out I have to cross my fingers."

"All you need is more experience, Jesse."

"I guess. I'll have a new instructor for the final check of A and if I get by him I'll go on to Stage B, which might be fun. Acrobatics! I got a taste of them at Glenview."

"Jesse, I'm so dumb about all these things you're telling me. Isn't acrobatics dangerous? Why do you need it?"

"You need it if you fly military aircraft. You fight up in the air. I'll be doing loops and chandelles and lazy-eights, short field work."

"I don't know what you're talking about, Jesse."

"I'll teach you. You just stay calm and happy at Mrs. Clayton's and I'll call you after the flight tomorrow and let you know if I graduate to the next stage. I love you and can't wait to take you in my arms on Saturday. I wish I could fly like a bird to your room tonight."

Daisy laughed. "I wish that too."

Alone in the SNJ, Jesse flew perfectly the next day for Lt. (jg) Hoover, takeoff to landing.

Excited, he spent another nickel that night to tell Daisy he'd move up to the next step.

Reality set in again on Friday. Zastri wrote:

```
Did not use enough forward stick in spin recov-
ery.
```

After they landed, Zastri said, "I have to remind you again. Spins and stalls can kill you. You better learn how to handle them. Now!"

He'd been told, all right, and he'd listened, and he'd tried to conquer the spin. Conquer it exactly and correctly, but somehow he'd always goofed. It was like playing fine music and missing one or another note each time.

That night he read and reread the flight manual:

Abnormal Spin: A spin developed by abnormal or severe use of the controls, or one in which the airplane will not recover to normal flight within a maximum of two additional turns after neutralizing the controls. In recovery from an "abnormal spin," it is often necessary to use opposite controls. Sometimes severe manipulations are required to overcome the spin.

On Saturday morning, after the white-glove room inspection, he got his weekend leave pass from the squadron office and took the crowded city bus into town, standing in the rear of it, holding on to a strap. Back there, as expected, he was the sole occupant with a gold anchor on his cap and on his shirt collar tabs.

Nearest to him was a rating, an aircraft mechanic first-class with several rows of battle ribbons on his chest. His skin was almost lemon-colored and he had intense dark eyes. Jesse estimated he was in his early thirties. He stared for a moment, then said quietly, "I've heard about you. You're Jesse Brown. Think you'll make it?"

"I hope so."

"I hope so too. Anyone giving you a bad time?"

"Not really. The guys have been very supportive. I deserve whatever bad times the instructors have given me."

"Oh?"

"I'm not a hot-shot student."

"Aren't many of those around here."

"I'm struggling," Jesse admitted.

"There's a lot of threat here, a lot of smoke, but not much fire. If they really wanted to, they could wipe out every class. You and I have one thing going for us. We're not in the cook-and-bottle wash department, Jesse Brown. Except for misbehaving, they kick us out and I think they'd have to answer to the Bureau of Personnel, in good old Washington, D.C. There's a new policy. That doesn't mean you don't have to truly qualify as an aviator, it just means nowadays that they can't play too many games because of our skin color."

Jesse kept quiet. He was disturbed by what the rating was saying.

"I'll be promoted to chief next year, do my twenty, retire, and take a job with an airline. I'll keep my nose clean until then, my mouth shut."

Jesse nodded.

"I hear things. I listen to the underground. It's like the old slave days. I hear there's a lieutenant instructor who said, 'If I go, I'll take that nigger with me.' That means you. A steward brother told me. In case you haven't met him, he's blond and skinny and his name is Tipton."

Jesse muttered a thanks. Oh, yes, he knew Tipton. Yes, he surely did.

"Good luck," the First said, and got off at the next stop.

Two stops later, Jesse went out the rear exit and began the walk to Mrs. Clayton's house, thinking about what the Aviation Mechanic had said. *Whatever this new Washington*

*policy is, I'd better keep my nose clean and my mouth shut. Most
of the problems have been individuals like Lieutenant Tipton, or
the captain at Ottumwa, not groups. And those individuals have
to be dealt with one-on-one, win or lose. The days of mob lynching,
even in Mississippi, are hopefully in the past.*

Daisy met him at the door, her smile radiant, her arms
open, saying, "I've been waiting for you since daylight. I
woke up waiting for you. . . ." They held each other a long
time.

Mrs. Clayton wasn't at home.

"You know what I've been thinking about? Us being seen
together on the street."

Jesse laughed. "I'm your best friend. I'm your boyfriend!
The Navy doesn't own these streets. Don't worry about that
for one moment. No one is going to come up and say, 'Are
you two married?' "

"But you have on your uniform."

"Of course, I do. That's all I have to wear, on-base or off."

Daisy said, "Okay" and then reported her week at Mrs.
Clayton's. "I'd go crazy here if I didn't keep busy. She took
me to a church social after the Wednesday night service and
introduced me as Daisy Nix."

"Keeping our secret," Jesse said.

Daisy nodded. "Yes, she's wonderful." After a beat, with
a wide smile, she said, knowingly, "She said you could
spend the night in my room. We can have our honeymoon
in Pensacola."

"She is wonderful," Jesse agreed.

Pensacola City

November 1947

They walked into town, holding hands, and Jesse showed her some of the tourist sights and then they went to two movie matinees, spending a dollar for the four segregated balcony tickets. Daisy was a film fan and had gone to a lot of "picture shows."

Since this was a "honeymoon," he decided to splurge and take her to dinner at the Cuban restaurant where he'd dined with Jack Keefer and Joan. An hour later, they left The Havana Cafe to begin walking back toward Mrs. Clayton's house.

After about three blocks, they were confronted by a pair of SPs, wearing armbands, dressed in winter blues, and each carrying billies at their left hips, flashlights in their right hands. One was a little taller than the other but both were strapping white boys. The tallest one asked Jesse, "That your uniform?"

"Yes, it is."

"You know you can be arrested, nigger, for impersonating a midshipman."

Jesse dug out his wallet and displayed his ID, burning inside.

"Pass?"

Jesse produced that paper, holding his temper.

The beam of one light encircled Jesse's face; the other light shone down on the ID card.

Jesse knew that Daisy was quivering beside him, her hand on his left arm.

"What are you doin', nigger boy, tryin' to be a pilot?" the shorter one asked.

Stomach tied in knots, fighting back inner rage, Jesse said, "I have every right to be a naval aviator."

The taller SP said, "The hell you do. You ain't the right color, boy."

The shorter one asked, "This girl got any ID?"

Jesse fought to maintain composure, to think carefully about what he was saying to them. "She's a civilian and not under Navy control." He could feel her fingers bouncing on his arm. He could lose it all—right now, tonight—unless he was careful.

"Well, well, you know what I think she is, I think she's a *whoor*," said the tall one. "Maybe we should call the police. They got records on 'em."

Daisy Nix Brown began to weep. Daisy Nix Brown couldn't believe those words.

Jesse laid his hand on hers and squeezed. "You've got no right to harass us. She's my girlfriend. You involve her with the police and I'll have your stripes tomorrow, believe me. I plan to file a complaint. I know who you are." He'd read their name tags.

The shorter one said, "You sound like a college boy, not a cotton-picker."

"I am a college boy," Jesse replied, evenly but freezer-

cold. He wanted to fight, to take both of these thugs out.
He knew he could do it.

"Tell you what, get your nigger-whoor off the street an'
quit disgracing your uniform. Go on. . . ."

Daisy was weeping loudly, head against Jesse's left shoulder. He thought she might collapse. With as much dignity
as he could summon, they went on.

After turning up a side street, Jesse found a bench outside
a closed shop. He sat her down and rocked her for a long
time, telling her to try to forget what had happened. "You
must, you have to. . . ." He knew she'd never forget it. Nor
would he.

Then they walked on to Mrs. Clayton's house.

She'd returned home and immediately saw Daisy's blood-
red eyes. "What happened?"

> Dearest Jesse:
>
> We received your letter saying that you had soloed
> that big airplane. The feeling of flying it all alone must
> have been something. We congratulate you and are so
> proud of you and all your accomplishments.
>
> Marvin came out to dinner with us last Sunday and
> we talked mostly about you. He always tells his stu-
> dents at the high school that he is your "big brother"
> and Mr. Burger constantly asks about you. He asked
> Marvin if you could please send a picture of yourself
> standing by your airplane. He wants to put it up on the
> school bulletin board, besides the one in your uniform.
>
> Daisy is so good about writing and fills in the lines
> about you, day by day. She's still frightened about be-
> ing discovered at that lady's house. I wrote to her yes-
> terday, telling her to place her faith in you and God.
>
> Lura and Fletcher are doing well in school and we
> hear from William now and then. He hates the Chicago
> winters, as you know.
>
> Papa's doctor has told him to slow down, but you

know your daddy. His heart isn't as strong as it used to be, but you'd never know it.

We think of you all the time and pray for your safety.

> All our love,
> Mama

Jesse flew with Lieutenant Zastri on the mostly clear morning of December 3, a Wednesday, and long before landing he knew he was again in trouble. As the days went by, the lieutenant was becoming less and less tolerant of mistakes; less patient.

Zastri had said, the afternoon before, "You had a solo flight three weeks ago. That should have told you I thought you were coming along fine. Now, you seem to be goofing off every time we go up. What's your problem, Brown?"

In the last few days, the lieutenant had written on the training form:

```
When dropping wing into the wind on crosswind
landing student did not use opposite rudder to
keep nose lined up down runway.
```

Mental error, of course. Will they never stop?

```
Student did not remember proper entry procedure
in steep turn stall.
```

Another mental error, of course. The brain guides the hand on the stick, the feet on the pedals.

```
Student did not observe wind direction.
```

I did glance at the wind sock, but it was only a glance.

```
Student didn't observe other plane in pattern.
```

Zastri had said angrily, "Mister, you could kill us both. . . ."

I did glance at the other planes. I saw several SNJs off to the sides, but the lieutenant pointed out three overhead.

Guilty. Maybe goofing off is the right term, Jesse thought. Stupid errors, dangerous errors. Jesse felt like he was riding a see-saw. For every good day, there were two bad ones. *Daisy is here, so that can't be the excuse. . . .*

After they were back on the ground, about ten-thirty, Zastri said tersely, "I'm putting you with another instructor this afternoon." He shook his hand. "Nice knowing you and good luck."

He walked away. Zastri was obviously disgusted and Jesse, moving slowly behind him toward the hangar with a hollow stomach, had no handy explanations. He wasn't purposely making the errors. There were no excuses, however.

He had no appetite and decided not to go to chow. He stayed in the hangar, had a chocolate bar and a soft drink, waiting for the afternoon flights to be posted. Undoubtedly, Zastri had arranged for a tough instructor.

Finally LIEUTENANT JOHN KNOX, USMC was chalked in beside BROWN, J. L. Jesse met the stocky pilot shortly after one o'clock and guessed immediately that Knox had flown combat in the Pacific. He was the right age and had the look of a veteran. Aside from a hello and handshake, Knox was silent as they walked toward the flight line. He had a rolling gait. Instructors didn't have to talk.

Jesse blew out an apprehensive breath. *Now I've got a Marine check pilot.* From Guadalcanal on to the Marshalls and Gilberts, then into the Philippines and Okinawa, Marine air groups had chewed up the Japanese and earned a brass-ball reputation during World War II.

Jesse knew the "jarhead" story and concluded that in all probability Knox had seen combat and would be tough, the kind of pilot who would want the very best on his wing; he'd demand the best. *That's what I'd want too.*

"How many hours have you had?" Knox asked, just before they climbed into SNJ 346.

"Sixty-one, sir. Ten of those at Glenview."

"Well, you ought to know how to fly by now," Knox said. "Let's get her up. I'm just a passenger."

Flight B17X, forever a part of Jesse's records, was off the ground in a few minutes and he knew he had to perform the full menu for his no-nonsense passenger.

When the altimeter read 5,000 feet, Knox said, "We're going to do it all, Brown."

> *Chandelle*: A climbing turn at high speed, during which the aircraft is suddenly turned so as to head in the opposite direction.

Jesse held his breath as the plane almost stalled, hanging too long in the air.

Knox asked, "You know the purpose of this maneuver, Brown?"

"I've read it, sir. In a flight manual, sir."

"Well, you sure as hell aren't acting like you know. It's to gain altitude at the same time the direction of flight is changed. Put that in your chandelle memory bank."

Sweat was again rolling down Jesse's face, even though the cockpit was chilly. The outside temperature was 20 degrees.

Knox said, "Okay, Brown, show me your stall. Power on. . . ." The Pratt & Whitney was roaring.

Jesse said to himself, *Oh Lord, help me now. Remember the manual.*

> *Stall with Power*: A flight condition in which the aircraft has been completely stalled with the power on and the preceding climb has been so steep that it seems to hang momentarily on the propeller because of the "power-on condition."

There was a sickening plunge and Jesse felt his stomach coming up into his mouth.

Knox said, "Stalls resulting from a full-stall condition with power are much more vicious and rapid and the aircraft is harder to handle than stalls without power. . . ."

The whole hour and forty-five minutes went that way, leaving Jesse drained as he set the 346 down on the runway and taxied it back to the flight line. Totally exhausted.

He'd "goofed" again and knew it.

A few feet away from the aircraft, Knox said, "Here, read what I've written."

He'd printed his assessment on the right hand side of the training form:

> *Stalls*: Lost excessive altitude in recovery from power-on stall. Let nose drop or fall it down to diving altitude. Did not drop wheels or flaps in doing an elevator trim-tab stall.
> *Lazy 8*: Poor drift correction. Doesn't bank up steep enough in downwind turns. Drifts away from point.

Jesse forced himself to go on reading.

> *Lo Altitude Emergency*: Unsatisfactory. Turned downwind when he could have easily turned into the wind.

> *Precision Landings*: Wide upwind in pattern, angles beam position. Speed generally fast downwind, slow in groove. Forgot propeller pitch on all occasions. Forgot prop pitch in precision landings and hi and lo altitude emergencies. Did not know flap settings for precision landings. Did not do a ''takeoff check-off.'' Student was 90° out of the wind at 200 ft. of altitude after takeoffs.

Jesse Leroy Brown,
Eureka High School, Class of 1944

Jesse's childhood friend Ike Heard at the Eureka
High School prom with his future wife, Gwen

Addie Nix,
Daisy Brown's mother
and Jesse's mother-in-law

Pamela and Daisy Brown

TD2 Vincent "Vic" Breddell, USN, Pam
and Daisy at the house in Rhode Island

LTJG Roland Christensen, USNR, Jesse's instructor at Glenview Naval Air Station

Courtesy U.S. Navy

Courtesy William H. Koenig

LTJG William H. Koenig, USN

Ensign Leland E. Nelson,
USN

Lee LaCroix Nelson

LTJG Thomas Hudner
USN

Jesse Leroy Brown being sworn in as the first African American naval aviator

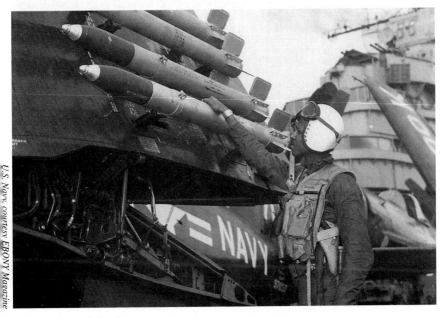

Jesse on board the *Leyte*

Ensign Brown and shipmates at work

Jesse enjoying off-hours on the *Leyte*

President Truman awarding the Medal of Honor to LTJG Thomas Hudner, USN

Jesse Leroy Brown, 1926–1950

I recommend extra time.

John Knox

Feeling ill, Jesse handed back the form which the chief instructor would soon read and which would become part of his flight jacket at the Chief of Naval Aviation Training Command. "I'm sorry, sir."

"You should be," Knox replied, ending any conversation, and began walking toward the hangar, as Lieutenant Zastri had done this morning.

Jesse wanted to throw up again, but there was nothing in his stomach. He felt the kind of illness that comes from absolute defeat: a dryness of mouth, a tightening of the chest, a dull ache all over. He avoided the hangar and went directly to the cattle car stop and waited for the ride to the barracks.

Once there, he was glad that O'Reilly was asleep, so he wouldn't ask, "How'd it go?" He quickly changed into shorts and a sweatshirt and went to the track. But even running would not take away the fear of losing it all within a day or two.

There'd be another check flight tomorrow and another unsmiling pilot. Once again, he knew it had nothing at all to do with the color of his skin. As his feet pounded the cinders, he knew it had everything to do with his ability as a naval aviation student.

He ran until his chest hurt, until each loud breath was a hot sword.

Jesse didn't think he slept more than an hour all night, going over stalls, wing-overs, chandelles, spins, small field landings, every lousy thing else, flying in the darkness in his bunk. He rolled and tossed, got up three times and went to the head, visited the water fountain in the hallway. By merciful reveille, he felt as if he had dry flu. His eyes stung.

Keefer said, "You look awful."

"No worse'n I feel. I keep making dumb mistakes."

They were all in different stages of dress, hurrying for assembly and breakfast, and the morning flight line.

Bingham, their new roommate, said, "Pal, don't talk to me about mistakes. I'm hanging on after three 'down' checks. My ass is on a quick slide out of here unless I fly better today than I did yesterday. You get no sympathy from me."

Jesse laughed ruefully. "I don't need sympathy, I just need a new connection between my brain, my hands, and my feet."

An hour later he looked at the assignment board in the hangar and saw LIEUTENANT TIPTON beside his name and muttered, "Why, why, why?"

There is only one instructor on the base named Tipton, Jesse thought. *Why do the odds, rotten enough anyway, have to be stacked against me at this point?*

But he'd gotten into this position by himself; couldn't blame it on fate or bad luck. Yesterday with the tough Marine was bad enough. Perhaps Knox had talked about him in the instructor's ready room and Tipton had overheard, asking for Brown, J. L., to be assigned as his student. Perhaps Tipton knew he was on his way out, like some other instructors, and would carry out his threat to take Brown, J. L., with him.

Seeing him in the lecture room or in the hangar or on the flight line later on, he noticed his blue eyes and high cheekbones. His face was long and narrow. It was a severe face. He looked a little like an actor named John Carradine, a character out of the Old West.

As Jesse walked up to him and saluted him, saying he was Brown, J. L., he said to himself, *Don't be afraid of this white man. Just fly your very best.* But he knew from the hostile stare in the blue eyes that "his best" wouldn't be good enough. Not nearly. A "down" check was inevitable.

Moments after the pre-start cockpit check, Jesse flipped the ignition switch. He again checked the instrument panel for fuel and waited a moment in post-start until there was a steady sound forward, the aircraft vibrating with the normal takeoff revs.

Thinking that at least he'd score okay on the takeoff, he taxied out at normal speed but blew it when he went past the signalman's "stop" by forty or fifty feet, causing Tipton to yell, "For Chrissakes, nigger, you wanna hit someone. . . ." They were close aboard other planes, almost colliding.

So the morning began going downhill even before they were airborne and he lifted the wheels up. Tipton wanted this one to be Brown, J. L.'s last flight.

> *Stalls*: Entry to stall nose too high. Student let
> his high speed steep turn to the left get away
> from him on recovery. We went over in steep turn
> to the right before he really broke the stall.
> Power of stall was too nose-down (40° dive) and
> he held it down and was slow to assume gliding
> attitude.
>
> Lt. R. Tipton

Jesse felt like he was riding a wild horse for the sake of the cowboy held behind him. This man, who might have vowed that no Negro would ever land a fighter on a carrier deck, was plainly his enemy. At the same time, he knew that truth was working against him. He was doing a lousy job. He could almost feel the animosity from the rear cockpit.

> *Wing-overs* border on pattern and speed. Speed
> faster on top—85 knots or over; 80 knots on an-
> other. Inconsistent.
>
> Lt. R. Tipton

Tipton said, "Small fields now. Nigger, you're the sloppiest student I've ever flown with."

Jesse fought off despair.

Small field landings, simply, were to teach pilots to land in small areas, usually on emergency. But the same skills were employed in learning how to land on carriers when those ships were tossing and rolling, matchsticks in the sea.

> *Unsatisfactory*. Pattern too close. As a result, we could not land and then get off in three shots. First shot was *wheels-up* pass. He made no move to correct for close pattern. On one pass we were high at edge of field with full flap down, gliding at 105 knots.
>
> *Headwork*: Not thinking and no planning. Weak judgment on small field work.
>
> *Air Discipline*: Flew over two fields at 1,000 ft. against traffic. Was flying in scattered clouds at 1,000 ft. until check pilot mentioned it. Student seemed oblivious to danger.
>
> Lt. R. Tipton

On and on it went, and to the side of the form was the black stamp of UNSATISFACTORY, with a thick arrow facing down. *"Down" check. Another one,* Jesse thought.

So much had been invested; so much of the future was invested. He felt Tipton, beginning with those "going home" painful words in the hallway, perhaps that card on his bunk, had psyched him out. But again, truthfully, he'd had this aircraft in *his* hands. He should have been able to shut out the words, as he'd promised Ike Heard and M. L. Beard; listen only to positive reactions. Not the negative ones.

Paperwork came down swiftly that afternoon, not long

after Lieutenant Tipton took his arrogant "goodbye" walk
across the tarmac.

Student's Name: Brown, J. L.   *Rank or Rate:*
                                    Mid.USN—9X—47P
Squadron: BTU-1 Corry   *Date:* 12/4/47 NATB,
                                    Pensacola, Fla.

Student to appear before SFB (Summary Flight Board) because of two B-17 check failures.
Down checks:
12/3/47   B-17X   Headwork—Air Discipline
12/4/47   B-17X   Air Discipline

                                        Lt. R. Tipton

Prior to appearing before the Board the next day, Jesse
was given a questionnaire to fill out.

To the Student:
In view of your difficulties in flight training to date,
you are herewith handed your flight record in order
that you may answer the following questions:
1. Have you any complaint or criticism to make concerning your treatment or training?

The room that Jesse was alone in faced out toward the
flight line. He looked at the aircraft taxiing, landing, taking
off. He could hear the guttural sounds of the engines as he
watched, knowing the throttles were two-blocked. He
watched as they lifted up into the air and he came as close
to quitting as the night Daisy was called a "whoor."

Well, he could write down that he'd been the target of
discrimination from Lieutenant Ross Tipton and others in
the past, beginning with the base commander at Ottumwa.

He could go on and on with small occurrences. He could
tell them what Daisy had been called. Those words he had
not been able to clear from his head. Perhaps words were
involved in the poor performance? They were no excuse.
He could write that Tipton had said, "Go home, nigger boy."
He could say he thought Tipton had left a card on his bunk
expressing the same thought.

Instead, he wrote down, "No." He had no complaints.

Another question asked if he would like to be retained.

He wrote down: "I desire very much to be retained."

An hour later he sat before the Board, which was composed of a lieutenant commander and four instructors. The
only one he personally knew was Lieutenant Zastri. He'd
seen the others around.

The lieutenant commander examined the questionnaire
and said, "You've thought about this statement of 'No' concerning treatment and training?"

"I have, sir."

The senior officer there nodded. "In view of these 'down'
checks and in view of instructor comments over the last two
weeks, I have to ask you whether or not you think you have
what it takes to be a good naval aviator?"

"I do, sir. I've had a bad two weeks. I admit it. I've
thought about it. I can't tell you exactly why. I've felt pressure, but that's no excuse, I realize. I'm a much better pilot
than what is in my flight record."

Lieutenant Zastri said, "May I comment, sir. I've been
Brown's principal instructor in Stage B. He is a much better
pilot than indicated. I think all of us went through a bad
period sometime. I know I did. I remember that after I got
into trouble and went before a board like this one, my flying
ability quickly increased."

Other instructors asked questions and then the senior officer said, "That'll be all, Brown. Wait outside."

He left the room, expecting the worst.

The final Board action was:

Recommend one increment of extra time; change of
instructors. If student fails two out of three
B-17 rechecks, he will be referred to COAB.

COAB (Commanding Officer's Air Board) was a totally senior officer board and usually meant a naval aviation career was over.

When Zastri came out of the room, he said, "You're retained, Brown. Don't let me down."

"I won't, sir. Thank you," Jesse answered.

He went out into the late-afternoon sunshine, feeling as if an SNJ itself had been lifted off his back. He went to a phone booth outside the barracks to call Daisy.

He now looked forward to the daily flights and immediate improvements were noted by the new instructor, Tompkins. Comments on his final two Stage B tests with check pilots were:

Good hop.

Good ride.

He'd regained concentration and confidence. Stages C and D, more acrobatics and instrument flying, would begin after the holidays. He knew he had a long way to go before wings would be pinned on his chest and "down" checks, and packing a suitcase, would be entirely possible any given week. But for now, he felt optimistic.

Jesse and Daisy went home on December 20. Money wasn't available for Christmas gifts and the families didn't expect any. Beaming Jesse, in his midshipman blues, and his bride were gifts enough.

16

Pensacola

April 1948

Jesse managed leave on most weekends and on a Saturday afternoon in April, while they were walking away from Mrs. Clayton's, Daisy said, "Stop and look at me. I have something to tell you."

He stopped.

Her eyes were sparkling and she displayed an ageless secretive smile, she said, "Jesse Brown, I'm going to make you a papa!"

Speechless, he finally yelped and took her into his arms. "When did you find out?"

"Yesterday. I went to Mrs. Clayton's doctor on Tuesday. I promised you four children and thought I better get started."

"You sure?"

"The doctor's sure."

"Man oh man."

She laughed. "Could be a girl."

The timing was not the greatest. There was always a certain risk of discovery when they were together, as the SP incident had proved, and midshipmen had seen them on Pensacola streets, had nodded to him, a few had even paused to talk to them, possibly to prove they weren't prejudiced. But when Daisy began to "show"—or perhaps before—it would be time for her to return home. It didn't make sense to take more risks.

Under other circumstances, as a declared dependent, she could have the baby in a naval hospital free of charge, including later pediatric service. Secret marriages had their penalties. Jesse would pay.

Late the next month, after talking about it again and again, both jittery, feeling like criminals on the run, Daisy returned to Hattiesburg to stay with her mother. The $10 room rent in Pensacola would be saved, although Mrs. Clayton offered to continue boarding Daisy without payment. Jesse wasn't comfortable with that idea and began traveling to Hattiesburg whenever he could by thumb and bus. They were back to writing daily love letters, his life divided into two separate worlds, the demands of flying and the thoughts of a pregnant wife back home.

Summer approached, with North Florida 90-degree humidity, mosquitoes, and afternoon thunderstorms, much the same in Hattiesburg. Daisy was working part-time at her old job, saving money for the baby. Jesse, combining ground school with the cockpit, was trying to survive.

> . . . another exam, sweet Daisy, to determine whether or not I know the safety procedures if the engine stops—is running rough—catches on fire; if my landing gear won't go down; if the radio goes out; if I lose my brakes.

Now in the final phases of basic training, he'd moved from the Mainside barracks to another cubicle at Saufley Field, with temporary roommates. He saw little of them.

There was a sense of urgency, a down-to-the-wire grind, for all of them.

Dearest Daisy:

Flying wide open on the tail of another aircraft twenty feet away, stepped-down about fifteen feet, is a thrill beyond belief. You've seen it in the movies, but to actually be in the plane is something else. At first, with an instructor in the lead plane (mine), there were two aircraft; the next day, four planes, flying smoothly and very close to each other, going through all sorts of maneuvers. Despite some crosswind trouble and over-controlling the aircraft, I passed formation flying.

Dearest Daisy:

. . . the four gunnery SNJs were equipped with a single thirty-caliber machine gun mounted on the upper cowling just ahead of the forward cockpit. Another SNJ towed the aerial target which was about twenty feet long. The tips of the bullets were painted different colors so we could see who scored the hits. We'd trained on a skeet range for this one. One after the other we dived on the target. The thump of the gun and the smell of gunpowder gave me an eerie sense of being in combat. The instructor wrote that I flew a good hop, on target most of the time.

Dearest Daisy:

I squeaked by bombing (average bomb hit 130 feet), but I lost sight of the target on one run-in. Then we started night flying, known here as "night frights." The field is as dark as a coal mine and flare pots are put on the runway to indicate the size of the field. Between the flare pots is the "carrier," blacker than coal. Eight of us did "touch-and-goes" in a simulated carrier pattern. At times, the plane in front of me was so close I could feel his prop wash. It's hard to judge distance and height at night. Reality becomes hidden in the ink and what is so obvious in the day must be searched out once day has gone. I could see the lights of Pensacola and other little towns, reminding me that I was still in a human world.

Someday, after the baby is born, I'll take you on a night flight. It is mysterious up there, especially in the rural areas of Alabama, where I flew my night solo. In all the darkness below, there'd be a single farmhouse light or the twin beams of a single car lighting up the road, then long stretches of woods that were solid black. Above, I was living in my own space of blackness. I felt lonely and vulnerable and was glad to turn back toward the base and the welcoming sight of the split beacon. I know I'll get used to night flying, but I'll never forget last night's experience in the void.

Ahead is more ground school, aerobatics review check, primary combat, navigation flights, dual instruments—flying "blind," flying by instruments only, a real attention-getter—and the Link trainer I told you about, tucked in that boxy, rocking simulator that has a mind of its own. One flight Jack Keefer had in the Link, he flew right into the ground, thinking everything was okay.

After watching films of carrier landings, including several fatal crashes, one flying into the stern, another making the deck but veering left off to drop eighty feet into the sea, Jesse listened intently to the instructor: "Unless you hack this exercise today, you'll never hack 'em at sea. And out there we'll have a carrier that can take care o' crosswinds. Jus' square up the stern an' head into 'em. Fly that baby all the way aroun' the pattern right to the 'cut.' Course, you don't have your tail hook down today, so it's the attitude, pattern, airspeed, and lineup that we'll be lookin' at. Are you gonna get that airplane in the 'groove' so it will catch the arrestin' wire? I'll tell you from personal experience sometimes it's harder to make these field landings than it is to land on a carrier. Not as dangerous, o' course, but harder. . . ."

Then the LSO, the Landing Signal Officer, came up in front to talk about his eighteen-inch wire-framed square cloth paddles and what they meant. The pink or yellow cloth was arranged in four-inch panels, allowing breeze to pierce through. If they were solid, a 30-knot wind would rip them from the LSO's hands. The paddles talked to the pilots bluntly, in a life-dependent language. *Ignore or misread and you can buy the farm.*

If the paddles were straight out to the side, it meant the landing attitude and altitude were correct. If the LSO's left paddle was horizontal and the right paddle lowered, the plane was too fast. If both paddles were snapped together several times, the plane was dangerously slow. Both paddles waved across his head meant "wave-off" and the pilot better *instantly* respond. If the LSO was satisfied that the plane could make a safe landing he would give the pilot a "Cut" engine signal by lowering the left paddle as he moved the right paddle across his left shoulder.

Jesse was furiously taking notes.

He'd already spent time out there studying the LSO's paddles, watching how the other students corrected. Taking your eyes off the LSO on his small stern platform for even a few seconds while landing on a carrier was an invitation to death.

The LSO talked about the "groove," the extension of the center, line of the carrier aft, the desired flight path of the landing aircraft, and talked about the aircraft being not more than twenty-five or thirty feet above the flight deck, not more than 10 knots above stall; nose-up for a three-point landing. He talked about absolute "faith" in the LSO; how the pilot's view would be partially obstructed due to the attitude of the aircraft when landing. "Gentlemen, your asses will be in my hands."

*   *   *

Walking across the tarmac to the flight line, parachutes bumping their fannies, exchanging remarks, trying for laughs, the qualifiers were all hiding the same everpresent fear of failure. Would it never stop until they got their wings? Would it stop then? Would they get more "downs" on this next to final phase? Would they be told to pack and go home?

Jesse had gotten another "down" in ground school recently. Navigation. He'd failed it and was hauled up, embarrassed, before another Board. He'd passed on the second try.

June heat waves rose off the runway of the outlying field. It was white-striped in the dimensions of a medium-sized aircraft carrier deck and Jesse was in the third SNJ of the four-aircraft division, awaiting takeoff on this first day of a week of field carrier practice landings.

Qualify here on dry land and he'd soon be on his way to try the real thing out in the Gulf of Mexico. The weather was good, sun out strong, skies blue, with the usual scattered clouds, but there was a crosswind that spelled trouble for those who had to sit down within the white outlines.

Props were spinning and the pilots patiently awaited the launch signal from the LSO, who stood by the edge of the runway holding his paddles in each hand. They were smaller than tennis rackets. On approach, the paddles "talked" to the pilots, an intimate language. Later on at sea, the language could be—could be—the difference between seeing the next sunset or crashing. Same language each time. Jesse knew he had to "listen" to those paddles and not question a single word.

The LSO was stripped to the waist, body deeply tanned from standing out there day after day, waving those paddles. The LSOs were veteran pilots, schooled in the art of coaxing airplanes safely to the flattop decks. They were, in effect, flying the oncoming aircraft for a few seconds.

Depending on velocity, crosswinds were often bad news for even the most qualified pilots and Jesse had battled them from the first day in the SNJ.

The wind sock at Saufley Field was almost limp, but that was no guarantee that cross or quartering winds wouldn't be blowing at the auxiliary runway thirty miles away. It was on uninhabited land, walking distance from a sound where instructors fished when no practice aircraft were landing. Jesse had seen it numerous times on prior flights. That patch of hewn-out palmetto began the final transition to Navy wings.

After the cockpit check, now as routine as brushing his teeth, he took off, mentally rehearsing the pattern he'd need to get into proper position. He'd be the fifth aircraft of eight allowed to land or be waved off by the LSO.

The eight planes soon formed overhead and one by one began the pass down the starboard side of the "carrier," toward the break where the simulated carrier dance began. The wind sock at the end of the runway was full, west to east, and whitecaps were flashing on the nearby sound.

He reported to the LSO, "Three Fox Niner Six Five, abeam, gear and flaps down," before beginning his approach turn. The LSO acknowledged.

All eight were waved off on their first approach, not unusual for Field Carrier Landing Practice.

Jesse made the turn okay but was too high and too fast in the groove, and both paddles waved over the LSO's head.

Caught in the crosswind, his biggest difficulty on other flights, he was overshooting the imaginary flight deck. The radio crackled with suggestions.

He was almost overwhelmed and soon realized he could only whip this aircraft if he broke it down into parts. He worked at getting a good start, looking for the right airspeed, attitude, and angle of bank to get into that elusive groove.

Jesse remembered the LSO taking a long curious look at him before they went out to fly, but he knew that what was happening in the air over the runway had nothing to do with skin color, once again. It was the miserable, damnable crosswind. And the other pilots were fighting it as well.

He learned some new lessons this bright morning: *Don't relax for a second. Stay trimmed up and on speed. Set up the pattern attitude at the start. Get set up for that final roll into the groove. Twenty feet off attitude is unacceptable.* He became truly aware of what the LSO wanted and discovered the bond with the paddles. All the other flying he'd done since Glenview seemed almost unimportant.

Finally he found the right final approach, got in the groove, made two touch-and-goes, as he'd be required to do at sea, then got a "cut" signal from the LSO and landed precisely where he was supposed to put the plane. He let out a yell of triumph.

Over the next two days, he was solidly in the middle percentage bracket of pattern and landings and final approach, and on the last day, the day he qualified, he rated in the top 20 percent in final approach, signals, and speed. The instructor had written:

```
Good hop. This student has the makings of a fine
pilot.
```

At last I've nailed it! I haven't had a better day since solo at Glenview.

12 June 1948

Dear Mr. Christensen:

It is always good to get mail, but your letter seemed

extraspecial. I'm glad that your family is doing okay. I guess Nancy Lee will soon be walking.

I hope to qualify aboard a carrier about Thursday of next week. So within the next ten days I should be on my way to Jacksonville for operational. I've requested fighters, either the Hellcat or the Corsair.

Sincerely,
Jesse

USS *Wright*

June 1948

For three anxious days, Jesse and Jack Keefer called the squadron duty office to find out when they were scheduled to "hit the boat": land on an aircraft carrier out in the Gulf of Mexico. The USS *Wright* was under way forty miles off Pensacola.

Finally Jesse and Keefer were notified that their group would rendezvous with the *Wright* at approximately 1030 in the morning, June 17, 1948, for "Charlie Time." They'd all learned the technique of putting their SNJs down on the practice field, but this platform would be moving at around 20 knots and on either side of it and at the stern would be the shallow blue-green Gulf.

Briefing, 0730; flight line, 0830; launch, 0900; Charlie Time, 1030. "Charlie Time" was such a matter-of-fact way to describe the few seconds when pilots were programmed to arrive at a carrier's ramp.

On this blue sky morning, white clouds again overhead, his job was to land on a portion of the *Wright*'s narrow 684-

foot flight deck without killing himself. As many Navy pilots before and after him would attest, the first carrier landing was often an ordeal framed in fear, as well as anticipation.

He'd seen the flight deck operations in training films. One narrator described carrier operations as the "most exciting show on earth." One book likened them to a theatrical performance and to dance because of the grace and coordination demanded. The activity of the plane handlers, identified by different-colored jerseys, was often termed a "ballet."

The sounding of "flight quarters" on a carrier casts a spell that seems never to lose its power in repetition. Pilots who are not manning planes or required to be in the ready rooms are often found lining the island railings, or Vultures Row, "flying" each plane off and sweating out the landings as incoming aircraft hurtle into the imaginary groove. They twitch and lean with body English, as if playing a giant pinball machine, mentally flying each plane as it seeks to get aboard safely.

It had been a year and almost three months since Jesse had flown at Glenview over those wet dark-earthed farm fields of Illinois. Behind him now were more than 150 hours in the air. If one wanted to be a naval aviator, carrier landings were inevitable, the supreme test of students. The wings of gold said it all. The fouled anchor at the base of the wings and shield meant sea duty; it meant carrier landings; it meant guts and balls. Carrier landings were a must, even to fly big transports.

The stories of aircraft crashing into flattop sterns had been told at Pensacola for years, testimony to the finality of a mistake. The bottom of the Gulf was littered with whole aircraft or parts of aircraft dating back to the mid-thirties and continuing through this year. Relatively few pilots had survived carrier collisions.

Jesse made his cockpit check carefully, even more carefully than usual, demanding that 6-Xray-273 be mechanically and electronically perfect. But on taxiing out he thought of all the mistakes he'd made during field qualifications. They were all too easy to make again. He thought of the midshipman who had made a mistake six weeks before and was now at the bottom of the sea. The plane had skidded over the side and dropped fifty feet on its back.

Takeoff!

Jesse, third aircraft of eight, meshed into the formation as they flew south, hunting the *Wright* at 6,500 feet. He noted now quickly land disappeared into the vastness of the Gulf stretching out in all directions without any landmarks. He suddenly felt uncomfortable being so far from land with just the chopping sea below.

It took less than thirty minutes to find her, a black miniature down below sliding along the water, trailing a white streak on the surface. She seemed so small to him between the fleecy clouds. As they circled, other planes were working the pattern, landing and taking off, looking like sun-flashed bees.

Long before dawn, Jesse had been rehearsing the landing in his bunk, thinking of the pattern, the speed, attitude opening the cockpit canopy. Vivid was the filmed landing of an aircraft on one wheel and disaster. Vivid was another aircraft with the LSO's shorthand notation:

```
OSCB, LUL, LL: Overshot the center line and came
back; lined up left; lousy landing.
```

Fastening his attention on the leader's aircraft, he switched radio frequency to that of the ship's and could hear the calm voice of the LSO as he instructed students who had never experienced that ultimate of thrills—a first landing on an aircraft carrier.

The requirements up here were to stay in formation, keep the formation looking good, fight the tendency to stare at the activity far below. Maintain self-discipline, with nothing out of order; everything in its proper sequence. Fly the plane; look good. *I'm here. I'll get my chance.*

Finally clearance came from *"Badger,"* code name of the *Wright*, and it was his turn to leave the orbit, flying at about 130 knots, finally dropping to 450 feet above the surface.

Jesse said a prayer, ending with "Lord, help me."

His mind became a space and time director, coordinating his hands and feet as he manipulated power, the angle of bank, the plane's attitude, and his position relative to the ship.

Now his mind accelerated. His palms began to sweat in his flight gloves. Everything switched over to mental automatic, a triggered repeat of the field carrier training. It was all happening too fast to linger on one thought. As his formation flew up the starboard side of *"Badger,"* he wanted to look good going into the landing pattern.

Separated out of the formation, he concentrated on the next step: *Gear down, flaps down, canopy open—position abeam the ship*. For a split second, the stark realization that *"Badger"* was going in one direction and his was the exact opposite. *A momentary distraction. Fly the pattern. Speed. Landing checklist*. His mental list rattled them off as the ship steamed on. He'd expected it to grow larger and larger, but that wouldn't happen until his final approach. He automatically coordinated his hands and feet as he manipulated power and the angle of bank.

He remembered what the field landing instructor had said: "Certain things won't look right, but fly it the way you were taught." *Trust the LSO*.

As he made the final turn, he could hear himself breathing in the headset and his hands were bathed in water as the ship's flight deck finally loomed larger and larger.

Too busy now to feel comforted by the increasing size of *"Badger,"* his eyes searched and locked on to the LSO on that tiny platform at the stern of the carrier, right where he should be. Red stripes of cloth covered his khaki flight coveralls. The square paddles of yellow cloth were in his hands. Veteran pilot, symphony conductor, mother and God, all in the same body, bringing his steel chicks home safely. *Trust him.*

The LSO's hands and the paddles dropped to his knees. Jesse was low and he nudged the throttle slightly to add power. *Too high now! Now a bit too much to starboard.* He corrected a little but not too much. He felt his breathing quicken. It was all happening so fast, yet he felt he had control of the roaring machine.

The flight deck, white stripes to indicate the touchdown spot, was a moving gray highway on that sea of blue.

Finally the right arm of "paddles" shot across his chest signaling "*cut.*"

Instantaneously, he closed the throttle.

There was a hard jolt as his wheels hit the deck.

I've done it, the first of two touch-and-go landings.

Without a second's hesitation, he added power and lifted off again over the water and began to search for the interval to get back into the pattern. Breathing became normal and his heart settled down and he murmured a thanks to God.

I've done it. Now that he had a moment to think, it wasn't so bad. He felt a surge of confidence and perhaps he could do better next time. That was what the touch-and-goes were all about, confidence builders. The old pilots who'd designed the program knew what they were doing. His second touch-and-go went well.

Finally it was time for the arrested landing, stop the plane in its tracks. Tail hook down was added to his landing checklist; shoulder harness locked firmly. He made the turn with precision and settled into the "groove" on target, saw the LSO's cut, pulled off his power, felt his wheels hit and the hook engage the arresting wires.

This time there was a body slam as well as the jolt, the aircraft hitting an invisible wall as the wires captured it, the eagle grasped by mighty steel hands. Unhooked immediately, he taxied forward to line up for a launch.

The Flight Deck Officer, body buffeted by the wind, pant legs flapping, rotated one finger, then two, waved his checkered flag and Jesse gave the SNJ full power, released his brakes and was airborne off the foredeck of the carrier, dipping slightly as he passed over the bow, glancing at the endless sea below.

I've done it.

Over the next hour, he sat down and took off another five required times, mixed in with two waveoffs. After the last landing, engine at idle, he heard the island loudspeaker boom out, "Midshipman Brown qualified."

I've done it.

He knew that for as long as he lived, there'd never be another moment like this one, surpassing that first flight at Glenview. He knew that he'd never be able to describe the drama of what had happened to Daisy or anyone else. Though the LSO had a lot to do with it, the act of coming aboard the carrier was singular and triumphant beyond description.

At the moment, relief of having successfully and safely qualified, feeling drained and exhilarated at the same time, it didn't occur to him that he was the first black man to ever accomplish that feat. He would think about it, at last, while flying back to Pensacola.

Within minutes after returning the aircraft to the Saufley flight line, he was on the phone to Hattiesburg, telling Daisy they "were rich." Overnight, he was eligible for flight pay of $35 a month, added to the original $82.

Jesse was now a Midshipman First Class, could belly up to the bar at the San Carlos Hotel if he wanted to; walk into the Officers' Club and own a car, an impossible dream for the time being. In all but name, he was now an officer. Of course, he still had to remain "single" until he was commissioned an ensign. It was a heady day for him, Keefer, and all others who had greased down on the deck of the *Wright.*

That late afternoon, in the Saufley Field barracks, the qualified students could bring out hidden brown shoes, badges of footwear separating them from the "black shoe, seabound Navy"; they could wear the naval aviator's green uniform; anchors on both collar tabs instead of one; a straight-across quarter-inch gold stripe on their shoulder boards.

Jesse did not have the money to buy the green uniform, but he splurged to buy the brown shoes. They were so special to naval aviators.

18

Wings of Gold

October 1948

In advanced training at Jacksonville Naval Air Station, he was looking forward to the Hellcat single-seater, a top World War II aircraft. With a twin-row, eighteen-cylinder engine, creating 2,000 horsepower, it could roar through the air at more than 300 knots. Now it was time to leave the trainers far behind and take on the rugged Hellcat, go from the kitten to the tiger.

Daisy was by his side again, and since he was First-Class, he had overnight liberty. A few days after reporting to the north Florida base, Jesse had singled out a Negro civilian employee a little older than he was and explained his plight.

Ralph Kennedy, a tall, long-armed, big-nosed electrician who wore overalls, said he thought the Navy's marriage policy was ridiculous. But he also opened his two-bedroom house in "cullud town" to Jesse and Daisy. She traveled from Hattiesburg, eager to rejoin her husband during the final weeks before winning his wings.

Daisy, early in the fourth month of her pregnancy, had not begun to "show" and they took long walks in neighborhoods where white faces were seldom seen. Unlike Pensacola, Jacksonville, a larger town, was a good place to hide a midshipman's wife. Almost every day, she went to the city bus stop around five-thirty to meet him. The station itself was in the city, bordered on two sides by the St. Johns River, in lush greenery.

So far as the command knew, Jesse's official residence was the Junior Bachelor Officers' Quarters, mostly transient living spaces for both unmarried and married pilots. His roommate was Midshipman Curt Carter, but Carter didn't see much of Jesse in the BOQ and had no idea why. Every possible off-duty moment was spent with Daisy.

Whenever he was on the station, he received waves and smiles from enlisted black brothers, his "rooting section," as he told Daisy. The attitude of the stewards had changed. They went out of their way at mealtimes to make sure that Midshipman Brown was well fed, at the risk of slighting commissioned officers.

As expected, midsummer high heat had followed them over from Pensacola and afternoon cumulus clouds often developed into thunderstorms that dumped furious rain, accompanied by lightning, plus icing and severe turbulence. The almost daily storms were usually short-lived but slowed down flight operations. Violent thunder heads rose to 30,000 or 40,000 feet over Jacksonville, treacherous air for any flying machine. The SNJs and Corsairs and Hellcats often stayed on the ground or diverted to safe areas. Jesse, having grown up with the Mississippi variety of thunderstorms, had no desire to play around with them.

J.B.O.Q., Box 27-A
NAS, Jacksonville
16 July 1948

Hi, Ike and Gwen,

Well, Junior, now that you've had your indoctrination, how do you like being married? Lovely, lovely!
You wouldn't trade it for the world, would you? I
wouldn't. If things go right, I should have my wings in
three months more.

> Your friend and pal,
> Leroy

Wartime, the Hellcat held belly tanks for a long-range
or escort mission and carried a ton of bombs. Six fifty-
caliber machine guns were mounted in the wings. Compared to the SNJ trainer, the Hellcat was an aerial
Rolls-Royce.

He went to the basic familiarization ground school on
how this airplane was put together, how to control it, how
to best operate it. He learned the basics of red line airspeeds,
temperatures and pressures that would be normal. At night,
with Daisy breathing gently beside him, he studied the basic
handbook of the Hellcat.

Four days later, after a lengthy preflight briefing, the instructor, sitting on the canopy rail, handed Jesse a blindfold.
"Okay, instrument check." On command, he touched the
altimeter, radio, airspeed indicator—every instrument,
every knob—any part of the cockpit used in operation.

"Okay, start her up."

With that, the instructor slid down the wing root.

The usual blue smoke spurted as the Pratt & Whitney
throat-coughed, the entire airframe shaking until the engine smoothed out into a steady staccato.

The machine was his—and his alone—for the next two
hours. After takeoff clearance, he murmured, "Let's get to
know each other," as he turned onto the runway, headed
toward the river. He pushed the throttle forward, calling on
the horses slowly, watching the manifold pressure, oil pressure, and RPMs. Several hundred feet down the runway,

he developed full power, thundering and feeding in more right rudder as the airplane began to swerve left as engine torque bit into the humid air. He corrected to the center of the runway.

It was glorious. Jesse felt the raw naked power in his feet, his legs, his hands, his arms—all over. The dark blue plane literally jumped into the air and he passed 1,000 feet quickly. He'd taken off many times but never in a machine that sliced into the sky. He let off his war whoop.

Attached to Squadron VT-2, a long way from that dirt field at Hattiesburg, the first two Hellcat flights were devoted to aerobatics and practice landings. An instructor flew in formation with him—behind him or below him—for observation.

```
Student did a split S on first power spiral;
rolled over on his back instead of a 60° bank.
```

"I'm a novelty," Daisy had said to Phylicia Kennedy with a smile. "Jesse is the first black Navy pilot and I'm his little black bride. I think that novelty may last a long time and I'm not sure what to do about it."

```
Spin out. Two turns to right and left. Recovery
technique satisfactory. Good landing.
```

"How are you going to fit in with all those white officers' wives?"

"Well, I just don't know," Daisy said with a laugh. "I guess they'll just have to get used to me. They are used to seeing people like me serve lunch and clean up the mess."

Phylicia laughed. "That could take some getting used to. Where will you go from here?"

"I have this baby to produce first and by that time Jesse'll probably know. I'll go with him wherever he goes except out to sea. He hopes for East Coast duty."

"You ever think you'd be a Navy pilot's wife?"

"I knew he was interested in aviation as a boy, but he didn't seem to get serious about it until he was at Ohio State. I had mixed feelings. I was hoping he'd be an architect and we could live in St. Louis or Chicago. He's got a brother in Chicago."

Good hop. Tendency to lose altitude in turns and patterns.

Jesse was being tested on such items as "evasive tactics" and "dives to 300 knots" and "steep landing descent" and Ralph Kennedy kept him at the supper table on many Saturday and Sunday nights just to talk aviation.

Ralph wanted to know how it felt to dive an airplane straight down.

Daisy and Phylicia listened, but Daisy, though she wanted to hear what he was doing, was still uncomfortable with the idea of him climbing into that powerful plane each day. She listened quietly and seldom asked any questions.

"The first time you do it," Jesse told Ralph, "you wonder if the wings won't come off when you pull out. As far back as preflight, the instructors tell you the wings only come off if you hit the ground or water. Yet the first time you dive like that you wonder if they're telling you the truth. They are. But you almost pee."

Good countering of attacks and positions at all times.

Jesse continued, "I ran out to the plane today and everything was in a mess due to the rain. All training aircraft were diverted to one area and soon the air was crowded with planes spinning, turning, diving all over the place. The combination of clouds, rain, and density of aircraft rattled me. I didn't do well. I was anxious, afraid of collision."

Speed control weak. Heading control weak.

J.B.O.Q., Box 27-A
NAS, Jacksonville
8 August 1948

Dear Lovers:

  I guess it won't be too long before you're beginning
school again, Ike, and you can bet your bottom dollar
that I'll be rooting for you all the way. You know I'm
a subscriber to the *Architectural Forum*. Every month I
get it I seem to fall more deeply in love with architecture. I sometimes envy the experience you're getting,
and boy, if I'm in the States come next May or June
I'm going to be there with bells on to see you get the
ol' sheepskin. *Smile!*

Your friend and pal,
Jesse

Daisy would kiss him goodbye in the morning and say a
prayer for his safety that day. The relationship with Phylicia
was close and warm, affording companionship for both.
There was four years' difference in their ages. They talked
a lot and went window shopping uptown, occasionally
splurging for lunch in a local Negro cafe.

  In mid-August Jesse went into the gunnery and bombing
phases of advanced training after scoring well on the skeet
range, telling Ralph it was the most fun he'd had since becoming a midshipman.

  He wrote to his family:

The tow plane, or tractor, pulled the twenty-foot target
sleeve, and we took off at thirty-second intervals and,
once out over the ocean, formed up in a column with
a separation of 1,000 feet. The first flight maneuvered
into a position abeam to slightly ahead and 3,000 feet

> above and perpendicular to the target. At a certain
> point, we formed an echelon about a half-mile away.
> No. 1 plane peeled off and dove toward the target, fol-
> lowed by the rest of us at eight-second intervals. I flew
> in No. 2 position usually and got a little scared when
> my turn came up.

With a machine gun hit rate of about 15 percent and
dummy bomb drops to within fifty feet of the target, he
qualified on August 24.

In early September Lieutenant Billie Spell, a Georgian on
temporary duty at Jacksonville for a fighter training refresher course, overheard talk in the instructor's ready
room.

The black midshipman he'd seen around the air station
was up for an "instrument chase hunt," flying certain patterns "blind," using special goggles to prevent seeing outside the cockpit. It was part of the advanced training
syllabus, but none of the instructors wanted to go with him,
monitor him, and keep him out of trouble aloft.

Spell volunteered, and the Operations Officer, a New Jersey commander, said, "You can't, Mr. Spell. You're from
the South."

"What difference does that make?" Spell replied.

"Up to you, man. I'm not going to help him get wings."

Spell didn't care to argue with the commander and
shrugged off the remark. He went out to the students'
ready room to meet Jesse, introducing himself, saying he
was not an instructor but would shepherd him out over
the Atlantic.

"You've been under a hood before?"

Jesse said he had.

Spell briefed him on the flight. "I'll be in a chase position
below and slightly behind you" and told him to switch to a
specific radio channel when ready to commence the blind
flight.

The Hellcats took off, heading east over the ocean to fly

the complicated patterns at 6,000 to 8,000 feet. The patterns would take more than an hour to complete, Jesse in semi-darkness the entire time.

Not long after they reached altitude, there was a May day not too far away. A Hellcat had gone into the ocean and Spell informed Jesse he was going to be a relay, as no one was responding to the help call. "Switch to guard channel, stay on your present course, continue your pattern. I'm switching to tower frequency, but I can hear you on the guard channel."

Spell trailed Jesse while relaying air-sea rescue details.

Jesse continued to fly blind calmly for another fifteen minutes at 150 to 240 knots. He'd coped with the difficult instrument maneuvers before in the SNJ cockpit. He didn't allow Spell's radio chatter to interrupt his concentration.

On landing, Spell returned to the instructors' ready room and said, simply, to all gathered, "I'll fly with Brown any day. He's a fine pilot." Then he walked out.

That night Jesse told Ralph Kennedy what had happened out over the Atlantic. "That Georgia stranger was my safety factor. He didn't tell me why he was flying with me instead of an instructor, but I think I know."

By now, Daisy was "showing," becoming barrel-sized around the waist and black kids who played near the bus stop made fun of her. She took it in stride but in early October, just before Jesse flew back to Pensacola, she took a train to Hattiesburg to await the birth of their child.

He checked into the BOQ at Saufley for the purpose of field qualifying the Hellcat at the same runway where he'd battled crosswinds to put an SNJ to the ground. Different aircraft flew differently, of course, and to drop a Hellcat on the *Wright* required practicing on dry land again.

```
Too fast.
Too flat.
Low start, also high start.
```

```
Pulls nose up at ramp,
Too high at 90°.
Too wide abeam.
Close overshoot.
Pattern trouble.
Okay. Good hop.
FIELD-QUALIFIED.
```

On October 13, 1948, his twenty-second birthday, over the Gulf of Mexico, Jesse flew the two required Hellcat touch-and-goes to the flight deck, then made six arrested landings without a wave off, and his training jacket was stamped:

```
Qualified this date in carrier landings aboard
the USS Wright.
```

He called Daisy from one of the phone booths outside the BOQ. It had taken almost three years of endurance. He knew he was not a "hot-shot" pilot and knew he had a long way to go, but he had survived and that was what counted.

"I wish you could pin my wings on next week."

Wives or girlfriends, sometimes either a father or a mother, did that. But Daisy, eight weeks at most from delivery, would cause raised eyebrows and quick questions by Navy brass at the ceremony. The secret was still safe.

"I'll repin them when you come home."

"That would be fine," Jesse said with a laugh.

The prized gold wings were attached to the chest of Midshipman Jesse Leroy Brown on October 21, 1948, by the commanding officer at Jacksonville. He made no mention of Jesse's color, but a photographer was on hand to record the event, and a public information officer released the story and picture the next day: FIRST NEGRO NAVAL AVIATOR.

The brief ceremony was carried over the Associated Press wire and his picture appeared in *Life* magazine.

He could not help but think of Lieutenant Tipton and others, who'd said, "No nigger will ever sit in the cockpit of a naval aircraft."

P A R T   I I I

Somong-ni, North Korea

December 4, 1950

Dick Cevoli sent his aircraft skyward to make sure his radio call for a rescue helicopter would be heard. Seeing the smoke drift out from wreckage forward of the cockpit, Hudner and Hudson began to circle Jesse. They both had the same thought—that gas tank just a few feet away from Jesse. An explosion could occur any second.

Hudner, Koenig, McQueen, and Hudson now began to fly the entire area close to Jesse, looking for any signs of enemy troops, ready to strafe and bomb them, attempt to keep them away from him.

At 8,000 feet, Cevoli added to the Mayday by calling for any listening fighters to come and help provide cover. One of their own was down. He gave the coordinates. Soon, another flight of Corsairs and a Skyraider flight were orbiting over Jesse.

At Hagaru-ri, where preparations were being made to receive the battered garrison troops from Yudam-ni, chopper pilot Charlie Ward was huddled over a kerosene stove in the pyramid tent attempting to keep warm when the Iroquois Flight Leader's call for rescue came in.

Marine First Lieutenant Ward had no idea that the man on the ground was the black ensign who'd talked to him aboard the Leyte *on the crossing from Hawaii to Japan. It didn't matter to Charlie who he was, white or black, or where he was. So long as he was within flying distance, Charlie would try to save him. His Sikorsky had a range of 161 miles and could make 75 miles per hour in the thin air.*

Dick Cevoli, circling high over Jesse, had pinpointed the site as being near the village of Somong-ni, north of Yudam-ni, about halfway up the Chosin's many fingers on the west side of the reservoir. Charlie knew the area, having flown over it several times within the past two weeks.

A few choppers were used experimentally late in World War II for observation and medical evacuation. The first Korean rescue had taken place in July when an Air Force plane crashed behind enemy lines. By now, the ''Angels'' were airborne daily on dangerous missions of mercy. The Sikorskys were still primitive aircraft, prone to mechanical problems; too few in numbers in the combat zones to handle all requests.

Of the six choppers that were ferried by the Leyte *to Japan, three had already been destroyed. A week ago, the* Leyte's *Ensign Wagner crash landed in enemy territory when hit by ack-ack fire. The chopper that rescued him was forced down by engine trouble and both pilots were now missing. Only yesterday, another Marine ''Angel'' close friend of Ward's had been killed attempting to rescue a downed pilot north of the reservoir, up toward the Manchurian border.*

Ward pulled on his flight boots and left the warmth of the tent to locate his crew chief and get the chopper ready to fly.

Fighter Squadron 32

December 1948

Early on December 22, Daisy entered Methodist Hospital in Hattiesburg, having gone into labor with a history of anemia. Late that afternoon, Addie Nix desperately tried to reach Jesse, who was on temporary duty at Norfolk Naval Air Station in Virginia. Addie wanted to tell him that Daisy was in serious trouble, that the doctor said it was now a choice between the baby and Daisy. She was not strong enough to undergo normal birth; she could die.

Jesse had already left Norfolk and was hitching rides on naval aircraft in the direction of Mississippi, coming home for Christmas. Now that he wore wings, it was a favorite and no-expense way to fly. Air stations were located throughout the country.

Addie soon made the decision for her son-in-law and Pamela Elise was born in late afternoon, December 23, by C-section. The baby was in perfect health, but Daisy was not. The long and difficult labor had drained her physically. She was very weak, a candidate for intensive care.

Jesse's brother William had arrived in Hattiesburg from Chicago several days earlier to spend the holidays with his family. Volunteering to give blood to Daisy, he was tested for type and the man with the terribly scarred face, arm, and hand soon found himself on a roll-in bed, transfusing her. He told her it was his Christmas gift.

After hops to Jacksonville and Gulfport, Mississippi, Jesse walked into her room on Christmas Eve afternoon and knelt by her bed to say, "God wasn't going to take you away from me." He had been briefed by Addie and William and her sisters in the waiting room.

They'd previously decided on the name of Pamela if the baby was a girl, and Jesse soon met his new daughter, spending Christmas Eve night at the hospital as well as most of the next day, unable to get enough of this Yuletide child. He held her and fed her while Daisy slept off and on, slowly beginning to recover.

He told her they'd be leaving the South. "We're headed for Quonset Point, Rhode Island. I'll be in Fighter Squadron 32. I hear it's a good one, flying off the *Leyte.*"

"Oh, Jesse, I'm so happy for you." She was, but she wasn't. Though she knew her husband was a good pilot, she was still wary of him taking off and landing at sea. "Where is Quonset Point?"

"I had to look it up. It's on Jamestown Island across from Newport, where all the rich people live, on Narragansett Bay."

"Where will we live?"

"I'm not sure. I've been told there are a lot of little towns near the base. I'll find us a house. It'll be different up there."

"How different?" Daisy had lived in Mississippi all her life except the time in St. Louis baby-sitting for her Aunt Laura. Pensacola hadn't been too much different than Hattiesburg.

"Well, I was told in Norfolk by the personnel officer that we'd be accepted in Rhode Island."

"I hope so," Daisy said.

"There may be a problem now and then," Jesse said realistically. "But not as many. At least we won't be riding in the back of the bus."

They talked a lot about the future until New Year's Day when Jesse began to hitchhike aerially back to Norfolk.

William continued to give blood and also paid the hospital charges. Even with the flight pay increase that Jesse had received upon becoming a Midshipman First Class, Jesse and Daisy were broke.

Papa John and Julia declared, individually, that Pam, their first grandchild, looked like them. They began timing their visits to attend the morning bath. Pam actually looked just like Jesse.

13 January 1949

Dear Daisy:

I'm settling in and finding my way around the air station, meeting the guys in the squadron and learning the routines. We're headquartered in a hangar and have sixteen Bearcats to fly as part of Air Group 3. Although we'll come and go aboard the *Leyte*, we are not part of the ship's company. We're just visitors while we're on her. Before she sails, we'll put all of our equipment aboard her and our squadron personnel, except for the pilots. The pilots and aircraft will meet her out at sea to begin operating.

"Do you want me to show you how to start that engine?" Vincent "Vic" Breddell, TRADEVMAN Second Class, asked. In Navy lingo, Training Devices Man 2.

Seated in the cockpit of a Grumman Bearcat for a photo shoot, which didn't involve flying, Jesse stared at the black enlisted man who appeared to be about his same age. The look on Jesse's face indicated his thinking: *How could you say that to me? What nerve! I've been in and out of aircraft for two years.*

Breddell was one of the few black enlisted airmen at Quonset Point. In fact, he was one of the few black airmen in the Navy. But Jesse, feeling his way along, seeing him around every day, had made no attempt to meet him. Breddell was an instructor, assigned to Operational Flight Training, presiding over a Bearcat flight trainer, akin to the Link trainer. Breddell had decided to make an approach to the aloof midshipman.

"Okay," Jesse said, frowning at the stranger, who had introduced himself with a half-minute background sketch. It broke the tension.

Pilots usually loved the Bearcat for its beauty, power, and speed. Power, power, power, with a four-bladed prop! It was like a sports car and flew like one. But what really made it different was the size of the cockpit. It was so cozy that even normal-sized shoulders brushed both sides. It was like fitting into a sausage skin.

He'd reported to the skipper of Fighter Squadron 32. Lieutenant Commander Earl "Chub" Willems eyed Jesse at length, then said, "Brown, you'll get no favors here. At the same time, I'll judge you solely on your flying ability and performance and not on the color of your skin." Jesse remembered almost the same words from Chief Shaw at Ottumwa.

"That's fine with me, sir," Jesse had replied. *That's exactly how I want it. Perfect.*

Willems said, "I'm going to work your butt off and that applies to all you new people. We've got a lot of different personalities here and it's my job to jell you together. Whatever your personalities are, whatever your personal problems, we're going to work together for the whole squadron."

Jesse said he understood.

Tall and slender, almost a stick figure, with blond hair and a narrow face, Willems smiled easily and had a broad sense of humor. This day, stuck with one more new pilot, he was unhappy and unsmiling. Too many rookies.

He was so tall that when flying the little Bearcat it appeared that he had the tops of his knees stuck up under his chin. Along with his pilots, he laughed at the contortions it took to jockey the machine.

Training for Jesse would continue, either in the classroom or from the Quonset Point flight line, or eventually at sea from the flight deck of the *Leyte*.

TD2 Breddell lived in the enlisted barracks almost directly opposite Jesse's BOQ quarters. The same restriction still existed. He couldn't bring Daisy and Pamela north until he was sworn in as an ensign. That might not take place for several months.

After the publicity shoot was over, Jesse asked Vic to come to the BOQ that night. He wanted to talk, having many questions about Quonset Point: about housing, about Fighter Squadron 32.

Even though the inhabitants of the BOQ were now 99 percent white, black stewards were in and out all the time, so Jesse ran no risks of a casual association with a black enlisted man. Call a steward if your bed wasn't made.

Though Breddell had been born in Manhattan and raised in Brooklyn, he viewed society through big-city eyes and had that common bond of race. He'd heard enough stories to know the difference between Mississippi and Brooklyn. He was also a Libra. The chemistry worked immediately. An honor student in high school, Breddell had wanted to be a naval aviator but didn't pass the eye exam.

"How is it on the base?" was Jesse's first question.

Vic knew immediately what he was talking about.

"Not so good."

"Off the base?"

"Not so good. Some restaurants will find excuses not to serve you, even if you're in uniform. Some clubs won't let you through the door."

"And this is the North?"

"This is the North."

Jesse didn't have many people to talk to on base aside from duty contacts. That was expected, no different than Glenview, Pensacola, or Jacksonville. He admitted to Vic that most of that situation was his own fault. He wasn't a partygoer, didn't hang out at the Officers' Club.

"I could, I know, to an extent. But I'm not comfortable. I don't drink and I don't want anyone to think I'm trying to ingratiate myself. I don't know how much social life there is in the squadron, but I think there's a lot. Some things I guess I'll have to go to."

They began going to Providence together. There was one nightclub, Filippi's, that welcomed them. Sitting at the bar, they drank ginger ale and bitters. It looked like scotch or bourbon on the rocks, so they'd fit in. In most white parts of the city, restaurants or bars, they were less than welcome.

They took Sunday walks along the Narragansett beach to watch the birds and just talk. Vic needed to talk as much as Jesse needed to talk. They shared the loneliness. For once, Jesse ignored the Navy's rule about officers associating with enlisted men. It wasn't his fault that more Negro officers weren't in the Navy. They wore civilian clothes and met off-base.

The squadron was then stationed in Land Plane Hangar No. 2, engaging in regular training as well as Field Carrier Landing Practice at an auxiliary strip not too far from Quonset. The Bearcat, with its huge prop, was capable of 450-plus knots and could climb from a standing start to 10,000 feet in record time, ninety seconds, another "sweet" plane.

10 April 1949

Dear Daisy:

There'll be a delay in mail for about four or five days. Tomorrow we move back aboard the *Leyte* for at least a week's training cruise, though I'm told we'll put into

New York for several days. I'll be making my first carrier takeoffs and landings in the Bearcat. Wish me luck.

Jesse was sworn in as an ensign on April 26 by the captain of the *Leyte*, which was moored to the dock at Quonset Point. The brief ceremony was not nearly as meaningful as the day he'd won his wings in Jacksonville. He rushed off the carrier and used a pay phone on the dock to call Daisy. They were now, at last, legitimate in the eyes of the Navy. No more hiding.

That night Jesse told Vic Breddell that he'd been married for more than a year and had a daughter four months old, that he'd kept it a secret both in Pensacola and Jacksonville.

Breddell knew of the midshipman restriction. "Man, you could have been kicked out."

Jesse acknowledged that circumstance with a laugh. He'd outwitted the rules and didn't want to break any others.

"You better tell Willems."

"I plan to tomorrow."

Willems took the news with a shoulder shrug. He had larger problems than an ensign's marriage.

The squadron conducted bombing, tactical, instrument, and ground-controlled approach training flights. The Bearcats took off almost every week day. Rocket training flights at the Roxy target area north of Otis Air Force Base; individual combat training flights; aerial gunnery training flights south of Block Island. Field landing carrier practice. Night training flights. Day after day. Willems hadn't been kidding when he said he'd work the butts off his pilots.

Dearest Daisy,

Your husband became an officer yesterday and we are "official" man and wife at last. No more sneaking around. I told Willems this morning and he couldn't have cared less.

I've already looked at want ads for two-bedroom rentals in this area and they aren't cheap. What goes for $25 a month in Hattiesburg is $100 here. Although we'll get a housing allowance and have commissary privileges, it's going to be tight for a while.

I'd love to tell you to get on the train tomorrow, but it'll probably be several months before I can save enough for your tickets and rent money. The way the wheels grind I won't get ensign's pay until next month.

All my love,
Jesse

He was given collateral duty as "log officer" for the squadron, meaning that he supervised the data entered in the aviator's flight log and the aircraft flight log, in addition to his flying. The flying he enjoyed.

Hattiesburg

May 1949

In late May Jesse took a week's leave to return to Hattiesburg, hitching aerial rides to Pensacola, then Greyhounding home. He hadn't seen Daisy or Pam since Christmas and planned to spend almost every hour with them. He couldn't believe the baby had grown so much in six months. He held and played with her whenever she was awake.

Aside from a bus ride to Eatonville, with Daisy and Pam, to visit his parents and brothers, Jesse devoted the whole leave to his family with the exception of attendance at the Eureka High baccalaureate service.

In his splendid dress whites he was the center of attention and gave a brief inspirational talk to the graduating class and their parents after being introduced by Professor Burger as an "illustrious son" of Eureka. Burger predicted that Jesse would be the Navy's first Negro admiral. Burger had no idea what it took to be an admiral, even a white one.

Then Jesse and Daisy, who was wearing a summer print dress and a hat, walked the ten blocks from Eureka's colored area back to the corner of Main and Pine to catch the bus to Daisy's mother's apartment.

As they were standing at the stop, a car containing four teenagers drove up and one stuck his head out the rear window to yell, "Hey, nigger, what yuh doin' in that officer's uniform? Yuh jus' stay right there. We're coming back. . . ."

Taunts and words of that sort were not at all new to them and they both believed the boys would drive on off, having had their fun. But a few minutes later the car returned. Eggs flew out of it, hitting both Jesse and Daisy in the body, one of them knocking his hat off.

Jesse chased the car for half a block. It stopped and one boy got out of the right-hand front door, only to be punched back inside. The right rear door opened and Jesse caught that occupant with another right hand.

The car shot forward and disappeared up the street.

Breathing in spurts, Jesse watched it go and returned slowly to Daisy's side, rubbing his knuckles. "Bastards," he said. "Four to one, and they wouldn't get out and fight."

"Are you all right?" she asked.

"Yeah. I just wish they'd come back."

The pristine uniform was ruined with yellow, as was Daisy's dress. They brushed themselves off silently as best they could and boarded the bus. The white passengers turned their heads as the couple went down the aisle. Jesse held Daisy's hand all the way home. There was nothing to be said. She put her head on his shoulder and wept softly.

The naval uniform had been disgraced and Daisy again fought tears as she washed and ironed it, knowing that she would also remember the corner of Main and Pine for as long as she lived.

The only person at Quonset to learn of the incident was Vic Breddell. Jesse did not even tell Ike Heard. On return, he said to Breddell, "I wanted to open all the doors to that car and drag them out one by one and beat them until they couldn't walk."

*   *   *

He'd returned to a saddened squadron.

On the last day of May the yeoman had written into the squadron daily log:

```
Lt. JG  R.G. Wittig, 437660/A3, USNR, was killed
this date in the line of duty when his aircraft,
F8F-1B, BuAer 121522, crashed, exploded, and
burned during a landing approach at Otis Air
Force Base, Mass. Cause of crash was established
as due to partial or total loss of power.
```

He'd known Wittig casually, had done formation flying with him. He'd thought Wittig was a good pilot, but he also knew that good pilots could not always cope with mechanical failures. Apparently, his engine had just quit running. Now, Wittig, at the age of twenty-three, had been burned to death. Jesse just hoped it was instant and out.

A death in the squadron was always devastating. Beyond the human loss, it put into question ability and aircraft performance. The temptation was always to blame it on the aircraft. But the hard truth was ability. These carrier aircraft did not tolerate many mistakes.

Jesse did not mention Wittig in his letter to Daisy that night.

On those beach walks with Vic Breddell Jesse had talked with Vic about death. He'd said, quite frankly, that he'd thought about the dangers of flying; that, like most pilots, he'd thought about being killed. Yet the thrill and joy of it outweighed the moments of terror.

In mid-August he met an ensign from Ashtabula, Ohio, who lived down the hall. The fact that Jesse had gone to Ohio State provided a quick handle to conversation with Leland Nelson.

Lee Nelson had heard of Jesse Brown before meeting him, he'd admired him for becoming the first black pilot in the

Navy against what had to have been considerable odds. There'd been bits of gossip about him being married through most of his midshipman training. He'd considered Brown "incredibly daring" for both feats.

Nelson, of Swedish descent, had grown up on the shores of Lake Erie, and from his room he could hear the surf on the beach, watch the ships and sailboats pass by, count the flashes from the lighthouse, and listen to the foghorns in bad weather. He was water-oriented from childhood and had planned to enter the Coast Guard.

Former newspaper boy, soda jerk in his grandfather's ice cream and candy shop, he'd been an avid builder of model airplanes and during the summer of 1943 learned how to fly a Piper Cub from Ashtabula's grass airfield. He'd been through Pensacola and won his Navy wings in 1947, first assigned to the carrier *Kearsarge*.

Jesse wrote to Daisy that not since Jack Keefer had he met a white man who was so receptive to friendship.

To that point, aside from his excursions with Vic Breddell, Jesse still had no social life. In the main this was still his own fault and it followed the exact pattern of Glenview, staying remote at Ottumwa, Pensacola, and Jacksonville. Though commissioned and eligible, he still didn't participate in Officers' Club events for the simple reason that he didn't feel he belonged there. He was the ultimate outsider.

Nelson soon introduced him to his fiancée, Lee LaCroix, a Northeast Airlines stewardess, and she invited Jesse to come to her parents' home in Newton Center near Boston for Sunday afternoon cocktails. Other squadron members had been there and this day an ensign named Frank Sheffield went along. "Sheff," a Texas rebel, was Nelson's best friend and roommate. He was also an exceptional pilot.

At the time, airline stewardesses were selected for youth, good looks, pleasing personalities, and some medical training. Lee LaCroix qualified in all categories. Petite and shapely, she was a brunette beauty. She'd been a medical technician for the Boston clinic that helped develop insulin.

Funloving, she liked to party and was usually in the middle of the action—wherever it was. In addition to all of the above she was compassionate. She immediately befriended Jesse as her fiancé had done.

Lee LaCroix's dad was an executive with New England Power and both parents were as cordial to Jesse as they were to Sheff in their spacious home. Dad LaCroix talked at length with Jesse and seemed to enjoy his presence. But a few days later Dad LaCroix took the Lees, Nelson and LaCroix, aside to say he believed Jesse was a fine young man but thought they'd made a mistake bringing him to upscale Newton Center. It wasn't a good idea in that "neighborhood."

Lee Nelson realized once again how subtle prejudice could be and appreciated even more the constant struggle. He repeated LaCroix's remark to Sheff, who said it didn't surprise him at all. "A lot of us Southerners get along better with Negroes. We understand the situation," Sheff said.

Big, built like a football player, with wavy brown hair and a perpetual grin, Sheff was proud of his Texas heritage, his Texas drawl, and possessed the best sense of humor in the whole squadron. He could laugh his way through almost anything.

Jesse wrote Daisy about the "nice time" he'd had at the LaCroix home, what wonderful people they were.

The Texan joined Nelson in being friendly to Jesse and was quick to react to any untoward remarks. In that, he was joined by most of the squadron pilots. Jesse was especially pleased that those born in the South seemed to accept him.

By late August, after sending money home monthly to support Daisy and Pam, Jesse had saved up $400, enough to pay a first-and-last-month rent, buy the train tickets, and bring his family to Rhode Island.

He began to read the local newspaper rental ads for the Quonset area and one night went to Nelson's room to ask if he could borrow Lee's Plymouth to check out possibilities.

By this time, he did not sound "black" on the phone. He'd

mostly purged his Lux manner of speaking in the five years since leaving Hattiesburg. He hadn't consciously done it. He still sounded "Dixie" but not necessarily black.

After making calls, identifying himself as "Ensign Brown," when he knocked on the doors of the prospective landlords or landladies, there was that moment of shock on viewing the face of this young "Ensign Brown." Then he was told the tiresome phrase: "It has just been rented."

One night, after experiencing three rejections, he came into Nelson's room, tossed his hat on a chair, and said, "I'm about to the end of my rope. Daisy and Pam are due in less than a week and no one will rent to me."

He'd been certain that would happen in Mississippi or Florida, but he didn't expect it in Rhode Island, though the Providence restaurant refusals were an indication. Finally a landlady in Apponaug, three miles from the air station, rented him a shabby but furnished three-room cottage in a run-down neighborhood.

At 140 Glena Drive, he became the first black resident of Apponaug, a tiny community of mostly weekenders. There were a few permanent residents and he disarmed them by ringing their bells and saying, up-front with a smile, "I'm a new resident, and my wife and daughter will be joining me," which was Jesse's way of saying that there would be no wild parties. He was wearing his dress greens, the shining gold wings above his coat pocket, gold on his hat.

Jesse and Vic Breddell soon shopped for a crib and other essentials, preparing the house for the new occupants.

There was a call from Jack Keefer, who was at Miramar Naval Air Station, San Diego, waiting for a carrier to come in from Pearl Harbor. They'd talked now and then since separating at Pensacola. Jack was flying a Panther.

"Ross Tipton was killed last week," Jack said. "The story is in this week's *Navy Times*."

"How?"

"Car. Head-on collision near his family home in Birmingham. Had a wife and four kids."

"That's sad," Jesse said and meant it. *There probably were some things to like about Lieutenant Tipton,* Jesse thought. *It's ironic that a holder of a Navy Cross was killed on the ground.*

Jesse talked with Jack for a while as they updated each other. He got off the phone, thinking about Tipton, wondering whether or not he'd been the one who'd placed the card on the bunk pillow. *Hopefully not.*

After riding a "Jim Crow" car from Hattiesburg, Daisy and Pam changed trains in Cincinnati and got into a berth for the night ride to New York. Pam had a cold and slight fever and was miserable. Jesse met them at Penn Station and they got on another train for the ride to Providence, then took a taxi home.

She'd heard a lot about Vic Breddell in Jesse's letters and they'd been practically inseparable since January, lonely in that sea of white. When Daisy reached the cottage in Apponaug, there was a bouquet of flowers on the table in the front room with a card signed: WELCOME, DAISY AND PAM, LOVE, VIC. She wondered if her arrival would change the men's relationship. She hoped not.

Within a few days, neighbors in Apponaug dropped by to visit the Browns. Some acted like they'd never seen black people except in the movies or on TV. Daisy thought it was remarkable. They seemed to be accepted by the people of Apponaug and soon had a white girl, Shirley, as a babysitter.

Jesse had little time off and Daisy asked why. He'd told her before but said again, "We're always preparing for war." She was developing the usually unspoken fear factor that most military pilots' wives are required to live with—the chaplain standing at the door, not smiling.

Jesse would come home exhausted. He loved to fly, but the type of flying he was doing was hard work. These weren't passenger planes with auto-pilot. They were powerful gunships. But he was never too exhausted to hold and play with Pam, to take Daisy into his arms.

Since arriving in the middle of September, she'd spent her days being a mother and homemaker. Vic Breddell had ridden a bus to Apponaug several times and she thought he was wonderful. He volunteered to baby-sit. They accepted the offer but not quite yet.

Daisy soon received an invitation from the Officers' Wives Club to attend the June bridge luncheon. Opening it, she said, "Oh no" and passed it to Jesse. "I don't want to go."

"You have to. You're the newest wife. You'll have fun. It's at the 'O' Club."

"I will not have fun. And I can't play bridge. You know I can't play bridge."

"We'll teach you."

"Who's the 'we'?"

"Vic and me."

"Jesse, I don't want to go. All those white women, drinking and smoking."

"You don't have to drink or smoke. You can have a Coke."

"Jesse, please don't make me do this."

"I'm just asking you to. The wives talk to their husbands and they'll say, 'She wouldn't come.' These are guys I fly with."

With misgiving, she agreed to go.

Several nights later Vic showed up with two decks of cards and after dinner the bridge lessons began. With a stony face, Daisy took her first lesson. Vic returned the next five nights and although Daisy improved she still had trouble remembering cards. Daisy brought up other problems. "What should I wear? And what about my hair? I have to have my hair done and only a colored operator will know how to do it."

On Saturday Jesse took a bus to Providence and stood by the main stop until a middle-aged black lady alighted. Walking up to her, in a scene reminiscent of Pensacola, he explained the problem and she solved it with the name and phone number of a Negro beauty parlor.

Daisy found other excuses not to go but nonetheless read etiquette books. "I know I can't be just good. I have to be more than good. I have to be better. I'm representing all black women."

"You're not either."

"That's what you think. I'm a woman."

The wife of an enlisted man took her to Providence to shop for clothes.

The big day soon arrived. Daisy was picked up at the cottage by a lieutenant's wife, who attempted to make her comfortable. They drove up to the station gate and a Marine guard waved them through. Daisy was certain that he thought a domestic was sitting in the car with the two-striper's window ID on it.

Inside the posh Officers' Club for the first time, she was introduced, thinking just how far she'd come from the streets of Hattiesburg.

She held her own at the bridge table, aware that eyes from other tables were constantly on her. They played two rubbers and lunch was served. The Negro stewards were amazed, Daisy smiling sweetly and a little triumphantly at them.

After bridge, the wives said that it was ritual that they all attend Happy Hour. Daisy sipped a Coke and listened to the chatter. After a drink or two, the ladies worked up courage to ask, "How does it feel to be the wife of the first Negro pilot in the U.S. Navy?"

She didn't need coaching to talk about how proud she felt and about Jesse Leroy Brown, the sharecropper's son.

On returning home, she told Jesse, "As long as you have a washing machine that doesn't work or a baby-sitter that doesn't show up . . ."

The next hurdle was the air group officers and wives' party. There'd be several hundred in the "O" Club and the Browns would have to mix with a lot of "brass": captains, commanders, lieutenant commanders down to the lowest rank of the three squadrons.

Jesse was as anxious about this one as Daisy was. Once again, the uncertain sea of white, drinking, dancing, making small talk, watching what they said, maintaining a special dignity.

"I wish we didn't have to go."

"We have to."

"What'll I wear?" *It's the same old problem, black or white,* Jesse thought.

"Well, it's summertime. Wear something with flowers on it. You'll look beautiful in anything."

"Jesse . . ."

While the band played on and drinks were served, the "whites" demonstrated they weren't racist. They overdid it, practically standing in line to talk to the Ensign Browns. Going home in the car Jesse borrowed from Lee Nelson, Daisy said, "You would have thought we were the President and his wife the way they were lining up." *Another victory,* Jesse thought.

John Brannon of Ottumwa and Pensacola days, Jesse's boxing opponent at Pre-Flight, now a member of Fighter Squadron 71, flying the new Panther jet off the *Bonhomme Richard,* showed up in Quonset Point. John was still a bachelor and Jesse invited him to Apponaug for dinner, their first guest.

Daisy was treated to almost nonstop pilot talk the entire evening. She'd begun to understand this special breed of man, doing their special thing, telling tales of derring-do, flying with their hands, as usual. What Jesse had told her before now had a theme. She felt and saw the comradeship that only pilots would know about. She felt lucky to hear the men talk, though it did not ease her fears.

Thomas Hudner

November 1949

LTJG Thomas Hudner of Fall River, Massachusetts, was about to put his flight suit on in the locker room of Hangar 2 when Jesse entered on a November day in 1949. Hudner hadn't been told that there was a Negro pilot in the U.S. Navy, much less in the very squadron to which he'd just been assigned. A look of mild surprise was registered on his face.

Jesse introduced himself, asking, "When did you get here?"

"Yesterday," Hudner replied.

"Welcome aboard," Jesse said, smiling cordially, extending his hand. Then he went on to his own locker to suit up for the morning flight. He did not attempt to make conversation, nor did Hudner. In that regard Jesse still hadn't changed. The Navy experience had not even slightly cracked the surfaces of reservation when it came to strangers, white or black.

Oddly enough, Tom Hudner had suffered air sickness as

a passenger. Less than two years ago on his first flight in an SNJ, before his training began, he'd thrown up in the cockpit. Now, he was a fully qualified naval aviator, a graduate of Pensacola.

Two years older than Jesse, Hudner was a former track star, football player, and lacrosse player. Movie-star handsome, Hudner's background was as different as the color of their skins. They were similar in only three ways—both were commissioned officers, both were pilots, both had been athletes.

Hudner's upper-middle-class family, of Irish ancestry, was well-to-do. His father, a Harvard graduate, worked for his grandfather's group of grocery markets in the Fall River area. Tom's mother was a college graduate and her father was once Chief Justice of the Pennsylvania Supreme Court. The Hudner family had a summer house in Westport Harbor, Massachusetts, and did a lot of sailing during the warm weather while the Browns continued their hoe work in the fields. Life was pleasant and rewarding for the Hudners and Tom loved to read nautical books, especially about four-masters and Captain Horatio Hornblower while Jesse was devouring aviation stories by lamplight. So the Navy became a mutual goal.

All four of the Hudner sons went on to the exclusive prep school Phillips Academy at Andover while Jesse was attending Bay Springs and Eureka high schools, cutting out cardboard insoles to cover gaps in his shoes. Two of Tom's brothers attended Harvard, the other Princeton. Tom graduated from the wartime Naval Academy, class of 1947, classmate of one future President of the United States and fourteen future admirals.

But backstream in Tom's bloodline was the self-educated grandfather who sold fruits and vegetables from a handcart before he opened a single grocery store and developed it into a chain.

There were few blacks in Fall River and only one in Tom's class in junior high. He'd never heard the word "nigger" used in school and certainly not within his family. By example, the four sons and one daughter were taught not to be biased against Negroes or Jews. He took that attitude into the Naval Academy.

Except for a midshipman named Wesley Brown, the only blacks on the grounds were stewards living aboard the USS *Cumberland*, a barracks ship. They marched to and from the mess hall and sometimes racist remarks were made about them by both Northern- and Southern-born midshipmen and by white enlisted personnel.

Rumor was that Eleanor Roosevelt had said, "Wesley Brown *will* get through Annapolis"—or words to that effect—a command from the White House.

A civilian English instructor teaching Tom's class said of Wesley Brown, "You know, there was another nigger who tried to get in here twenty-five years ago but never made it." Legend had it that he ended up tied to a buoy in the Severn River at Annapolis.

Tom Hudner viewed Wesley Brown as making history and soon felt the same way about Ensign Jesse Brown.

There was another difference that ran through the entire officer corps bottom to top. Tom was a grade higher than Jesse and associated with other "jaygees"; he was also a bachelor and the single men tended to flock together, especially the Annapolis graduates.

Beyond that, Tom had served in the fleet aboard the cruiser *Helena* and had come to aviation, by choice, a year later than Jesse. He'd entered the Academy with the idea of making the Navy a lifetime career and was well prepared to do so. He had, in all ways, the right material to go up the ladder.

Hudner became the squadron's assistant maintenance officer and spent much of his time involved with the engines and aircraft mechanics, the most important department of all. The lives of the entire squadron depended on whirling propellers. Laymen often thought that the pilots sat around all day playing pinochle in the ready rooms, hangars, or carriers. Actually, they were usually busy with paperwork when they weren't airborne.

For quite a while, Jesse and Tom Hudner saw each other in the ready room and on the flight line at Quonset; later in the *Leyte* mess, ready room, and on her flight deck. Both were swallowed up by the huge carrier and the 3,000 men who rode her. They were shipmates but not close friends.

Hudner had flown the F4U-4 Corsair in advanced training at Corpus Christi, one of the few squadron pilots who'd had experience with it. When it became known that the Corsair was the squadron's plane of the future, Jesse had a lot of questions about it.

Just when he thought he'd mastered the Hellcat and the Bearcat, here came another aircraft with a reputation for making widows. "That's not true," Hudner told him. "In the early days but no longer. You have to learn to handle it like any other type you haven't flown before. With that long nose, you can't see very well ahead. In flight, you have to turn a little to see what's up ahead. On a carrier, when you're coming up on final, you're sticking your head out as far as you can so you can continue to see the LSO. . . ."

Jesse asked him what that "widow-maker" was about.

Hudner replied, "At first, it didn't give you much warning of a stall in slow flight. It had a characteristic where it would stall and spin almost instantly without warning, so that for a carrier approach you didn't have enough time and enough altitude to be able to safely recover. But they fixed that with a little spoiler, a piece about six inches long on the starboard wing. They made a few other changes and now it's a fine aircraft."

Jesse still had reservations.

Hudner continued, "It's a good gun platform. It's steady. I've fired rockets from it. You don't have dive brakes, so you just drop your wheels when you bomb. You do sixty-degree dives and hang off your shoulder harnesses. The steeper you dive, the more accurate you are, of course."

Jesse would soon find out about the Corsair.

Life out of the cockpit or ready room or squadron office continued dawn to dark for Jesse, although frequently he'd be late in getting his logs up to date and Willems would call him to the mat.

"Damn it, Brown, can't you get your work in on time!"

"I'm trying to, sir. I'll try harder."

"You damn better try harder."

Jesse was a typical ensign, not yet up to speed with paperwork, hating it.

Lieutenant Commander Dick Cevoli, a senior pilot who would pick Jesse to fly in his division, said, "Yeah, Brown, you better try harder!" Another laid-back party man, World War II veteran, he was liked by everyone in the squadron. Cevoli was the executive officer.

Throughout the early fall, a priceless time in New England, the squadron trained at Quonset Point and nearby outlying fields, occasionally flying out to work with a carrier for refresher routines. Jesse sometimes flew three to five hours a day. The squadron was awarded the coveted Battle Efficiency Pennant. It was all going smoothly on the ground and in the air.

Daisy was enjoying the moderate weather, little humidity, no mosquitoes, and walks with the stroller in the village. She wouldn't have minded staying in Apponaug for a long time. Jesse shopped at the station commissary for food. Vic Breddell often came over to spend the night on the front room couch.

One pretty weekend Jesse borrowed Lee Nelson's car and told Daisy that they were going to Providence, taking Pam, Vic, and the baby-sitter along. She wanted to know the purpose. "It's a surprise," he said.

On the outskirts of Providence he turned into the airport road and went to the rental area. "I'm taking you up. I promised myself I'd do this. Just to show you how good a pilot I am."

Daisy was leery of climbing into the Cessna with the baby.

But wherever Jesse led, she followed. Up they went for an hour, Jesse continually looking back at her with a wide smile. The air was gentle and the trees were golden and the sea was blue. Cape Cod, a place she'd long heard about, was suddenly beneath them. She shouted over the engine clatter, "Now, I know what you're talking about!" Jesse had thought maybe a ride on a nice day would ease her fears. Maybe it would. He hoped so.

Then there was Lieutenant Dick "Dad" Fowler, squadron operations officer. In civilian clothes he looked more like an insurance salesman than a fighter pilot. But every stick jockey in 32 agreed that they'd fly on his wing anytime, anywhere. He had a flashing smile and used it frequently. He'd won the Navy Cross in "the big war" just ended.

Not long after Jesse reported for duty, Fowler had said, "We're so proud to have you with us. That goes for the whole air group."

Those few simple words sent Jesse skyward without a plane. He felt very much at home in Squadron 32.

But he still continued to avoid the partying if at all possible. One Friday afternoon in early December he was standing outside the "O" Club with Lee LaCroix while she waited for Lee Nelson to show up for a date. It was "stag" Happy Hour time and they were both dragged into the bar by squadron bachelors. Jesse quietly sipped a soft drink until Lee showed up and then vanished.

The Lees soon went to dinner at the Brown's cottage in Apponaug. Though run-down and poorly furnished, it was immaculate and Daisy entertained and cooked as if it was the captain's house.

10 December 1949

Dear Ike and Gwen:

Your announcement really knocked us back. Gee, but it was good news. Hardiest congratulations and a

"Well done" to all hands involved. Sure hope that mother and baby are still doing fine.

Again, congratulations, and best wishes for the Yuletide season and the coming year.

Jesse and Daisy

Wanting a car, needing a car, Jesse scrimped throughout October and November, taking the bus to work. A commissioned officer hitchhiking, especially one so noticeable because of color was a Navy no-no. By Thanksgiving, he still didn't have the money.

But one early night in mid-December, Daisy heard a car pull up in front of the cottage, Jesse got out and went inside.

"Who brought you home?"

"One of the guys."

A little while later the car came back.

"Who is that?" Daisy asked.

"Don't know. Let's go out and see."

Vic Breddell was there with a 1950 green Dodge Wayfarer.

"It's your Christmas present," Jesse said proudly. *Papa John has never owned a car and probably never will,* Jesse thought.

Daisy didn't know how to drive but was thrilled over the new "wheels." They were now independent. During the next months, no automobile in all of New England was babied more than the green Wayfarer. Jesse and Vic brushed snow off it as if it were human. They washed and waxed and inspected under the hood when no inspection was required. When the roads weren't icy, they taught Daisy how to drive.

Jesse showed up alone at the squadron's Christmas party, Daisy declining because of baby-sitting problems, a semilegitimate excuse. He talked briefly with Lee Nelson, Tom Hudner, Sheff, and a few others and departed, anxious to return home.

*   *   *

The usual familiarization program with the Corsair was under way not long after the holidays: briefings, cockpit checks, instrument flying, field carrier landing practice. Anything and everything to do with that aircraft.

At night, Jesse often huddled with Vic Breddell in the cottage to go over the pilot's handbook, page by page. He quizzed Jesse on the aircraft and emergency procedures, every phase of the Corsair's operation. Jesse told Breddell it "wasn't as responsive as either of the Cats." He wasn't happy with it.

About this time, another pilot experienced in the Corsair showed up at Quonset. An Iowan, LTJG William Koenig had been a surface ship officer, thought that flying might be fun, and went through training at Pensacola with Tom Hudner.

Scrubbed-face, blond-haired, blue-eyed, cigar-smoking, sea-booted Bill Koenig was another of those under-six-foot fighter pilots. They seemed to be of one mold, trim at about 150 pounds. There were only two above-six-footers in the entire squadron. "Junior" was an appropriate nickname for Koenig, an Iowan. As a senior in high school, he'd wanted to fly the Corsair. He'd first slid into a U-bird cockpit the previous year and was a staunch believer in the aircraft.

He met Jesse while checking in but was not surprised at the ensign's skin color. There'd been a picture and short article in the fall 1949 edition of *Naval Aviation News*, a service publication. Koenig was impressed with the seeming "underwhelming" ease that the Mississippian displayed in the squadron.

Meanwhile, there was a new skipper aboard for Squadron VF-32, Lieutenant Commander Dugald T. Neill, USN. A new commander was always a cause for some apprehension. What kind of guy would he be in the stress and strain of bossing sixteen aircraft and their pilots? A good squadron is always represented by the personality and skill of the No. 1 leader. Neill came to Squadron 32 with high recommendations. Naval aviator for twelve years, distinguished fighter pilot in World War II.

Feisty, dapper in dress, the dark-haired Neill, who kept his mouth-wide mustache trimmed precisely, was different in style than Willems. He paid attention to military bearing, a matter not a priority for all pilots. What mattered to them was how he would run the squadron. He soon proved to be a thorough professional, one who also partied well and frequently.

Jesse thrived on a spit-and-polish appearance and told Daisy how impressed he was with Doug Neill. The new leader seemed to be totally color-blind.

Squadron 32 was beginning to change from the Bearcat to the Corsair F4U-4. Some pilots still thought that the gull-winged Corsair was a ''man-killer'' and they weren't talking about enemy action. Others thought the exact opposite. An aircraft was needed for Marine close support missions, ground fighting missions, and the Bearcat was not the ''bird'' for the job. The rugged long-nosed Corsair could do it.

''Honey, the *Leyte* got orders today. Five months in the Med! Italy, France, Portugal, Sicily,'' Jesse said excitedly.

''The Mediterranean?''

''Life on the Riviera. All those French girls who just go mad over chocolate skin.''

''Are you telling the truth?''

''I swear it. That's what you join the Navy for, to see the world.'' He couldn't stop grinning.

''That isn't fair.''

''I just follow orders.''

''Five months? That isn't fair. What'll I do?''

''Go back to Hattiesburg with Pam.''

''That's just great.''

''Honey, I'm going to miss you every day and night.'' Yet he sounded to Daisy Pearl like he couldn't wait to head overseas. He looked like he couldn't wait.

"When will you go?"

"Sometime in late April. We'll do some flying en route."

"That's fine, Jesse. Enjoy it! I've heard this is what happens. Suddenly you're gone for a long time."

"Well, it does happen and all Navy wives know it."

"This is the first time for me. What do we do with this place? Is the ship coming back here at the end of five months? Do we move everything to Hattiesburg? It's so simple for you. You take your airplane and go off on that ship. . . ."

"I think the ship will come back here, but I don't know that it will. So you take everything to Hattiesburg and we'll rent another place when I come back."

"Are you going to drive me home?"

"Daisy Pearl, I don't think so. I've got a full schedule. I'll ask Vic to do that."

"Suppose he can't."

"Well, I'll pack everything for you and ship it. Then you take the train . . ."

It was the first real argument they'd had and Daisy Pearl retreated into silence.

"Honey, this affects more than just you. Thousands of people. Everyone in the squadron, the whole air group, a thousand men, everyone on the ship, all the wives and children. . . ."

"Well, forgive me for just thinking about myself and Pamela."

"I'll do everything I can to make it just as easy as possible. . . ."

Air Group 3 would have two squadrons of Corsair fighters, one squadron of the heavier Skyraider bombers, and a squadron of Panther jets plus a mixture of night fighters, night attack bombers, early warning aircraft and two plane-guard rescue helicopters, the much-loved "Angels," eighty-six aircraft in all.

Three weeks into the new year Midshipman E. W. Byron, USN, not too long out of Pensacola, crashed on takeoff during a field carrier landing practice at the Naval Auxiliary Station, Charleston, Rhode Island, and Jesse's yeoman entered the mishap into the squadron log. Byron was not injured. Each crash without a fatality buoyed the squadron.

Daisy Pearl said, "Doesn't that bother you? Doesn't that make you think about quitting?"

"Look, it's scary every time something like that happens but then you think, 'Well, he isn't dead.' Someone has to fly these airplanes."

"But he could have been killed," Daisy Pearl insisted.

"Yeah, he could have been killed!"

Wittig's death had cut to the heart and soul of Squadron 32 and now, six months later, Byron could have easily been another sad casualty.

"But he wasn't," Jesse added emphatically.

Daisy Pearl refused to be philosophical about it and Jesse hadn't found a way to shield her from the rare incidents.

The Flying Midshipmen program was being phased out but they were in cockpits on every carrier, risking their lives daily alongside ensigns and higher ranks. Six, including Byron, were in VF-32.

"What happened at Charleston?" she asked.

"It's being investigated. What's left of the plane will be inspected and Byron will be asked every possible question. They'll find out exactly what happened this time."

A long sigh was the reply. The trip to the Med hovered over the Apponaug cottage.

Jesse turned on the record player and took Pam's hands. They danced to Glenn Miller's "String of Pearls" and "Moonlight Serenade," little Pam's face in a perpetual smile. He often danced with and sang to her.

22

USS *Philippine Sea*

February 1950

On the first of February, sky bleak, ocean gray and tossing, wind raw and cold, the *Philippine Sea* was under way off Rhode Island for carrier qualifications. The *Leyte* was tied up down at Norfolk, undergoing repairs.

The squadron had flown out from Quonset the day before and would spend the night aboard while qualifying. It was not uncommon to utilize any of the available larger flattops for the landing tests. It would be Jesse's first crack at sitting a six-ton "Hog" down on a flight deck.

For operations, all carriers were divided into two halves: after half for landing; forward half for launching. Prior to launching, the planes are parked aft. During landings, aircraft aboard are pushed or taxied forward.

If the nine arresting wires did not halt the landing aircraft, then "barriers," three or four strong wire cables strung about five feet above the deck, were employed to stop it. The four barriers were on steel stanchions, swiveled at the bottom, raised and lowered continuously while aircraft landed and taxied forward. The barriers were always in an "up" position during landings and were quickly dropped after the plane came to a stop. In bad landings, it was better to crash into the barriers, damage the plane, than plough forward into the parked aircraft or hit the island.

On this day Jesse came in high and fast at the LSO's "*Cut*," dropping hard on a tooth-crunching landing, bouncing ten or twelve feet into the air. His hook didn't catch the first arresting wire and everyone on Vultures Row and on the bridge expected him to slam down again and probably crash into the barrier fence. His plane was almost out of control.

But then they heard a roar as he went to full throttle, breaking the No. 1 landing rule: "Cut" meant pull off the power. *Now! No exceptions!* Disregarding the signal threatened the pilot, as well as almost everyone on the flight deck, could destroy not only his aircraft but any other planes on deck, cause a gas fire that might threaten the entire ship.

When Jesse added full power to go around again, several things could happen: catch a late "wire" and crash into the barrier; settle into the barrier itself before regaining flying speed; clear the barrier with his airplane only to catch it with his tail hook and crash into the forward area where a few planes were parked or simply flip over the side.

Observers watched with astonishment as he cleared the first barrier without hitting it or hooking it. He came down hard again, past the fourth barrier, engine thundering, prop whirring frantically, and bounced back into the air, just missing the forward end of the island structure and the windows of the navigation bridge and disappeared over the starboard side, settling toward the water. Mouths were open.

Nelson, Hudner, Koenig, and others, standing on Vultures Row, held their breaths, looking aft as the ship steamed on, awaiting the likely death of Jesse Leroy Brown, who'd obviously hit the water on the starboard side. From their angle, they couldn't see over the edge of the flight deck.

The Sikorsky rescue chopper, always airborne about a quarter-mile astern of the ship, well out of the way of landing aircraft, was already moving up to the scene of an almost certain crash.

Instead, incredibly, the blue Corsair came into sight again, barely above the sea, propeller whipping up water. Jesse slowly climbed for altitude ahead of the ship. He soon joined the pattern and made a routine landing, leaving everyone on Vultures Row shaking their heads.

Unbelievable heart-stopping luck allowed him to climb out of the aircraft in one piece.

He was called to the bridge and chewed out by Doug Neill and the captain of the *Philippine Sea*, who'd never seen anything like that happen in all his years as a pilot. The latter yelled at him, "If you'd done one thing right, you'd be dead!" The LSO also had some unkind words for him.

Acknowledging he'd made a terrible mistake and would never make it again, his only other comment was, "God wasn't ready to take me," rephrasing what he'd told Daisy on Pamela's birth. Booed loudly, he was carried into the wardroom for a "kangaroo court" and forced to pay for the week's coffee mess.

Daisy Pearl's mother was suddenly ill and needed surgery. Plans were made for a trip to Hattiesburg in the Wayfarer. Jesse and Vic Breddell applied for emergency leave and got it, Vic to share the driving back and forth.

They left for Hattiesburg the following day, stopping only to eat or sleep in the car. Negro motels were scarce along the way. They managed to go from Apponaug all the way to the Hattiesburg city limits without being checked by the highway patrols of five states. Jesse thought they were lucky. No tap on the window, no flashlight beam.

But when they arrived, even before turning up Daisy Pearl's street, they were stopped by a police car. Any black person driving a new vehicle with out-of-state plates was immediately suspect. The usual occurred—produce IDs and driver's licenses, auto registration. The cops looked long and hard at Jesse's uniform, his wings; Vic's uniform. Sometimes they wore them as protection.

"You a pilot?" There was disbelief in the cop's voice.

"Yes, I am." He did not add "sir."

After ten minutes or so, they were allowed to proceed to the apartment of Addie Nix.

Jesse and Vic were in Hattiesburg only a few days, visiting the Browns and friends. Jesse paid a call on Professor Burger at Eureka High, always a must. Then the Wayfarer got on the road back to New England, practically nonstop. Daisy Pearl and Pam stayed on for a month.

On many days while she was gone, Jesse was up in the air, flying the same Corsair that he'd barrier hopped on the *Philippine Sea*, getting more comfortable with it each time.

> If my wingman is on my right, I look right to see him and beyond him through a 180-degree arc . . . up and down too . . . watching for enemy fighters or any other hazard. He, in turn, looks left to see me and protect me . . . we support each other against air or ground targets . . . if we don't, one of us may die.

No matter personal progress and brotherhood, neither Jesse nor Daisy Pearl could escape the matter of race. Nor did they expect to. It was always there, around the next corner, under the next rock.

She'd flown back to Rhode Island with Pam to spend the rest of the time with Jesse before the *Leyte* sailed. One afternoon she got into the Wayfarer to go to the station and pick him up at the hangar. Once, on the base, she'd turned the wrong way into a one-way street. She didn't have a driver's license, an item she planned to take care of soon.

Instead of passing her through, the main gate guard waved her over to the side. "Now, what are you doing driving that officer's car?"

The Quonset Point officer's sticker was clearly visible in the left-hand corner of the windshield.

"That officer happens to be my husband."

Corporal Lakeman said, "Who are you kidding? We don't have any colored officers on this base."

"How long have you been here?"

"Long enough to know that we don't have any nigger officers on this base. Let me see your ID."

She displayed it for him.

He examined it and said gruffly to her, "Go on through."

Shaken, she drove to the hangar to meet Jesse.

In the car Jesse asked her what was wrong.

She told him and as they drove back through the gate, "Which one did it?"

She pointed him out. "Did you get his name?"

"Lakeman."

"I'll take care of him."

It was the first overt act at Quonset Point involving either one of them.

Daisy Pearl said, "We haven't had any trouble here. Let's don't start now."

"He has to learn."

Next day Lakeman was summoned to the office of the Marine major commanding the guard detail. When he entered, he saw Jesse standing by the major's desk.

The major looked at Lakeman, saying, "I need some coffee." The door closed behind him.

"Stand at attention, Corporal. Yesterday, you gave my wife a bad time simply because her skin is black."

Lakeman opened his mouth to explain.

"Shut up.

"I've put you on report. Your mind and your mouth will have cost you money. I think you better tell me what you had in mind."

"Sir, I thought she was a maid and thought she'd stolen an officer's car."

"She told you she was an officer's wife."

"Sir, I didn't believe her."

"Did you apologize after she showed you her ID?"

"No, sir."

"Do you have anything against black people in general? Is there something about our skin that upsets you?"

"No, sir."

"You're a liar, Lakeman. Hopefully, within a week you'll be Private Lakeman and will have to start your Marine Corps career all over again."

"Yes, sir."

"One more thing. I want you to write my wife a letter of apology. Give it to your major."

"Yes, sir."

"Stay here at attention until he returns."

One evening a few days later Jesse and Vic were reading in the living room. Daisy was with Pam in the bedroom.

Jesse looked up. "You know, Vic, I think that Corsair will kill me. I just have that feeling."

Vic answered, "Come on, Jesse."

"I have it," he said and went back to his book.

Vic decided to stay away from the Browns so they could enjoy each other in the time remaining.

The *Leyte* sailed from Quonset Point May 2 for Hampton Roads, Virginia, and Daisy Pearl was on the pier with Pam, along with hundreds of other wives and children. They waved goodbye as equally hundreds of officers and enlisted personnel lined the flight deck as lines dropped away and diesel tugs, horns blowing, guided her out into the channel.

There was a new captain aboard, Thomas U. Sisson, a tall, slender Mississippian, distinguished-looking and reserved. As occurs on every large ship, Captain Sisson, up in his command roost on the island, would remain largely unknown to the pilots aboard—in fact, to 99 percent of the personnel. No one wanted to be summoned to the bridge for a lecture,

Jesse least of all. He remembered the chewing-out from the *Philippine Sea*'s four-striper.

Two days later the Wayfarer was again headed for Mississippi, Vic Breddell behind the wheel.

Daisy said, "He keeps telling me he won't make more than five or ten carrier landings a month over there."

"That's about it unless they're in joint exercises or heavy training. . . ."

"Why does everyone keep lying to me?"

"No one is lying."

"But any one takeoff or landing could kill him."

"That's true, but Jesse is a very good pilot."

"I know that but someone else had to tell me when he bounced over the barrier and almost hit the *Philippine Sea* island. He didn't tell me. Not Jesse!"

"Why worry you? He didn't even get scratched."

Soon they crossed into Connecticut on Route 95 South.

Jesse was living in a so-called "Boys Town," a dormitory space on the *Leyte*, along with eleven other aviation midshipmen and ensigns, juniors of all the pilots from Air Group 3. Rank always had its privileges. Make lieutenant junior-grade or else become a "senior" ensign and the door would open for three in a room.

The man in the bunk directly overhead was Ensign Herbert Sargent, a New Englander. They'd gone through both Ottumwa and Pensacola together but had little contact at either place. Herb had seen him both places. Jesse's skin color made no difference to him, as was the case with the other ten occupants of "Boys Town." Flying was on their minds.

Life on board the *Leyte* for Jesse revolved around Squadron 32's cluttered ready room. Each squadron had its own ready room for flight operations, training operations, communications, mission briefing, mission debriefing, socializing. Flight gear was stowed there.

When not busy with squadron activities, Jesse could usually be found writing letters, studying, or skeet shooting off the stern; going to the nightly movie, attending boxing matches or jam sessions. He always attended church services on the hangar deck. He didn't participate in the all-night "red dog" card games or in the penny-a-point bridge games in the wardroom. He was invited. He wasn't a gambler.

Jesse found time to write to Daisy almost nightly and about weekly to his parents. He also wrote to Ike and Gwen Heard and Martin Luther Beard and occasionally to Professor Burger. He told all of them that the Negroes aboard had adopted him and aside from royal treatment in the wardroom found places in the superstructure to cheer each launch and landing. He always waved to the black faces when he cranked back the canopy.

Whenever he found Lee Nelson writing to Lee LaCroix, Jesse always said, "Tell her hello for me," or he'd write a note to her on the edge of the letter, perhaps send her a postcard. She was the only white woman who'd ever befriended him.

After evening chow, Jesse was often found on the *Leyte*'s foc'sle "front porch," the open space at the bow, above the main deck but below the flight deck, deep in thought, watching the sunset in silence, watching the porpoises careen off the waves, watching the escorts as the ship sliced the water. The big flattop was a moving city for her temporary birds. Jesse was discovering that carriers were truly remarkable ships.

13 May 1950

Dearest Daisy:

We're anchored in Lisbon harbor, a place I never dreamed of going to. We can see the hills of the old city and the river traffic of the famous Tagus sweeps by us. So there's something else besides flying airplanes to this duty. We had air operations crossing the Atlantic, but since you don't particularly like to hear about them, I'll just tell you that everything was fine and dandy. A swan in a pond couldn't have been any safer than I was.

I have liberty in the morning and I'm just going to walk around over there and take some pictures. I didn't know you'd put a Mediterranean guide book in my bag until after we left Norfolk. It will come in handy when I do the museums. I can't wait to go ashore. I plan to buy you a hand-embroidered Madeira blouse.

We'll be here two more days, then off to Sardinia and Sicily. I think we'll pretty much stick to that twelve-port schedule, two or three days each place. I promise I'll take you to all of them someday. . . .

On the afternoon of May 22 Ensign Charlie Mohring, USN, of VF-32 was lost at sea when his Corsair crashed while making an approach for a landing. The plane sank in sight of the *Leyte,* about 100 yards away. It was obvious Mohring was knocked unconscious on impact and the aircraft disappeared within seconds. A rescue helicopter and plane-guard destroyers found nothing but an oil slick in the wake of the ship.

Jesse had already come aboard safely and was standing on Vultures Row, the usual pilots' observation areas, when it happened. Accidents had to be expected, but they never were; they were pushed back into that area of the brain that houses denial and fear. Planes were launched with the full expectancy that they'd land without harm or loss of life. On this day all ships personnel were again reminded that life in carrier airplanes was deceivingly fragile. At the memorial service, the sad notes of taps lingered in the air. Again, there was that pall that would last for a few days or longer. Pilots seldom told their wives or parents.

Captains of the ships and squadron commanders always faced the possibility that some pilots would be afraid to fly.

There was nothing worse than sitting strapped in the cockpit on the flight deck, engine roaring, awaiting launch, knowing a crash had just occurred.

For a while, Jesse was numb. So was everyone else in Squadron 32.

25 May 1950

Dearest Daisy,
Here I am in Augusta, Sicily, and everything is going well on the ship and in the squadron. . . .

There were foreign government social receptions in most of the ports and Jesse attended some of them in his whites, attracting attention because in past visits of United States naval vessels, all of the officers had been Caucasians.

He wrote Daisy that the diplomats picked him out for a welcoming handshake, that he enjoyed it. He said, "I'm showing the color. . . ." His sense of humor was always subtle.

Naples, Italy
11 June 1950

Dear Ike, Gwen, and Ike Jr.:
Was nice to hear from you three again. At least I know I'm not completely forgotten. This is the fourth day in Naples and I don't have any trouble finding my way around. The people are quite friendly. I have a ticket to go to Capri and Pompei.

After we leave here on the sixteenth, we go to Leghorn and then on to Cannes, France, then Athens, Istanbul, Beirut, and back to France again, showing the flag.

But I'll give you a small clue. The happiest moment

of the whole cruise will be when they say, "Let's go home."

Bye for now.

Your Ace Boon Coon,
Jesse

War

June 1950

Two weeks later, on June 25, 1950, Tokyo time, Vice Admiral Turner C. Joy, Commander, Naval Forces, Far East, received a call in the resort Hotel Fujiya in Myanoshita: "North Koreans have crossed the thirty-eighth parallel and are moving south. . . ."

In Washington, D.C., minus fourteen hours, Admiral Forrest Sherman, Chief of Naval Operations (CNO), was notified that the North Koreans had invaded South Korea.

A few minutes later every three- and four-star admiral involved in air operations anywhere around the world received a message marked OPERATIONAL IMMEDIATE. It said:

```
Due to Korean incident, place 30 percent of all
naval aircraft on one-hour notice and remainder
of all aircraft on four-hour notice.
```

The meaning was all too clear: Would China become involved? Would the Soviet Union, known to be hard at work on an atom bomb, become involved?

The *Leyte* was anchored off Leghorn, Italy, having partic-ipated in war games with several European nations. The "Boys Town" door opened not long after midnight. Jesse, a light sleeper, turned on his bunk light. The other occu-pants groaned.

The visitor said, "We've got a problem. North Korea has invaded South Korea. CNO says to put some planes on one-hour notice. Up and at 'em."

"Hey, we're in the Med. Korea's a long way off," Herb Sargent said.

"CNO knows that. So does the old man." The door closed again.

Lee Nelson, who'd gone to bed early, having skipped the movie and the coffee and bull sessions in the wardroom, was awakened when his light came on and a voice said, "We're at war and we're getting shot at. Get your ass up. Wake up your ordnance crew and load ammunition. . . ." Lee was the squadron ordnance officer.

Nelson dressed in less than a minute and ran to the ward-room barefooted.

Tom Hudner soon joined Jesse and the crowd of other sleepy, puzzled pilots in the wardroom: drinking black cof-fee, trying to find out what had happened, thinking that the *Leyte* might soon be involved, even though she was an "East Coast" carrier.

In Hattiesburg Daisy listened to the local radio station, wondering if the *Leyte* would go to the Far East. Jesse had said that his job was always to "prepare for war."

Doug Neill had no other information aside from the brief Far East announcement, but selected 30 percent of his pi-lots, including Hudner and Brown, to stand by; the others could go back to their bunks until dawn.

Soon Captain Sisson spoke, repeating what little he knew, only adding, "The Seventh Fleet is standing by for orders. At this moment, I do not know what the mission of the *Leyte* will be. However, as of this moment, *Leyte* goes on combat-ready status." The Seventh Fleet was on duty in Far Eastern waters. The *Leyte* operated in the Sixth Fleet.

As he spoke, the carrier's exterior lights went out and the big ship vanished into the night.

"Isn't the *Valley Forge* the only carrier out there?" asked Jesse. He knew that Jack Keefer was on the *Valley Forge*. *Keefer has gotten his war*, Jesse thought.

The communication officer confirmed.

Jesse and Herb Sargent were on standby until 0800.

By 2 A.M. Nelson's ordnance crew was loading ammunition for the Corsair's six fifty-caliber wing guns. They carried a mixture of armor-piercing and tracer cartridges.

The next day President Truman told Secretary of State Dean Acheson that he was prepared to "draw the line" against further Communist encroachment.

The day after that, even before the United Nations Security Council was to vote on actions against North Korea, Truman ordered United States air and sea forces to "give the South Korean government troops cover and support. . . ."

Jesse listened to all the talk in the wardroom. The ship's daily mimeographed newspaper contained a brief roundup of stories off the Associated Press wire. The main concern was what the Soviets might do, if anything. Moscow was only a few hours' flight from the Mediterranean.

In early July Jesse was summoned to Doug Neill's office. "Think you can handle assistant operations officer?"

"As well as anybody in the squadron."

"You've got it, Jesse. Don't let me down."

"I won't."

That means I'll be working for Dad Fowler.

Meanwhile, troop landing exercises and air operations continued off Crete, Athens, and Turkey, all places for mailing letters home. Jesse stuffed half a dozen letters into single envelopes and mailed them from each next port. In the last one he again admitted he'd had enough of the exotic places and was ready to come back to Hattiesburg. The mail from Daisy was mostly about Pam, with photos.

The *Leyte*, in company with the new carrier *Midway*, dropped anchor in the late afternoon on August 10 off Beirut, Lebanon. During the night, there seemed to be a lot of activity and the wardroom scuttlebutt said something was "going on." Communications people were busy.

A helicopter was ferrying admirals between the carriers and soon Captain Sisson announced that the *Leyte* was going home and then to Korea. Ten days in the Norfolk area for overhaul, loading stores and ammunition.

Excitement swept the carrier. This was what they were all about. War was the culmination of all the training, all the days in schools, all the hours in the air, all the gunnery practice, all the narrow escapes. A shooting war was why they wore gold wings. Jesse was caught up in it as much as anyone aboard.

Three days later the *Leyte* was detached from the Sixth Fleet and off-loaded a contingent of Sixth Division Marines in Crete before heading for the Virginia Capes at best speed, no interruptions for air operations. The Marines were bound for Korea. Mechanics worked night and day to prepare the aircraft for combat. The aviators got paperwork done.

The Lees had discussed getting married when the *Leyte* returned to the United States. With Korea ahead and the possibility of getting killed, Lee Nelson talked the captain and air group commander into letting him send a message to his fiancée saying the wedding was "off." It sounded to Lee LaCroix as though the message was coded and her fiancé was headed home. Her mind wasn't changed by it.

Jesse was launched from the *Leyte* with the rest of the squadron on August 23, flying to the Naval Auxiliary Air Station at Oceana, a few miles southwest of Virginia Beach.

The next ten days would be used to prepare for war. The other pilots scattered.

At twilight, after a flight to Pensacola, a Greyhound glided toward Hattiesburg. Jesse was looking out the window toward the fields, which were at the peak of their summer growing season. Though he was in khaki uniform, the gold stripe on his shoulder boards, the gold wings on his chest, he was again in the back of the bus. The driver had sent him there with a toss of his head. He had passed rows of frowning white faces. *No problem*, Jesse thought. *I've got other things to think about.*

On arrival in Boston Lee Nelson tried to postpone the ceremony until Korea was over, reminding Lee LaCroix that fighter pilots had a high casualty rate. "I'd rather have a few days together than none" was her response. In a few busy days at Newton Centre the LaCroix family managed to pull together a complete church wedding, with bridesmaids, music, and a reception; an ivory satin gown for the bride. Frank Sheffield was best man. The Lee Nelsons headed for Virginia Beach for a five-day honeymoon.

Jesse walked up to the front door of the Nix apartment on Robinson Place and rang the bell. Sister Lillie opened it and shouted, "Jesse, we didn't know you were comin'."

Daisy was in the tub, sudsed to her chin, reading a magazine. The magazine flew up into the air. She was not fully inside the robe and suds were still up to her chin as Jesse swept her into his arms.

After he kissed her, hugged her, held her close, he asked, "Where is that baby?"

Daisy answered, "Asleep, of course. It's eight-thirty. What kind of mother do you think I am?"

"You're a good one, but wake her up."

Jesse, holding the sleeping Pam in his arms, told her he was going to Korea.

Tears suddenly welled up. "I knew the minute Lillie yelled."

"It may all be over before we get there. We're putting in troops and more carriers, more aircraft. But let's don't talk about all that."

"You know me."

"I'm taking you to Norfolk."

Her mood changed. "Do we take Pam?"

"No. I love her like life itself, but the next nine days are for you and me."

Daisy thought a moment. "You know, we could just stay here and talk."

"No, we can't," Jesse said. "Pack what you need. We're going to Norfolk tonight. Nonstop."

"Tonight?" Daisy was stunned.

"Right now."

"How are we going to get there? Fly?"

"That green Dodge that's parked out in the street."

"We're going to drive all night, Jesse?"

"Yep. I've got four days of duty in Norfolk and then we'll come back here for five days. We'll spend all that time together."

Daisy clapped her hands and jumped up and down.

Jesse drove by the slums of Brambleton Avenue, on by Broad Creek Road, then east on Lincoln Avenue. Few white faces were to be seen.

Stopping in front of the DeYoung Hotel on the fringe of the ghetto, Jesse said with a grin, "Best hotel in town." The clientele was all black. They had little choice.

As they signed in, the elderly clerk drawled, "You sure you belong in that uniform, son? That's an officer's uniform. Don't get into trouble."

Jesse smiled back. "That's what I am, an officer."

"Well, you sneaked in, didn't you? I know we have cooks an' bed-makers an' broom handlers but nevah any braid. Top o' that, you a pilot, ain't cha?"

Jesse was pleased with this conversation, as always.

The old man continued, "I swear I didn't know one of us was a pilot anywhere on earth."

"I got lucky."

Daisy said, "You did not. You earned those wings."

Jesse carried their bags upstairs. The DeYoung didn't have an elevator.

The room was clean but Spartan. "They're all full at the Monticello," he joked. The sedate old Monticello on Granby Street was *the* hotel in town. Negroes could not be guests.

Looking around, she said, "This is fine with me. The Monticello is not exclusive enough for a honeymoon. You realize we never had one."

They spent a few minutes in each other's arms, then he said, "I'm going to Oceana where the squadron is. Take a nap. I'll be back about five."

She'd slept off and on during the ride through Alabama, Georgia, North Carolina, and on into Virginia. They'd talked whenever she was awake, Jesse telling her about all the foreign ports. She was weary from the drive and took his advice. She went to bed.

Jesse returned before five and she was still asleep. He sprawled out beside her and neither awakened until well after midnight.

"A night wasted," she said.

"Oh no, we're together," he said, pulling her close.

He drove back from Oceana the next day to take her to lunch and on leaving the cafe steered her into a jewelry store on Brambleton. "Why are we going in here?" she asked.

"To buy you the diamond ring you didn't get two years ago."

"Jesse Brown, I don't need a diamond from you." She held up her hand, plain gold band gracing her ring finger. "I wouldn't part with this for anything. I don't need anything added."

"We can afford it now."

The black clerk asked, "Can I help you folks?"
Daisy answered firmly. "No, you can't."

Korea was on Jesse's mind when he went to work the next day. Pages of the *Norfolk Virginian-Pilot* were filled with what President Truman still called a "police action." Political nonsense aside, full-scale war was being waged from near the tip of the South Korean peninsula up to the thirty-eighth parallel, which divided the Communists from the southern democracy. Carrier attacks had begun July 3 with the USS *Valley Forge* and the British *Triumph* destroying Communist-held airfields with rockets. An ensign flying off the *Valley Forge* had been killed July 22, Jesse noted, thankful it wasn't Keefer. Norfolk was a Navy town, a carrier town, and each day brought bad news.

The next afternoon they went to the Negro beach at Cape Henry. They'd borrowed towels from the hotel and Daisy had packed a picnic lunch. Though the day was sunny, not many people were on the sands or splashing in the low surf.

Hand in hand, they walked south until confronted with a sign that said: NEGROES NOT ALLOWED BEYOND THIS POINT. Beyond the sign was sacrosanct white sunning and bathing territory. They turned around without discussing the restriction. Talk about it would lead nowhere.

After playing in the surf, they returned to their towels. During lunch, Jesse said, "If something should happen to me, I want you to go to college and get a degree. All right? It's the only way for us. If I get the chance, I'm going back to get mine someday. The Navy will pay for it." The Holloway Flying Midshipmen plan guaranteed two more years.

Frowning, Daisy said, "Nothing is going to happen to you."

"I'm talking this way only for your sake. Carrier pilots have a high casualty rate and you better know it. If something does happen, you'll have enough money so you don't have to remarry right away just for support."

Daisy said, "Please don't say all these things" and began to weep.

"Now stop that. We have to talk about this. If it does happen, I want you to go to college. I want you to become a teacher. Promise me."

"I promise."

"I want you to bring Pam up with a lot of love, and I also want her to have a good education. . . ."

"I promise."

"Okay, we won't talk about it again the whole time."

An Associated Press story out of Tokyo quoted General Douglas MacArthur, Supreme Commander, Far East, as saying he did not think China or the Soviet Union would become involved. An aide quickly denied the quote.

Before they returned to Norfolk, Jesse said, "I want you to meet the Nelsons tomorrow. They just got married."

"They're black?"

"No, white as Pam's baby powder. Lee's my best friend in the squadron. I wrote you about him. A great guy. He's an ensign, my age. He knows all about you. I made a date for lunch with them tomorrow."

Not long after noon the next day, they were at the maître d' stand of the posh Hotel Monticello dining room when the manager called Lee aside, saying, "I'm sorry but we can't seat your friends. We can't serve them."

Lee was embarrassed and furious, but kept his voice low. "He's an officer of the U.S. Navy. What's wrong with you?"

"I'm sorry, sir. We have other guests."

Finally Jesse stepped forward, not really surprised, saying, "Come on, Lee, let's go." He had to get back to Oceana.

On the sidewalk he grinned tightly. "Don't let it throw you."

The next day Jesse asked Lee to join them for lunch and Nelson raced home to pick up his wife at their tiny surfside apartment in Virginia Beach. She'd just come off the beach and was still in her wet bathing suit. She was concerned about what to wear to lunch. He said, "This is a beach resort. Wear shorts."

Jesse took them to a restaurant they'd never heard of and Lee quickly understood why. The staff and customers were all black.

Jesse spotted an empty table and they all sat down. The table was bare except for salt, pepper, and sugar. They waited for service, but it didn't come. The waitresses stared at the mixed foursome.

After waiting for at least ten minutes, Jesse was furious and walked over to the manager, demanding to know why they weren't being served. The manager looked at Lee's wife's bare legs and said he wouldn't serve anyone wearing shorts. But the reason was obvious. Whites weren't welcome.

They left immediately, went to a nearby drive-in, and managed to recover their dignity and sense of humor while eating barbecued spare ribs in the car.

> *Norfolk Virginian-Pilot*, Associated Press (Delayed): . . . after the glide-bombing attack on the bridge, Ensign Thompson of the USS *Valley Forge* called to say he was losing oil. Apparently, he'd been hit by small-arms fire in the engine or accessory section. He immediately went to full power to try and reach the ocean forty miles to the south. He got halfway there when his engine froze up. He jettisoned the belly tank and made an excellent landing on a dry sand bar in a river bed. "Wasn't that a damn good crash landing?" he said on his radio. Neither Thompson or anyone else on the *Valley Forge* knew he'd landed in enemy territory. He was later reported to be a prisoner of war. . . .

Those are the risks, Jesse thought.

"Did you see this newspaper story?" Daisy gave him the page.

He shook his head. He had seen it. He thought about Jack Keefer flying off the "Happy Valley."

The days passed quickly—too quickly—and early Wednesday the Wayfarer began the long trip back to Mississippi. Daisy, always the talker, was subdued most of the ride, and Jesse didn't talk about the *Leyte* or flying. They listened to music.

"Mr. Yates, you remember me?"

Corley Yates shook his head. He was standing outside his building at the private side of Hattiesburg Municipal Airport. The sign above the doorway said: YATES AVIATION. His red hair was gray. He was an old man now.

"I was the kid you chased away when this was a dirt strip. You threw a wrench at me one time," Jesse said. "I never took it personally."

"Well, doggone, I do remember you. Pesky kid. An' look at you now. You got wings." He extended a hand and Jesse shook it. Corley Yates had mellowed from those days in the 1930s. "I'll be doggoned. You learnt to fly, didn't cha. You're an officer now. What'cha name?"

"Jesse Brown."

"Where'd you live 'round here?"

"Dewey Street, Palmer's Crossing, Lux, Kelly's Settlement . . ."

Yates laughed. "Jus' spots in the roads then."

"I fell in love with airplanes," Jesse said, feeling comfortable with Corley Yates at last.

"I'm still foolin' 'round with 'em. Got my own service an' rental business. I spent the war at Maxwell Field with the Air Corps, fixin' engines, an' saved enough money to get this goin' . . ."

Jesse said, "This is Ike Heard and my younger brothers, Lura and Fletcher." Lura and Fletcher were still teenagers.

Yates shook hands with them.

"I went to school with Ike at Eureka. We've been friends ever since. A long time ago I told Ike that when I got my wings I was going to fly over Main Street an' Market Street an' Pine Street an' Front Street an' Mobile . . .''

Ike was smiling and nodding his head.

Ike had come to Hattiesburg to visit his parents and heard that Jesse was in town. He'd graduated from Hampton Institute and was teaching at Mary Allen College in Crockett, Texas. His wife Gwen was a Galveston girl.

''I said I was going to circle the whole town at three hundred feet and fly up the Bouie River till I found out where it started. So what I'd like to do, Mr. Yates, is rent that pretty four-place Cessna standing over there for an hour. . . .''

Yates looked at the red plane, and then back at Jesse. ''Tell you what I'm gonna do, Jesse Brown. Just pay for the gas. Come on in the office an' fill out the rental form.''

While Jesse was inking the agreement, Yates said, ''One thing, jus' don't fly over town at three hundred feet. Things 'ave changed here. One o' them deputies might shoot you down.''

A little later there were wide smiles on the faces of the passengers and a wider one on Jesse's face. He'd offered to fly Papa John and his mother. They'd declined.

He went over the town at a respectable 1,000 feet and over Lux and Eatonville and up the Bouie River until it was just a creek.

> *Task Force 77 Air Intelligence Brief*: On August 7, Ensign Elmer McCallum, Jr., of Squadron 54, the *Valley Forge*, was hit by ground fire after bombing a railroad bridge at Seoul and then ran into power lines. He fluttered for twenty miles to a point off Inchon harbor and then got rid of ammunition and rockets, ditching in the sea. He swam for two hours and found a rock at low tide which was reduced to about four by eight feet at high tide during the night. A North Korean gunboat searched for him, but after dawn the next day a British destroyer rescued him.

There was a revival going on at Shady Grove Baptist and Jesse took Daisy and Pam, collecting Papa John, who was still a deacon there, and his mother from Kelly's Settlement for the preaching and singing each night.

On Friday night, last night of the revival, Reverend Woullard said, "One of our long-time brothers, Jesse Brown, will fly to Norfolk Monday morning and join his ship to go to Korea and fight the Communists. Jesse has been the outstanding member of our church and community for quite a while now. We're all so proud of him, and his wife Daisy and daughter Pam, of Deacon John and Julia, and his brothers, Marvin, Lura, and Fletcher, all of whom are here tonight. Jesse, could you come up and say a few words to us?"

Julia was holding little Pam in her lap and tears came into her eyes each time she looked at Jesse. He seemed so young in his uniform with those wings on his chest. He seemed so vulnerable to her.

"You don't know how happy I am to be here. I grew up in this church and have so many memories of Sundays here, of going to school here, even of teaching here when I was a teenager. So I'm home with all of you, and I love all of you. Within a week my ship, the USS *Leyte*, will be sailing for Korea to join the fight against the North Korean Communists. I've been training three years for this and it's my duty to go. We are professionals on the *Leyte*, our pilots are among the best on earth, and we are not at all afraid of the North Koreans. I ask you to pray for my squadron so that we can return safely. I ask you to pray for me so that I can again join Daisy and Pam and my parents and brothers. Thank you."

Comments of "Amen" and "Say it, brother" punctuated the short talk.

Outside the church almost the whole congregation came up to shake Jesse's hand and touch Daisy and Pam and murmur words of support to Deacon John and Julia and Lura and Fletcher. A black son and brother was off to war.

By Sunday morning there was a hurricane raging in the Gulf of Mexico, moving in the general direction of Gulfport, Biloxi, and Mobile. The nearest open airport was Birmingham and Jesse booked an afternoon flight out of there.

Ike and Gwen offered to go along in the Wayfarer so that Daisy would have someone in the car on the drive back to Hattiesburg to share the wheel. The distance was several hundred miles.

Daisy's mother and aunt were going to Meridian, Mississippi, that same morning, taking Pam with them. Jesse followed them all the eighty miles to Meridian, then continued on to Birmingham. Pam stood up in the backseat looking at them, smiling and waving occasionally. Sometimes she'd sit down, then pop up again to wave and smile. Jesse watched her continuously. It was a day and scene that Daisy would remember forever.

At Birmingham Airport Ike and Gwen walked around for almost an hour to give Jesse and Daisy time together.

Enroute North Korea

September 1950

Repaired and resupplied, Air Group 3 aboard, plus six Sikorsky HO-3S-1 helicopters, with their ten Marine pilots, the *Leyte* sailed for Korean waters. The Marine choppers were the same models as the Navy's "Angels," the planeguards that flew astern of the carriers during air operations. In Korea they were to act as observation platforms for the ground forces in combat and rescue work. Chopper tasks—on land and at sea—grew daily.

More than a year had gone by since Jesse had joined the *Leyte* and he felt altogether comfortable aboard her, felt that he was an integral and worthwhile part of the air group and ship family. There had not been a single word or incident that he was aware of that involved the color of his skin. The invisible line had vanished.

Jesse flew four times while crossing the Caribbean, with routine takeoffs and landings as the squadrons practiced for combat. He and the other ensigns aboard were very much aware that only the lowest-ranking pilots had been involved in mishaps to date. Two, both nonfatal, had occurred at Oceana. "This was to be expected," Bill Koenig said. "Lack of experience," he said. "Get more time in the cockpit if you can."

As one of the more senior ensigns, Jesse had graduated from "Boys Town" after eight new aviation midshipmen and ensigns came aboard in Norfolk. He was now rooming with Koenig and Bobby Schabacker, "jaygees," three to a room. Schabacker flew an attack bomber.

The *Leyte* scraped the sides of the Panama Canal on September 11 with her ninety-three-foot beam and then stopped in San Diego for high-level briefings with more air operations en route.

At Sea, Pacific Ocean
Wednesday Nite, 13 Sept. '50

Dear Ike and Gwen and Junior:

I've thought about you quite a lot since I left, despite all the paces we've been going through. I guess you'll soon be on your way home and back to work on that apartment building.

Allow me to say thanks so much for all your extreme kindness in helping me out of my difficulties. Your kindness meant that I could spend a few more hours with Daisy that I could not have done otherwise.

I had the excitement of being home and among relatives and close friends, and the knowledge and accompanying dread of knowing that I'd be leaving it at a distance only too soon. But I'll trust God and turn my case and myself to his keeping. At times like these, I feel most the incompetence of men, and especially myself. . . .

Your friend & pal,
Jesse

Korea was closing in, but Jesse didn't mention the word in the letter he mailed to Hattiesburg from Pearl Harbor. "All is well," he wrote. "Smile."

The squadrons, the F4U-4 Corsairs, the bigger, heavier AD-4 Skyraiders, and the 797-2 Panther jets, operated around the Hawaiian area over the next three days, then the *Leyte* got under way for Japan. The aircraft, both those shackled on the flight deck and those below on the hangar deck, stayed aboard for the crossing. But there were preparations going on the entire time. Work on the planes, intelligence briefings, squadron talks on tactics, ready room lectures.

The *Leyte* had taken on additional aircraft in Hawaii and was jammed with extra flying machines. Their pilots were transients and would not operate with the *Leyte* aviators. They'd be detached in Japan. Although they seldom visited the air group ready rooms, they ate and chatted in the officers' mess. There were always men in there drinking coffee and talking.

Jesse was particularly impressed with one of the Marine chopper pilots, First Lieutenant Charlie Ward, a compact prematurely gray-haired man in his early thirties. He'd heard Ward say, "Ah don't know the meaning of the word 'fear,' but not because Ah'm brave. Ah jus' don't understand big words." The minute Ward opened his mouth Jesse knew he was from the deep South. He had an Alabama/Mississippi drawl.

Ward talked on about the choppers: how they were still in infancy, how they couldn't operate at night because of lousy instrumentation, how lousy they were in the mountains above 5,000 feet. He grinned. "Yuh guys gonna crash, do it at sea level. I'll meet you there. . . ."

After he left the wardroom, Jesse asked one of the other Marines about Charlie Ward.

"Ol' Charlie? He's got the guts and determination to make him the perfect chopper pilot. Got in as a teenager before Pearl Harbor, wound up as a drill instructor at the boot camp in South Carolina. Got into flight training, got his wings in '43. He flew dive bombers in the Pacific in '44 and '45. Then he joined the first Marine chopper unit in early '47, tenth man to qualify. Get him to tell you about dead-sticking an SBD in a Florida swamp after an engine failure. The only thing left of that sucker was the cockpit and Charlie Ward still strapped into it. Man is fearless. . . .''

Flying their flimsy, underpowered whirlybirds, the chopper pilots were treated with great respect by fixed-wing aviators aboard all the carriers.

Several days out of Pearl Harbor, Jesse, Koenig, Hudner, Nelson, Sheff, and other junior officers sat mesmerized as a three-striper, a commander, air intelligence officer, veteran of World War II, said, ''It's a little different than it was in the last war. These people don't fight the way the Japanese did. The action is scattered. They hide tanks and trucks in haystacks and houses. They literally drive the tanks through the front end of a house and force the occupants to move outside as if nothing is going on. You look down and see the peaceful cottage. They use horses like jeeps. They camouflage ammunition carts as hay wagons pulled by horses. Then somebody like you, in a flip mood, decides to strafe a hay wagon and it blows sky high. Their soldiers use the peasants for gun fodder, pushing them ahead of columns. You'll never fight a meaner, trickier war. . . .''

Jesse was taking notes.

''You all-suffering pilots, let me tell you something else. The gutless left-wing politicians are playing games with it. In fact, some members of Congress are arguing whether or not the Chinese are shooting at us. Well, you'll find out for yourselves at Sinuiju and elsewhere. Across from there is the Chinese city of Antung, and there's a MiG airfield southwest of that town. As you all know, the Soviets have provided the Chinks with the MiGs and everything else, sometimes even pilots. They come up when they see us. From high altitude they dive down through our jet cover, take potshots at us, then turn left and cross the Yalu, home-free. We can't shoot back, because of the yellow-belly politicians, sitting safe and comfortable on their asses in Washington. It's a lousy way to fight a war. Frankly, I don't think they want us to win. . . ."

Tom Hudner asked, "Are Chinese troops fighting so far?"
"Only in the air. . . ."

This was another subject Jesse wouldn't touch in the letters he'd mail to Daisy from Yokosuka.

During the Mediterranean cruise, he'd volunteered to help the chaplain when he wasn't flying. Now, the best he could do was attend church services on the hangar deck when not in the air. He barely had time to keep up with the correspondence course on international law, take care of the log, fulfill his operational chores, and write home.

Now part of famed Task Force 77, a unit of the Seventh Fleet, the *Leyte* would operate with the *Valley Forge* and the *Philippine Sea*, the carrier of Jesse's barrier bounce. The escort carriers, *Badoeng Strait,* also known as the "Bing-Ding," and the *Sicily*, were also on station. The weary *Valley Forge*, the "Happy Valley," had been out there since July and needed a rest. Jack Keefer was already a "war vet."

Jesse had seen films of huge World War II task forces, but the array of Task Force 77's vessels, including the battleship *Missouri*, four cruisers, countless destroyers, and other support vessels, gliding along, maneuvering as a unit like a drill team, was breathtaking, he wrote Daisy. The carriers were perhaps a mile apart, usually abeam of each other except in diamond formations, always into the wind during flight operations. Circling above was the CAP, the lookout combat air patrol, two or more aircraft according to proximity of land. They kept an eye out for Russian submarines always observing the operations or for MiGs that might play dangerous games. Jet CAP was as high as 35,000 feet.

The *Leyte* had steamed at 22 knots most of the time from the Med out here to the Sea of Japan. But the first day of combat always had butterflies zooming around inside most stomachs. The feeling sets in the night before. Pilots worry about ground fire, ack-ack, and about nose-to-nose or tail-to-tail combat with the enemy; worry about their aircraft, mostly about the power plants. *Will that engine keep turning the prop*? They all had those concerns, very much including Ensign Brown.

There was shoptalk in the wardroom, not designed to frighten young aviators like Jesse, but simply combat case histories. "Guy off the 'Happy Valley' named Curry was the first pilot shot down out here. Back in July. He was strafing a gunboat in Wonsan harbor and got hit. Corsair caught fire and he bailed out through flames two miles offshore. Got burnt bad, but inflated his raft and got picked up by the *Hollister*. He's back at Bethesda, I hear. Looks like a piece of toast, but he's alive. Maybe he rode that sucker too long before leaving it. . . ."

The basic unit of naval fighter tactics was a two-plane "section," the leader and his wingman. Most of the Korean operations would be conducted with a group of four aircraft, "a division": the division leader and his wingman, the section leader and his wingman. The two sections of aircraft would work together and protect each other.

It had been explained to Jesse as early as Ottumwa that this arrangement was a natural to encourage competition between individual pilots, sections, and divisions. Competition to be the best! The best-looking formation, best carrier landings, best gunnery, rocket and bombing scores! It was the same as physical competition in preflight. And he felt it was a constant challenge, as a black man, to his ego and ability, he'd written Ike Heard. Though he had trained for it, he'd never really expected to be tested in actual combat. Now he would be and he hoped he'd perform in a professional and correct manner, make anyone with a black skin proud of him.

Leyte history records that Squadron 32's first strike against the Communists occurred October 10 in the Wonsan area with a lieutenant named Frank Cronin as division leader and "Sheff" as a section leader.

Just past dawn, Jesse, along with Tom Hudner, Bill Koenig, Herb Sargent, and others selected for the second morning strike, two divisions, eight aircraft all together, were in the squadron ready room for the briefing by the air intelligence officer. Each had a clipboard to jot down information. A teletype at the front gave them the latest weather conditions. A large chart was central in the room.

"Okay, we're operating in support of General MacArthur's Wonsan invasion forces and here's Sindu Island. Used to be a Japanese fortress honeycombed with huge tunnels. There are a lot of shore guns and the idea is to put them out of business. We'll be hitting them this morning along with strikes from the *Philippine Sea* and *Valley Forge*. We'll be coordinating attacks with them, but watch yourselves. A lot of our planes will be in the air. . . ."

Wonsan was a major port on the west coast of North Korea, 100 miles above the South Korean border.

Jesse asked, "Suppose we meet MiGs?"

"I doubt you will. All I can say is good luck."

Nelson asked, "What kind of guns do they have?"

"Four twenty-three mms and two thirty-seven mms [millimeters], we think."

"How fast?" a pilot asked.

"Fast. It'll climb forty-five thousand feet in eight minutes. Estimated speed over five hundred and sixty knots. Avoid them if at all possible." That got a laugh. "But I don't think you'll run into them around Wonsan. They're staying up north."

Doug Neill said, "If a plane goes down, that's one down. We don't need any Hollywood stuff." He was referring to *Fighter Squadron,* in which Robert Stack landed beside his shot-down skipper, picked him up, and flew him to safety, a silly World War II film. "We won't do that. If we lose one, that's one. We can't afford to lose two. . . ."

The PIM, "point of intended movement," the point

where the *Leyte* should be at their return, was posted. Jesse noted it down. All they usually had to do was plot it and figure the course to steer from North Korea back to the ship about 100 miles off the coast. But sometimes the carrier was not at its probable location or hidden by snow squalls or fog. They'd have to search for the task force. They were being tracked by radar, outgoing or incoming. Neill or Dad Fowler would lead them home.

Then Jesse went into the locker room adjacent to the ready room to put on a rubber survival "poopy" suit. The waters off Korea were icy. Even with the rubber suits, survival didn't stretch much beyond several hours in ideal situations.

He was already wearing longies and two pairs of socks. The poopy suit had a neckband to keep out freezing water. Then he pulled on the bulky Mae West, adjusted the parachute harness straps and the hip knife, plus the pistol. Using the ladder to the flight deck, he'd carry the flight board, with its navigation data, codes, and plots, to strap on his right knee after he climbed into the cockpit. He felt like a sausage and was sweating profusely.

After he was settled in, the flight deck bullhorn blared, "Start your engines!" There was a sudden roar. Then the white flag, signifying the beginning of flight operations, broke out from Primary Flight on the island superstructure, fluttering in the chill wind. For every knot of wind across the flight deck, the temperature was lowered one degree.

It was harvest time in North Korea, but there was enough sting to the wind to cause the flight deck crews to button up their jackets and wear heavier gloves. Those who'd ever served on ships or ashore in the Far East knew that savage winter would soon visit. The ballet was about to begin, movement of the armed Corsairs to a spot opposite the island.

Soon Jesse sat in his aircraft, waiting tensely, having gone through the cockpit check. Now it was lock brakes, apply full power, and wait for the signal from the launch officer, then takeoff. The usual swirl of activity, the green and yellow and purple and red, painted the ballet.

Out to the sides of the *Leyte*, the escorting destroyers plunged along in the blue gray seas.

On the wing of the navigation ridge Captain Sisson was looking down, his face a red oval in the fur of his flight jacket.

Engine at full throttle, propeller a blur, rings of vapor around it, aircraft trembling from the tail tip to the nose, Jesse waited for the downward sweep of the checkered flag held by the Fly I officer.

He glanced up toward the island. The usual gallery of black faces looked down. They were making the victory sign, sober-faced. He waved and smiled.

Behind him, in another division, Tom Hudner was waiting to be directed to the takeoff spot, his engine idling.

Fly I whipped the flag down and Jesse's plane flashed forward, traveling about 400 feet, and then lifted off into the sky gracefully, turning out and up to join Dick Cevoli, Bill Koenig, and Herb Sargent.

After the fighters, the bombers would roll. The Skyraiders could carry three 1,000-pound bombs, ten 250-pound fragmentation bombs, rockets, and napalm, as well as 200 rounds of ammunition in each twenty-mm cannon, depending on what load was selected. The Panther jets, with their high speeds, were catapulted last. The ballet would be over for a while.

Soon Jesse's four-plane division had assembled and was flying toward the Wonsan area, which was still held by the Communists.

Jesse's right hand was on the control stick, which was configured with a "pistol grip." On the front was the trigger, on the left-hand side of the grip, convenient to the thumb, was the firing button for the wing-mounted rockets, and on the top of the grip was the release for the centerline stores: the 500-pound bomb or napalm or external fuel tank.

Soon they were over target and the Army ground controller was saying, "Navy, I have you in sight. Over."

Dick Cevoli replied, "One division, four Corsairs, each carrying one five-hundred-pound bomb, eight five-inch rockets, and a full load of ammo. Second four-Corsair division coming in behind us, carrying one napalm each, eight rockets, full loads of ammo. We're ready to work. . . ."

The ground controller acknowledged Cevoli's report and called out the coordinates of their assigned target, a gun emplacement atop a high hill about five miles from the division's position.

This is it, the supreme test, Jesse thought. Within minutes, Jesse pushed the Corsair over and dropped a 500-pounder on the North Korean heavy artillery position, located on the hill. Orange winks responded from the ack-ack guns below, then the black puffs in the sky. The bomb exploded as targeted, and he climbed to safety and got ready to send his rockets down and then begin strafing runs. Pensacola and Jacksonville flashed through his mind.

He hadn't known what his own reaction would be to this first combat mission. He'd expected all the training to kick in and it had. He'd felt anxiety like every other pilot launched that morning, but was it fear or the gray line between. He'd felt relief on completion of the runs and thought he'd performed in a professional manner. His division rendezvoused off the coast with other strike units and proceeded toward the task force and *Leyte.*

Back aboard for debriefing over coffee, Jesse joined the pilots of the day's strikes in the smoky ready room to talk about what happened, where and when. It was ritual. It was a joint decompression session, a letting down from the tensions. Every safe landing after a strike was an individual victory.

Flight operations were secured. The *Leyte* and her escorts eventually faded into the dusk. Jesse stopped by Lee Nelson's room for a moment. "Next time you write to Lee, ask her to send me some wedding pictures. I want to see the grins on your faces."

Nelson said he would.

On Thursday night, October 12, Jesse was writing to Daisy when Lee Nelson dropped by the stateroom. "You know what tomorrow is?"

Jesse nodded. "Friday the Thirteenth, 1950."

"You superstitious?"

"You ever heard of a black man who wasn't superstitious?"

"You're the most religious man in this squadron. Say a prayer for us tonight."

"That's what I had in mind. Consider it done."

As Lee walked away, Jesse called after him, "Why don't you try praying yourself?"

Tomorrow would be Jesse's twenty-fourth birthday. He didn't mention it.

Lee came back and sat down. "You going to make a career of this?"

Jesse laid his pen down. "I was. Now I doubt it. What future is there for someone like me? Going all the way to admiral?" He shook his head. "Only a fraction of you white guys ever make admiral. I certainly won't. . . ."

Lee nodded. "That's being realistic."

"I think so."

They talked on about both of their careers, and Jesse finally said, "I'm going back to Ohio State as soon as I can. I'll fulfill my obligation here and then get out. I've got a buddy in architecture and I hope to join him sometime. I love to fly, just as you do, but the commercial airlines aren't about to put a black man on the flight deck anytime soon. So what do I do?"

Lee nodded and returned to his own stateroom.

On the cloud-covered night of October 15, crack Chinese Communist infantrymen began to cross the Yalu bridges in secrecy. They took cover in the frigid bleak high mountains of North Korea and silently awaited orders to move south. Hundreds of thousands of them were poised to follow the token force. Though reconnaissance pilots sometimes flew over the areas, seeing smoke from isolated campfires, none of them had any idea what was below them.

But Washington was nervous about Soviet reactions and from the Pentagon came orders to cut off tops of the maps that showed the Yalu so that if a pilot was shot down over Chinese territory, the excuse would be that the pilot inadvertently strayed beyond the sanctioned limit. They were then "politically correct" maps, even if that term wasn't in use. A few planes *had* already strayed into Manchuria.

Doug Neill laughed in the ready room, "Yeah, we shot up a couple of camels and knocked a few bricks out of a walled city."

At Sea
21 October 1950

Dear Ike, Gwen, & Ike Jr.:

It certainly was a real pleasure to get your letter a couple of days ago. It is always good to get mail, but a letter from real friends is quite a treat.

Yes, the news has taken a turn for the better, but being a little close to it all, I can still see that all the danger is not all yet past. However, if China doesn't get into it, there is a chance that a few more days may end all except mopping up and guerrilla warfare. Even if it does end right now, and I certainly hope so, we have no assurance we'll be coming home soon.

Since we got over here, I've flown quite a few missions. Some routine and unexciting—others deep into North Korean territory where I think we were a bit unwelcome. They were shooting at us, and I consider that downright unfriendly. I'm glad we didn't get shot down because they have a special torture for aviators they shoot down.

Day before yesterday I got a very fine Rolex watch as a birthday present. It was a gift from the stewards and they brought it in with a cake. I thought it was darn nice of them and I appreciate their gift and the spirit of their giving. They seem to think well of me and I hope I never let them down. There was a little item in the ship's newspaper that my birthday was on the thirteenth and that on that day I flew in Event 13.

Guess I'll call it quits for now. I've got to eat early chow and get ready for a flight.

So be good and be careful and write when you can spare a few minutes.

> Your ABC (Ace Boon Coon),
> Jesse

For the next five days during daylight hours, Squadron 32 flew combat operations against enemy forces at Chonjin, Hapsu, Hyesanjin, and Kilchu. Despite heavy ack-ack over each target and aircraft coming home with holes in them from flying too low, not one was lost.

Bill Koenig was flying wingman on Jesse near the Yalu above cloud cover at about 18,000 feet. They let down through the undercast to about 3,000 feet above the ground and suddenly heard the distinct *KAHWOOMP* of cannon fire and saw the black puffs. Koenig looked ahead and down, seeing little holes in Jesse's tail, thinking, *Hey, we better separate.*

Jesse said, "Calm down" and got on the air: "This is Two Zero Three taking departure for the recco route. . . ." He'd been taught radio discipline long ago. *Let your brain take over, key the mike, engage your mouth. Be concise.*

On October 24, when there were just a few snow flurries in the North Korean mountains, a general named Barr had said confidently to his 27,000 troops, "We are going to the

Manchurian border, destroying any enemy along the way. . . ." The border was seventy-five miles north and the North Korean armies had been defeated. MacArthur, the fabled Supreme Commander, had issued orders from Tokyo to make that statement possible, thinking that the Allies had almost complete control over the country. Neither Barr nor MacArthur nor other generals knew what was waiting for them on a high plateau below the Yalu, alongside a reservoir called the Chosin.

Japan

November 1950

Just before the *Leyte,* the *Valley Forge,* and the *Philippine Sea* sailed for Japan on October 28 for rest, recreation, and replenishment, Jesse wrote to Daisy, saying he "definitely thought the war was winding down." So did the admirals. They had no idea that thousands of Chinese had already crossed the Yalu. General MacArthur was still saying the troops would be home by Christmas.

While Jesse slept or flew, the *Leyte* went about its business of being a floating airport, an aviation city on a war footing. Flight operations continued from dawn to dusk, maneuvering on various courses and speeds, but every two or three days she'd rendezvous with the replenishment fleet for food, fuel oil, aviation gas, and ammunition. The other carriers alternated.

Heavy bombs—2,000-pound, 1,000-pound, and 500-pound—and rockets and rocket motors and rocket fuses and thousands of rounds of fifty cartridges and thousands of pounds of napalm were delivered from the *Paracutin* and the *Chara*. There'd be another delivery in two days. The *Leyte* steamed, night and day.

Supplies and personnel, both officer and enlisted, came and went on lines rigged between the carrier and the delivering ship, the sea sometimes licking at their heels. Precious mail came by the sack and went the same way by one or another destroyers, a postal service just as good as any in the U.S.A.

Sick Bay received half a dozen patients a day, anything from galley knife cuts to head contusions from not ducking a towed aircraft. Court martials were held and guilty parties went to the brig for up to thirty days.

There were more than 1,000 separate jobs to occupy the more than 3,000 men aboard. Even at midnight, up to 500 were on duty.

One late afternoon in Hattiesburg, after the mailman arrived, Daisy opened Jesse's first letter about combat.

> I thought I'd be nervous when we got over the target, a gun battery, but then all the training kicked in and it was automatic from then on. I dove the plane, guided it and dropped the bomb, saw it explode and pulled up. You would have been proud of me. . . .
>
> Yesterday I flew low over a road deep in enemy territory after a strafing run. I'd hit three trucks, setting them afire. Suddenly, down there was a woman and a little girl, walking along peacefully. How strange it was! The little girl looked up and waved just as I put on power and climbed. I'd left death behind only a few seconds ago. I thought about the little girl last night and about you, Pamela. I pray that she'll survive. . . .

Daisy copied it, almost every word, to send to Snook Hardy in Louisiana.

*   *   *

The *Leyte* and the *Valley Forge* were anchored off Sasebo in southern Japan, while the *Philippine Sea* had put into Yokosuka, the naval base about twenty miles from Yokohama. Liberty boats ran back and forth between the gangways and the Japanese shore as thousands of sailors and officers ate, drank, shopped for Christmas, tried to pick up girls, and otherwise enjoyed themselves.

Shops and cabarets and restaurants and bars anywhere near the waterfront were doing turn-away business on this night of November 4. Those serious about Christmas shopping could start with lacquer ware and silk garments and go upward to pearls and furs.

After dinner, Jesse and Lee Nelson were in a gift shop haggling with the owner. Nelson wanted a pair of pearl earrings for his wife Lee and Jesse was trying to decide whether or not he could afford a pearl necklace for Daisy.

"Let's try another place," Nelson said and they left the shop. They hadn't walked more than thirty feet when two shore patrolmen approached, asking, "Are you from the *Valley Forge* or *Leyte*?"

"*Leyte*," Jesse replied.

"All liberty has been canceled, sir. You are to go back to your ship immediately. Sorry."

"Thanks," said a depressed Nelson. He turned to Jesse. "You want to go back to that shop?"

"Next time."

As they hurried toward the docks, Jesse said, "I thought we were going to wind this war down."

"Something's happened."

What had happened was an urgent message from the Commander, Naval Forces, Far East, to the Commander, Seventh Fleet:

```
Task Force 77 proceed east coast Korea. Destroy
all installations and troops within North Ko-
rea, but be meticulous about not crossing bor-
der.
```

Wide-open war, Jesse thought. *What else is new? The carriers have been pounding the east coast for months. We've been warned about not crossing the Yalu for months.*

Jesse said, "I've got a hunch this has something to do with China. I sat beside one of the communications guys at lunch a couple of days ago. He said he read between the lines that the Chinks were gathering on the North Korea side of the Yalu. . . ."

Not long after seven the next morning, the *Leyte* and *Valley Forge* moved out to sea and into the Korea Straits, then on into the Sea of Japan, with their usual escorts. Even the ship captains were baffled by the urgency. The crews had needed every minute ashore. Then word was passed. Intelligence estimated 500,000 Chinese troops were staging at the Yalu and moving south. There was alarm in the Pentagon and in the White House.

Jesse flew his war with a mixture of fear and thrill. He flew on the edge of constant danger and sometimes enjoyed it.

There were two types of bombing missions. In one the strike pilots would be briefed on a particular target before launching, given coordinates on it in the ready room—photographs if they were available. In the other type they'd gone out with certain bomb loads and reported in to a task force control ship that was current with the situation ashore. If they were lucky, they'd get a target assignment without having to circle around the command ship. If not, they'd soar around like buzzards until the code-named controller below would tell them where to go.

Targets were anything from utilities to bridges to roadways to tanks, railroad terminals to truck parks to troop concentrations. Bomb them, rocket them, strafe them, destroy them. Then there were armed "recco" [reconnaissance] missions, flying over particular areas searching for targets of opportunity.

The strike pilots were all learning, the hard way, why the

navigation courses at Pensacola had been so tough. They now wished it had been even tougher. Jesse wished that.

There were no radio beacons, no airways, no ground communications aside from Army or Marine target controllers; no aids of any kind to navigation over North Korea. The maps were based on old Japanese surveys and targets were often well away from where they were supposed to be.

It was all visual, they discovered, dead reckoning by identifying a river or town or railroad tracks often wrongly labeled, then flying a course from that landmark according to a pencil line drawn on a chart. It was a navigational nightmare, and Jesse agreed with the intelligence briefer of two months ago. All wars were mean, but this one was turning into the "meanest."

To get to targets, they were looking for bends in rivers and highways or railroad tracks that disappeared into tunnels. Sometimes one set of hills looked exactly like the next; one valley was no different than the next.

Jesse marveled at the bleak beauty of the upper plateaus, the wide expanses where there were no buildings larger than the primitive mud houses. The houses passed beneath the throbs of the Corsair engines, taking them deep into enemy territory, ending in dives on targets, explosions erecting giant red mushrooms. In treetop attacks there were trucks and trains to be blown up with streaming bullets and soldiers shooting back at them with rifles. Then the red splotches of napalm.

Aside from the enemy's antiaircraft guns, the black puffs, and the *KAWOOMPS*, there were several natural hazards. A lot of Manchuria's electric power came from the Chosin Reservoir area. High-tension wires carried electricity to the Mukden, Port Arthur, and Darien industrial centers.

The ready room briefer of two months ago had said: "Don't fly up any valley unless you check it carefully for high-tension towers. It will be easy to follow a road or railroad track around a bend at two hundred and fifty knots, but you won't see those wires. *Goodbye!* So far, two aircraft have been destroyed, two pilots lost because they didn't watch for the towers. [They were probably decapitated.] There are no orange balls on the wires." It was easy to forget the briefer and the towers.

In a moment of attack, turning a corner in a valley, Jesse caught sight of several Chinese soldiers in their cotton-quilted jackets staring at him from a mountainside road about level with his aircraft. He expected them to jump into a ditch for cover. But they just stood there. He decided to teach them a lesson and strafe them, pulling up sharply, intending to roll to his right and come back down to spray them with bullets. Then, to his horror, he saw high-tension wires flash not more than a yard beneath him.

The soldiers had stopped to watch him fly directly into the steel trap, and his own heart stopped.

As he climbed for altitude, his hands were shaking and he knew, for as long as he lived, he would never forget the split-second vision of the wires. He looked back and saw, for the first time, the towers that carried the treacherous cables. God had let him live.

Sixty thousand troops of the "People's Liberation Army" were already deployed along the battle lines below the Yalu, according to intelligence, and General MacArthur issued a communiqué:

> While the North Korea forces with which we were
> initially engaged have been destroyed or ren-
> dered impotent for military action, a new and
> fresh Chinese Communist army now faces us,
> backed up by the possibility of large alien re-
> serves and adequate supply within easy reach to
> the enemy but beyond our present sphere of mil-
> itary action. . . .

The Yalu.

The communiqué, a report to the U.N. but directed toward the American public, was read aboard the *Leyte* in the wardroom, the ready rooms, and the crew's mess, courtesy of the ship's daily mimeographed newspaper, with a sinking feeling. The wily old soldier, hero of World War II, was still insisting they would be "home by Christmas," but his words now rang hollow.

26

The Bridges Over the Yalu

November 1950

Late in the afternoon on November 9 Jesse sat in Squadron 32's ready room listening to the air intelligence officer talk about bridges.

There were seven major bridges over the Yalu and the Chinese were already using them to send troops and tons of supplies into North Korea to drive out United Nations forces, primarily American. The two major bridges—one railroad, one vehicular, side by side—were located at Sin-uiju at the western end of the Yalu, which would soon be iced over.

The intelligence briefer said, "We estimate fifty thousand ChiCom troops are already south of the Yalu and there's likely two hundred thousand or more waiting to cross. So those are your targets for the next week or ten days."

The bridges had to be dropped. Air Force B-29 bombers couldn't do the job without entering Manchurian airspace, so the carriers had received the assignment. Precision bombing at the south end of the bridges in North Korean territory. *That part sounds okay,* Jesse thought.

"Same restrictions, gentlemen. Do not go over the middle of the river."

Across from Sinuiju was the Chinese city of Antung and southwest of it was that airfield, home to MiGs, that the intelligence briefer had talked about.

"So those bastards can shoot at us from their side and send up the MiGs," one pilot said.

"You got it. You want to fight a MiG, do it south of the Yalu."

Jesse told Tom Hudner he didn't like the odds, Corsair against the swept-wing Russian jet. "Neither do I," Hudner replied.

"You'll have the Panthers to give you cover."

"How many?" Sheff asked.

"Twelve. Four to chase the MiGs and go in with the props, four to protect the Skyraiders, and four to cover your pull-out and withdrawal."

"Bless the poor Panther drivers," someone on the back row said.

"Are the Panthers a match for the MiGs?" someone else asked.

"A pilot off the *Phil Sea* shot the first one down yesterday up where you're going. Depends on the driver, I guess. By the way, they're a hundred knots faster than the Panther."

When the briefing was over, few pilots left the ready room. They stayed to talk about tactics for tomorrow. Fighting an air war against an enemy that had stacked the political deck was going to be almost impossible. *At four hundred knots, don't cross the river. What a joke.*

Tom Hudner departed to go down on the hangar deck and make sure the maintenance crews would have the aircraft ready for launch in the morning. Maintenance and repairs were crucial.

Just before the evening meal, a long message was received from Admiral Joy. It ended with:

> Our naval pilots have been given a most difficult
> task. May God be with them as they accomplish it.

It was remembered that Sheff shouted, "Amen!"

In the magazines ordnance personnel worked all night fusing bombs.

For the new pilots such as Jesse, Sinuiju represented the full test, not only ack-ack but the possibility of dogfights with jets. In the eleven combat missions thus far he'd flown through flak twice. That was unnerving enough at 1,000 feet, the escape level. Even the senior Corsair drivers didn't look forward to tangling with the MiGs, whose Chinese pilots were trained by the Soviet Air Force. Most likely, Russian pilots were also jockeying the MiGs.

There would be task force strikes of Corsairs and the heavier Skyraiders from the three carriers, up to thirty or forty planes from each carrier at one time. To avoid getting hit by "friendly bomb fragments" or colliding with each other, the strikes had to be closely coordinated. After bomb release, the planes had to haul tail to the rendezvous point in a defensive attitude and return to "Home Plate," their carriers, and rearm for the next mission.

Jesse's division arrived over the target at 20,000 feet and set up for the first bombing run. There were flashes of sunlight from the Antung base as the MiGs took off and climbed lazily to 20,000 feet on the north side of the river when the strikes began.

A black puff appeared in front of him, then another. Soon the whole Manchurian side was a shooting gallery: orange stabs from the ack-ack batteries, black puffs everywhere in the sky. Black smoke from the first two bombs.

He concentrated on airspeed, angle, then pushed over and dove at about 50 degrees, releasing his bomb at 1,000 feet, and then flew on the deck southwest down the Yalu, taking evasive tactics, "jinking" against more ack-ack and small-arms fire.

This time the MiGs decided to interrupt the bridge-busting party and dove down through the Panther cover from high altitude, shot at the Skyraiders and Corsairs, including Jesse's, and dropped down to the deck, crossing back to their side of the river, avoiding the chasing Panthers. The Panther frustration was massive at not being able to cross the imaginary "dotted line." But a *Valley Forge* jet got a MiG during the bridge-busting campaign.

There was a great temptation for every pilot to fire into Manchuria and accidentally toss a bomb on Antung. But the Chinese were daily complaining at the U.N. that American planes were violating their airspace and some Congressmen, aware that the Communists had entered the war, though not declaring it, believed them.

Over the next nine days, on Lee Nelson's advice, Jesse learned to wait until the MiG was almost at firing range, then turn hard, directly toward it. He was almost turning on a "dime" with the much slower Corsair in comparison to the MiG's speed. This would hold the Chinese pilot inside his high-speed turning radius, and Jesse would slide by without getting shot at.

One day Lee almost got a MiG but misjudged his own tactics. He turned too soon and wound up head-on with the jet, closing at very high speed. The MiG had a twenty-millimeter in its nose and Lee had the six fifty-caliber machine guns in his wings. All his gun switches were on and he was ready to fire, but he didn't hit the button and neither did the Chinese or Russian pilot. They would have gone through each other's wreckage in midair. It made a fine ready room account.

Jesse asked Lee, "Does all this scare you?"

"Oh my God, yes. All of it. I think it scares everyone, including the old guys. Every time I dive down, seeing all that ack-ack, I wish I could just cut and run, but it wouldn't be the right thing to do. Wouldn't be fair to you or anyone else ahead of me or behind in the dive. I can't chicken out."

"I feel the same way," Jesse said. "For a few seconds, if I think about it, I want to cut and run, but I'm okay after I deliver and pull out."

"Ask anyone here and you'll get the same answer."

Jesse nodded and went up the ladder to man his plane.

He scarcely knew these white men as friends, but there was an unspoken bond between them which, in an odd way, was stronger than friendship. They were kin to him in combat, blood brothers. Up in the air, flying beside them or ahead of them or behind them, he would die for them, and they would die for him. He knew that by now, and out here, on this ship and in the grim skies, facing death every day, color meant nothing.

> Dear Daisy,
>
> I've had fun the past week trying to knock out some bridges over the Yalu River. We (Americans) built one of them; the Japanese built the other one. They are sure rugged.
>
> We're all still hoping and praying that the Chinese, facing much superior air power, will pull back across the Yalu, but that's maybe wishful thinking. Smile.
>
> I've told you about Herb Sargent, the guy who bunked over top of me in "Boys Town." Yesterday he made the 28,000th landing on the *Leyte*. Can you imagine that, 28,000 times pilots have put down on our flight deck. The cooks made a cake for him. . . .

He tried to keep the letters light and short on combat details, didn't tell her that LTJG Roland Batson had crash-landed his Skyraider behind enemy lines after a strike at Sinuiju. He was seen to walk away from his plane. Rescue Combat Air Patrols scouted the area for four days without success. Soon Batson's next-of-kin would be notified he was missing in action.

Yet to Jesse it seemed that for every unsuccessful rescue mission there was a triumph. On November 21 an ensign crashed into the sea and was recovered, uninjured, by a *Leyte* chopper. Nine days later a Panther crashed off the starboard beam and the pilot was pulled out of the freezing water within five minutes by a whirlybird. Such swift rescue work by the "Angels" heartened Jesse and every other pilot in the ready rooms.

Thanksgiving Day flight operations were suspended while the carrier took on fuel and ammunition. The ship's crew worked until about noon, then an elaborate feast was served. Most of the pilots then took sack time thinking about home.

Jesse's letter to Hattiesburg that night admitted homesickness. "MacArthur's dispatch to all commands wishing us happy turkey day again claimed we'd be home for Christmas. Nice thought, but I think the odds are a hundred to one we'll make it. . . ." He'd fought back tears in the desk light thinking of Daisy and Pam. They splashed on the paper.

Another two days passed, with strikes at places with crazy-sounding names—to American ears—like Tongmongni and Chang-Tien Hokou. Jesse's yeoman bitched about trying to get them down correctly for the squadron's log. He had to depend on the intelligence yeoman to even come close to correct spelling.

The intelligence briefer said the next place there might be trouble was the Chosin, located sixty-five miles south of the Yalu. There were frozen inlets and fingers of the great lake that sprawled for almost thirty miles in a general north-south direction. Back from its rocky cliffs and snow-mantled shoreline trees was terrible terrain on which to fight.

At the very south end of the Chosin was Hagaru-ri at the intersection of two roads that led around both sides of the reservoir. It had grown from a peaceful farming village of boarded-up mud huts and small wooden commercial buildings into a base for the march to the Yalu. Guarded by

artillery pieces and battalion-strength troops, tents and con-
struction equipment and hundreds of men were spread over
the desolate snow-covered acres, mountains rising to the
west. Many families had fled.

The westernmost dirt road, narrow and steep-banked,
had been named the MSR, the main supply route to the
border of Manchuria. Thousands of Marines, with their
jeeps, trucks, tractors, machine guns, mortars and artillery
pieces, plus a lone tank, had already struggled up-hill over
its icy surface, past Hagaru-ri.

In addition to a landing strip for transports, to bring in
supplies and fly out wounded, engineers had carved out a
pad for chopper operations. Charlie Ward and another
chopper pilot, flying Sikorskys, were stationed at Hagaru-
ri, waiting for calls to rescue downed pilots or "fly brass" or
whatever missions they were assigned. They had been passengers on the *Leyte*, of course.

On October 25, the main body of Marines, the Fifth and
Seventh regiments, had tramped into Yudam-ni, another
mud-hut village that sat fourteen miles above Hagaru-ri.
Cattle stood unattended in the fields. To the invaders it was
another of the poor hamlets they'd passed through going
north from their sea invasion. Yet it seemed especially om-
inous.

The young riflemen, many younger than Jesse Brown or
the *Leyte* pilots, shivering within their parkas, were wary of
enemy guns that might be inside the silent dwellings and
few wooden commercial buildings. They bobbed and
weaved as they'd been taught to do, ready to flatten out at
the spurt of a bullet. Some sensed, they later said, an over-
powering danger lurking in the valley of Yudam-ni. As the
raw wind moaned, they could look west across the barren
landscape and not see a trace of the enemy, yet they sensed
he was out there in the mountains beyond.

The enemy *was* out there, 120,000 of him, Chinese infantrymen in white cotton-quilted uniforms. They were
called "volunteers," the People's Liberation Army, the PLA,

by the Beijing government. They were equipped with light and medium artillery, tanks, rocket launchers, grenades, machine guns (burp guns), and rifles. They were veteran troops, under veteran officers, not a single volunteer among them.

At 9:00 P.M., November 27, with the temperature 20 degrees below zero, the Communist troops probed the newly arrived Marines at Yudam-ni, awakening them in their tents and fighting holes with grenades, accompanied by shepherd's horns, whistles, bugles, and bells. It was terrifying for those who'd never been in battle. There were red and green rockets and star shells and tracers and spitting burp guns and red streaks from the bigger ChiCom guns.

Bullets whined all night. When dawn came, the wounded and dead were strewn over every Marine position. For two days, night and day, the 10,000 defenders of Yudam-ni fought around the clock outnumbered twelve to one, and finally there was only one way to go—retreat back downhill on that miserable narrow lane sixty-five miles to the sea, then evacuation at captured Hungnam.

The fleet would pull closer to Hungnam and the huge guns of the *Missouri* would open fire if the PLA ventured that far south. A hospital ship was enroute full speed to aid the wounded and frost bitten.

Troops, jeeps, trucks, tractors, guns, and the medium tank that had rolled to Yudam-ni with the regiments started back single-column on December 1. They were being shot at from hills above the MSR, from behind roadblocks. On the downside of the slippery road was a steep falloff, so steep that a tumble could cause death.

The Marines were completely surrounded, fighting fiercely as they retreated; wounded riding the trucks, walking wounded slogging and stumbling along. More killed, more wounded. The Chosin retreat would go down as one of the most agonizing yet most successful in military history. Bravery and heroism went with each painful step. Those who survived became known as "The Chosin Few."

Never in the long history of the Corps had there been such a brutal winter ordeal as was happening now to the foot soldiers on the twisting mountain road, the long column of trucks and walking wounded slowly making their way south, dying under enemy fire, freezing to death down there. Fingers and toes turned purple and black from frostbite, soon to be amputated. Frozen corpses of the dead were stacked like cordwood in some of the trucks; seriously wounded were stacked the same way in other trucks. They rode fenders, even the hoods of the jeeps and trucks.

Their only help and salvation was from the air.

The MSR

December 1, 1950

In the Squadron 32 ready room Doug Neill said, "Fellows, we're going west of the Chosin Reservoir this morning to save as many Marines as we possibly can." Using a pointer, he continued, "Poor bastards are coming down this road from Yudam-ni, outnumbered at least fifteen to one, and the only chance they've got to stay alive is close air support. Us! So it's an all-out effort by every carrier, every land-based Marine aircraft—every fighter the Air Force has. There's a foot of snow on the ground over there. With lousy parkas and rotten boots, they're in an outgunned icy hell. . . ."

Though Jesse had seen it from 10,000 feet, he studied the photo blowups of the villages and that killer road, the MSR. He thought this was the exact kind of mission for which he was trained. He wanted to participate. This time he could help someone with his bullets and bombs and napalm. It was a mission God would want him to make, he wrote Daisy that night.

The wind from Siberia howled across the *Leyte* as she launched aircraft. Destination: the MSR and the ground controllers.

"Navy flight, this is Raspberry One. I'm in the lead jeep. I've got black stripes on my hood. Rock your wings if you see me."

Koenig rocked his wings.

Raspberry One said, "I've got you."

Jesse could see the Chinese troops on either side of the road and up ahead. Some wore white capes, blending in the snow.

There were aircraft all over the place. At least eight flights were operating, stretching back five miles. Bombing, strafing, tossing down the jellied gasoline. Sometimes it spread for a block, roasting the ChiComs.

Raspberry One said, "Come over me on a heading of one hundred sixty degrees. Then push over and commence firing."

It was easy enough to see the targets.

The four *Leyte* planes lined up and began strafing.

Jesse squeezed the gun-button knob on his control stick and the six wing guns shuddered and roared, jarring the Corsair as he corrected, watching the stream of bullets rip bodies, then he pulled up as the division reformed for another run.

Raspberry One said, "Good enough. Let's go with napalm."

Jesse, following Koenig, who was flying wingman on Cevoli, dropped his first tank of napalm, then climbed out, glancing back at the red splotch, knowing the ChiComs he'd hit were burning alive.

This is no time or place for pity, Jesse thought. The Chinese were firing with automatic weapons and throwing grenades, backed by machine guns up on the icy ridges. All the way back to Yudam-ni, the snow was pink along the road from American blood.

So it went day after day. *Launch, fly, kill, land back aboard the carriers. Launch, fly, kill. Reload for tomorrow.* The land-based Marine fighter-bombers were relentless and after dusk the night fighters again took over, screaming down on each side of the still moving column, answering the white phosphorus markers sent skyward by ground controllers.

In his cockpit above the MSR Jesse realized how lucky he was not to be down there shuffling along in rubber-soled shoe pacs, not to be the target of burp guns, artillery, or mortars. All the pilots were comparatively safe up in the air, the MiGs not interfering with this land battle, comfort-spoiled. The airmen hadn't been sleeping in frozen foxholes or carrying wounded comrades on their backs, blood splashing down their dirty green parkas. Ice was on their beards down there and even saliva froze. Some hadn't even been scratched, but they were half-dead from the bitter cold and exhaustion. He wrote Daisy about them that night. This was one battle that Jesse enjoyed. There was no choice but to try to help his Marine comrades in the snow below.

On December 3 the regiments advanced two miles toward Hungnam against incessant Chinese fire and roadblocks composed of abandoned or shot-up vehicles. The Corsairs flew around the clock, so many of them in the air that they had to await their chance at the targets.

Koenig and Schabacker, exhausted, were already asleep when Jesse, equally exhausted, hit the sack. His mind kept repeating what he'd seen after Hudner dropped his napalm that day, a lone Chinese soldier running away, his back engulfed in flame. It was like a loop of film.

To get away from the flaming back, Jesse directed his mind elsewhere, searching for something benign. He'd brought his drawing set aboard, thinking he might design a house for his family. But he hadn't been able to find time and inspiration for architecture. *Perhaps this weekend, after the Marines are safe. Then I'll make time*, Jesse promised himself.

Jesse thought of Daisy. *We've been married three years, but we've spent very little time together. First she was hidden in Pen-*

sacola, then again in Jacksonville. Then we had a few precious months at Quonset Point. Added up, every day and night of it, we've had less than six months in three years together.

He got out of his bunk just before midnight and went to the desk, sitting a moment listening to the usual ship noises, feeling the motion of the carrier as it sliced through the night, surrounded by the dark shapes of her escorts.

Perhaps it was what had happened during the day, the awful blood baths along the road; whatever it was, he felt different this night. And he needed to tell Daisy how often he thought of her and how much he loved her.

At Sea, Sunday Nite
3 December 1950

My own dear sweet Angel,

I'm so lonesome I could just boo-hoo. But I try to restrain myself and think of the fun we're going to have when we do get together, so only a few tears escape now and then. I love you so very much, my darling.

I've been trying to get a chance to write you for the last three days but without much success. I'd like to write you every night. I love to tell you that I love and adore you, and, although I never quite succeed in getting it across, I like to try and tell you how much I care and how much you really mean to me. So you see, my darling, not only do I like to hear you tell me that you love me but I like telling you also that you're the sweetest woman in the world. I love you, Angel, and I want you to know that my heart belongs to you.

It was a little past midnite when I started this, but who cares. We're in love and that's what matters, not the time. Right, darling?

The last few days we've been doing quite a bit of flying, trying to help slow down the Chinese Communists and to give support to some Marines who were surrounded when the Chinese launched their big drive. Knowing that he's helping those poor guys on the ground, I think every pilot on here would fly until he dropped in his tracks. This morning we were flying in weather so bad we could hardly see each other at times—snowing—yet the air was full of planes. Navy planes for close support of the troops. Air Force transports dropping supplies by parachute, etc. We know a few of the Marine officers down on the ground because they were with us in the Med. But my biggest hope still is that somehow, thru the mercy of God, this war can come to a close without us getting into an all-out war with China.

Know what, darling? I love you with all my heart and soul. I'm so deeply and completely in love with you until nothing else in life matters to me at all except you, Angel. Occasionally Lee Nelson will show me a certain portion of one of his letters from Lee. The reason I mention that is because her letters to him always remind me of yours to me and mine to you. I guess people who are really and truly in love do think quite a bit alike—different couples, I mean. As for us, our thoughts and mind seem to run exactly alike and I know that it isn't just a coincidence. When we were married, darling, our bodies, minds, hearts, and souls were also wed. I guess that is why making love to you is such an exquisite joy, because we belong to each other and we give ourselves to each other without reservations at all. In Lee's letter to Lee she was telling him how she needed him and how she was praying and trusting in God to bring him home soon.

Darling, heaven alone can know how much I need you and how badly I want to see you. I need you and want you, Angel, for more than I have the ability to express. If only my heart could talk—if only my hungry, lonely, arms could enfold you—darling, I love you with a passion that is beyond description. I love you

with a true love, an everlasting love, a love that says
that I am yours alone, only yours, darling, and that I
always shall belong to you. Sweetness, my very soul is
dedicated to you.

I'm so lonesome for you and I need you so much,
darling. I guess you've always thought I was a big cry-
baby, but honest, darling, you're my weakness and I
can't help it. I love you so much, darling, and even
though usually it seems that instead of tears flowing
from my eyes they flow down into my heart and stay
there and hurt, sometimes this loneliness just wrings
the tears of my aching heart. Often when I climb into
my rack at nite all the loneliness of the day seems to
descend upon me and I'm haunted by seemingly a
thousand sweet memories of you. Then all the tears
that I've been holding back all day long refuse to be
held any longer, and I just lay there in loneliness and
misery and cry my heart out. I pray so earnestly to God
to see my tears and grant that thru his pity and mercy
we may be together again soon. Then I feel His comfort
and yours and I go to sleep.

Oh, darling, please, please try and realize what you
mean to me and try and understand how much I care.
I need you so much, darling. Please help me, Daisy,
please, my darling.

Don't be discouraged, Angel, believe in God and believe in Him with all your might and I know that things
will work out all right. We need Him now like never
before. Have faith with me, darling, and He'll see us
thru and we'll be together again before long too. I want
you to keep that pretty little chin up, Angel, come on
now, way up. I want you also to be confident in this
and that is: Your husband loves his wife with all his
heart and soul—no man ever loved a woman more.

You know how I feel now? I feel like I feel when
we've just laid in each others arms a long time, just
talking. We usually kiss and whisper sweet words of

love to each other. . . . That is one of the times when our loving is sweet and gentle. That's the way I'd like to love you right now, Angel, sweet and gentle. I'd like to whisper sweet things in your dainty ears, kiss your sweet lips, play in your hair and caress your smooth skin, frame your beautiful face in my hands—hold you close and enjoy the thrill of you taking my breath away—raise up at times just so I can look at you and admire you.

Darling, I'm going to close now and climb in the rack. I honestly dread going to bed, but I usually dream of you, so I'll manage to make it until we'll share our bed together again—darling, pray that it'll be soon. I have to fly tomorrow. But so far as that goes my heart hasn't been down to earth since the first time you kissed me, and when you love me you "send" it clear out-of-this-world.

I'll write again as soon as I can. I'll love you forever.

> Your devoted husband
> lovingly and completely yours
> forever
> Jesse

P A R T   I V

Somong-ni, North Korea

December 4, 1950

Tom Hudner came around again, a 360-degree turn, low and slow, risking ground fire if enemy guns were nearby, and saw that Jesse had pulled the canopy back and was waving, but it appeared he'd made no attempt to get out despite that smoldering fire. Pinned in there some way, *Hudner thought.*

Hudner called Cevoli to report what he saw. It was easily apparent to Tom that any quick help would have to come from someone orbiting the wreckage. Put the fire out, extricate Jesse; wait for the chopper.

In the five cockpits above there was a throat-

grabbing, gut-wrenching fear of the Corsair blowing up before their eyes, Jesse still in it. With a stab of bad luck any of them could be down where he was.

There was radio cross talk.

"Jesus, why doesn't he get out of there?" someone said.

Someone else said, "That plane's gonna blow up before the chopper gets here."

Jesse began waving again.

Without hesitation, at 2:45 P.M., Hudner made the decision to crash-land beside Jesse. No permission was sought from Dick Cevoli. He doubted that Cevoli would give it. No consideration of the fact that he would destroy a costly naval aircraft. No consideration of the fact that he might be taken prisoner of the ChiComs. All of that could be sorted out later. A fellow pilot was down and might burn to death, which was unthinkable.

Hudner informed Cevoli, "I'm going down . . ."

Cevoli rogered the transmission without comment, though he'd heard Doug Neill say, "If a plane goes down, that's one down. We don't need Hollywood stuff."

Hudner felt he was indestructible and with the Corsair and its big engine and nose up there acting as plow, he could put it down and walk away to save Jesse's life. He also knew it was possible that he could end up trapped in his own cockpit or be killed outright. Crash landings were not predictable.

Flight operations are never routine, but the Leyte *was steaming along routinely with the other ships of Task Force 77. Her log book for the hours of 1200 to 1600 shows:*

```
1411 changed course to 180. Changed speed to 15
knots. 1420 Lt. D. R. HARRIS, USN, sat to try the
case of C. T. HUEGENOT, Fireman 2nd, 655 26034.
1522 changed course to 310. Changed speed to 10
knots. Received accident report of DIXON,
W. T., who struck his head on a hatch while walk-
ing under it. . . .
```

No mention of Jesse Brown.

Those aboard the Leyte, *more than 100 miles away, had no idea what was happening on the mountain slope at Somong-ni. They were out of radio range. Even if they had known, there was nothing at all they could do to help him.*

Hudner *went around again, another 360-degree turn firing his rockets and ammunition into the mountainside to lighten the plane. There was still no sign of enemy activity, though there were footprints in the new snow. He reduced power and lowered his flaps to slow down to about 85 knots, descending to within a few feet of the ground, intending then to add power and fly up parallel to the slope, settling gradually into the snow, wheels up. His watch showed 2:50 P.M.*

The earth underneath the snow, at 20 degrees below zero, was like solid concrete, and he hit the ground hard, the foot-deep snow doing nothing to lessen the impact. The windscreen, brittle from the cold, shattered. The plane stopped about a hundred yards away from Jesse. But Hudner was alive, thank God, and could now try to pull Jesse out.

Hudner believed that without power to control his aircraft, Jesse had smashed down with the force of a flying bulldozer, the landing ripping the engine off and twisting the fuselage at cockpit point.

Turning off all switches, he clambered out, slip-sliding in the snow.

Jesse, bareheaded, was sitting in the cockpit, obviously in great pain, but spoke clearly and calmly. "I'm pinned in here, Tom!" He was about six feet off the ground, so Hudner tried to climb up on the wing to see exactly what might be done.

Because the soles of his boots were packed with snow, getting a footing, especially on the sloping gull wing, was almost impossible. But grabbing handholds and the canopy track, he managed to pull himself up and look inside the trap. Hudner saw the bent fuselage had jammed Jesse's right knee against the control panel, straddled by his feet, so he couldn't move. Again, calmly, Jesse said, "We've got to do something to get out of here. . . ."

"Don't worry, Jesse. We're getting a chopper in."

Jesse had taken off his helmet, a modified plastic football helmet with holes cut out for headphones, and his gloves. Apparently, he'd tried to get out of his parachute which had three buckles, two in the groin area on each leg and one across his chest. Likely, he'd dropped his gloves in trying and already his hands were probably frozen. Anything dropped in a Corsair cockpit went under the seat and down into the floor. The only way to retrieve it in flight was to invert the airplane, and have it fall back. Even on the ground, retrieval was difficult.

Hudner took off his scarf and wrapped it around Jesse's hands, then got his wool watch cap out of his flight jacket pocket and pulled it down over Jesse's head, who had yet to complain about his situation, though he didn't appear to be in shock. Hudner had never seen anyone as totally imperturbable.

Then he reached in and attempted to pull Jesse's leg loose, knowing the pain had to be excruciating. Yet there was not a single outcry.

He slid to earth again and yelled up, ''Back in a minute. . . .''

Returning to his aircraft, he got on the radio and briefly explained the problems to Cevoli, requesting the chopper pilot to bring an axe and a fire extinguisher.

''He's got all the heart in the world,'' he told Cevoli and the other banking pilots. Hudner found himself drawing on that courage and returned to Jesse's side, tossing snow on the stubborn magnesium blaze. Had the altitude been lower, the tank would have already blown. The snow did little good.

All the while, he was trying desperately to think of a way to extricate Jesse. Single-fighter cockpits are seldom easy to deal with. You sat almost on the deck in the Corsair, feet out in front. There was no way for him to squeeze down in front of Jesse and pry or lift the rudder pedals away. Though Tom was strong, he knew he could not get enough leverage to do that, even if he could slip partially into the opening. There was no way to straddle the cockpit and attempt to jerk him out.

Not once did he think of the possibility of enemy troops closing in. He was confident that the aircraft above would drive them off.

*   *   *

Ward quickly had his crew chief check the machine for a mountain rescue, then went to operations for the coordinates.

He wasn't airborne five minutes when Cevoli called to say another aircraft (Hudner) had crash-landed. So now, his passenger load would be two people and he hoped they weren't big ones. The Sikorsky might not be able to lift even one passenger at the 5,500-foot height, plus himself and his crew chief. He returned to base and off-loaded his crew chief.

He even off-loaded the tool box, rifle and ammunition. Figuring he could carry a payload of 300 pounds if he burned some fuel off, he was soon back on his way to the Somong-ni area.

Jesse had now been on the ground about thirty minutes.

Yesterday, December 3, in Kelly's Settlement, the regular Sunday services were held at Shady Grove Baptist Church, attended by Deacon Brown, Julia, Lura, and Fletcher. Ever since the revival meeting in September and Jesse's departure for North Korea, the Reverend Woullard had asked the congregation to join him in prayer for their special son and brother who was off fighting a war. Christmas music had begun at Shady Grove and the choir sang ''Sweet Little Jesus Boy'' and ''Go Tell It on the Mountains.'' They were among Jesse's favorites.

In Hattiesburg a week before Daisy, little Pam, and Addie Nix attended services at Antioch Baptist Church, corner of Fredma and John Streets, and the Reverend Woullard again asked the congregation to remember Jesse Brown and pray for his safety. He preached at Antioch on alternate Sundays.

Jesse was quiet, his eyes closed, and Hudner believed he was going in and out of consciousness.

Another ten aircraft had joined the original five sweeping over the downed planes, but there was still no sign of enemy activity on the ridges. The problem was now daylight. With sunset less than an hour away, the dimness, combined with the overcast, raised the possibility of collision, fifteen aircraft now orbiting.

Hudner talked to Jesse while they awaited the chopper. Again, no sign or word of pain. No Hollywood stuff. There wasn't much to say. Just a few words to let him know his fellow pilot was still there, still hoping, still praying. Could he hear the planes above? Hudner thought Jesse knew everything possible was being done. The Navy, Marines and Air Force did not easily give up their aviators. But Hudner's mind was racing: What else can I possibly do? Actually, the chopper was the only hope. If it didn't come, they were both doomed from the cold. He'd seen a farmhouse not far away, but probable capture wasn't very inviting.

In roughly ten or twelve minutes, Hudner heard the Sikorsky coming up the slope. It circled for a few minutes, Ward being careful of the landing spot. Part of Hudner's survival equipment was a red smoke flare. He ignited it, so the pilot could see the wind direction.

Ward had other problems. The chopper he was flying had no brakes and he was deathly afraid that while he was trying to help the downed pilots his machine would start rolling down the hill. Also, the one he was flying had a cantankerous engine. If it quit, he probably couldn't get it started again at this altitude. So, putting it down at 3:30 P.M., he decided to let the rotors slowly pat the icy air, hoping the machine would stay put.

As soon as he stepped down, there was mutual recognition between Hudner and Ward. They'd talked several times on the way out aboard the Leyte. Hudner thought Ward was the most welcome human being he'd ever seen. Carrying the axe and fire extinguisher, they went up the slope, Hudner saying he didn't think there was any way to get Jesse out of there if the axe didn't work. They both had hunting knives strapped at the hip, but for the moment the idea of cutting his leg off wasn't even an option.

Hudner shouted up, "The chopper is here!" Yet he knew it might not lift three bodies at this altitude, another dilemma.

Jesse replied weakly, "I heard it." Then he repeated, "We have to get out of here . . ."

Hudner had a back pain from his landing and could only guess that Jesse had serious internal injuries, perhaps vertebrae crushed from his much harder slam to earth. Time was now a factor in several ways. Whatever his physical condition was, there was little they could do except extract him. Jesse had to be half-frozen by *now. His exposure suit was developed for water. More than an hour had passed since he went down.*

The fire extinguisher lessened the smoke for a moment, but the metal embers remained alive, slowly eating toward the tank. The axe was useless. It would bounce off the blue riveted aluminum skin, barely making a dent.

"You have any tools of any kind in the chopper?" Hudner asked Ward.

"No, I took them out to save weight."

Though they teamed up, there was just no way to remove Jesse from the Corsair. They couldn't get firm footing to grasp him and heave up. There was nothing in either aircraft, no crowbar or jackhandle type piece of steel to use. They had to stand there, helpless, discouraged, desperate.

Although there were probably cutting torches at Hagaru-ri, fifteen miles away, there was not enough daylight left to return and bring one in. Jesse had the bad luck of getting hit at the exact time of the year's earliest sunsets. The other chopper at Hagaru-ri wouldn't start. Mechanics had been working on it all day, another terrible dealing of bad luck. Had Jesse crashed on the morning launch, there would have been a chance to recover him.

Hudner and Ward conferred for a few minutes, well away from Jesse. Due to the height of the fuselage above the ground there was still no way that they could physically reach down and jerk him out. They had nothing to stand on. Even if they could find a way to pull him out, Hudner didn't think he could handle the pain.

At one point, Ward said shaking his head, "We can stay with him another twenty minutes. Then we have to go. I can't fly that thing at night. . . ." Hudner knew about the lack of night instrumentation and the resultant risks in that mountain-top terrain.

Meanwhile, fuel was running low on some of the circling planes and there was the problem of not being able to make it back to the Leyte before dark. Koenig and McQueen departed the scene to head for Yon-po, the captured field five miles southwest at Hungnam, to refuel and overnight.

Dick Cevoli and George Hudson headed back for the carrier. Both were qualified for night landings and could sit down on the blacked-out Leyte *with a measure of confidence, there to tell the sad story of Somong-ni.*

Hudner went back to Jesse who seemed to be fading rapidly but he did open his eyes to say, ''Cut my leg off, Tom.''
''I can't do that, Jesse. I don't have a knife that will do it. . . .''
Even so, without footing neither Hudner nor Ward could have reached in to perform the operation, cut the bone, stop the bleeding.
Accepting that decision stoically, Jesse nodded and closed his eyes again. Whiteness had set in around his lips and under his eyes.
Hudner stayed up on the steps, heartsick, determined to remain there until Jesse died. To have him die alone up here on this treacherous frozen ground, in this miserable Communist nation, was something that Hudner could not abide.
Another few minutes passed and Jesse opened his eyes again to say, ''Tell Daisy how much I love her . . .''
''I will.''
Soon he took a shallow breath and then his head slumped down on his chest. Battle-hardened Tom Hudner and Charlie Ward wept.

Only faint light remained when Ward ran the Sikorsky down the hill and lifted off for the ride back to Hagaru-ri, soon to be overrun by the ChiComs.
To risk a morning chopper run back to Jesse's side, to risk Ward's life or another helo pilot just to rescue the body with a cutting torch would be something that Jesse would not want, Hudner truly believed. By then, the crashed aircraft would have attracted enemy attention. If he could speak, Jesse would have told them not to go back. Air cover would have to return, risking ground fire.
On the short flight he thought about the gallantry and guts of Charlie Ward, who had experienced the loss of squadron mates while they were trying to save pilots such as himself. The first one had been killed on September 6. They were heroic, selfless men.
He thought about Jesse Brown, who had made his dream come true, who had won his fight, gained his wings, flew off carriers,

defying those who attempted to keep a black man out of cockpits. He was gone now and certainly in heaven, a kinder place in which Jesse truly believed and had said so. His country and his Navy could be grateful tonight; so proud tonight.

Aboard the Leyte *there was shock, disbelief, and sorrow. The early information was mixed: Jesse had been rescued, Jesse was dead. Then the latter was confirmed. The Negro stewards wept openly and Lee Nelson put on his parka to go to the "front porch" and stand above the bow, letting the wind slash at him, cursing the war, cursing the ChiComs.*

Lee had great admiration for what Tom Hudner had done, but like most of the other pilots questioned himself as to whether or not he would have had the guts to crash out there in enemy territory. As the hours passed, they wondered whether or not Hudner would get a medal or a court-martial for demolishing an aircraft, endangering a combat operation.

A bugler played taps and Marines fired volleys over the stern in tribute to their shipmate.

Hattiesburg

December 4, 1950

It was now December 5 on the Sea of Japan and the weather—sleet and driving snow—was so bad that all aircraft remained aboard.

It was still December 4 in Hattiesburg. Daisy and her mother had gone out about eight-thirty to buy groceries. As Daisy drove the green Wayfarer into the store parking lot, a white man raced for the same spot and, losing it, yelled, "Nigger bitches. . . ."

He got out of his car and shouted, "What are yuh doin' drivin' a car with Rhode Island plates?"

Then he said, "Ah'm gonna beat hell out of yuh" and other terrible things.

Addie said, "Don't say anything to him. Let's go inside."

He followed them inside and kept up the angry talk until M'dear Miz Addie said, "You're making a lot of threats, but if you hit either one of us we'll hit back and one of us'll be hauled away. . . ." They proceeded to buy food and departed.

It was not a good start for the day.

Daisy had received a letter from Jesse written in late November telling her the things he wanted Pam to have for her birthday two days before Christmas, chiefly a tricycle.

So late that morning Daisy and sister Katherine went to Western Auto to buy the trike and then shopped for a small table and chair. They did a little more shopping and then went on to Snook Hardy's house for a quick visit. Snook was home for Christmas. They stood outside Snook's house laughing and talking. Then her phone rang. It was Addie, who said, "Someone wants to see you. Come on home." Her voice sounded strange.

"Who?"

"M. L. Beard." Daisy knew he was in town again working for money to continue medical school at Toogaloo.

She and Katherine got back into the Wayfarer, but it wouldn't start. It had always started easily. Daisy tried and Katherine tried and finally Snook got the reluctant engine to turn over.

Arriving home, Daisy began taking the packages out of the car. Jesse had told her to start putting a wardrobe together. He wanted to take her down to the Caribbean after the *Leyte* came home. Addie was acting strangely, as if she didn't want to see what Daisy had bought.

"What are you doing here?" Daisy asked Martin Luther Beard.

"Well, I thought I'd come over here and see how you were doing."

Then she saw a Red Cross worker and a stranger, a woman who said she was from the *Hattiesburg American*.

Daisy was baffled for a moment.

M. L. crossed the room and drew a telegram out from under the scarf on top of the stereo. It was from the Secretary of the Navy. Now realizing what it was, she opened it, resenting the presence of the Red Cross woman and the reporter.

With Addie's hand on her shoulder, she held on to her

emotions, asking M. L., "Do Jesse's parents know?" They still didn't have a phone.

"I'm not sure."

"Drive me there." She ran out of the house and into the Wayfarer, weeping as they went to Kelly's Settlement.

The Browns had been notified as well. John Brown's heart trouble had gotten worse while Jesse was in the Navy and Daisy and Julia took him to the doctor. Returning to their house, they talked awhile and then M. L. drove her home.

Once back at her mother's house, Daisy said goodbye to M. L. and then started up the stairs, passing out halfway up.

Many white people came to the house over the next week to pay respects.

On December 7 in the Sea of Japan, after the two-day halt for bad weather, the aircraft were again furiously attacking the Chinese as the weary column of Marine infantrymen plodded on the MSR toward Hungnam, closer every hour to safety.

It had taken Tom Hudner two days to return to the *Leyte* due to the bad weather. He'd spent the first night with Marines in an icy tent, shivering, unable to sleep, thinking about what had happened, about Jesse. The second night was spent at Yon-po, the captured airfield outside Hungnam. He'd talked to Bill Koenig, expressing his disappointment and sorrow at not being able to save Jesse. With the weather clearing, Koenig and McQueen flew their planes back to the carrier.

A Skyraider from the *Leyte* went to Yon-po to pick up Hudner and soon Tom was reporting to Captain Sisson, relating exactly what had happened in the mountain bowl near Somong-ni and his reasons for the crash landing.

The distraught skipper listened, thought a moment, then said, "I'm ready to take this ship as close to shore as possible, put up eight aircraft for cover, launch a chopper with a flight surgeon, and recover Jesse's body."

Hudner replied, "I wouldn't do that, sir. Jesse's dead and I don't think he would want you to do that. It would be a symbolic act that would risk the life of the surgeon and the helo pilot. The danger far outweighs the chances of success. . . ."

Sisson stared out to sea for a long time, sighed, and finally said sadly, "I agree, Hudner. We'll send out two divisions and give Jesse a warrior's funeral."

Within an hour, seven aircraft from Squadron 32, all piloted by Jesse's friends, took off for Somong-ni, six carrying full loads of napalm. The sun was out, the sky was blue.

Reaching the site of the downed aircraft, making several low passes, the pilots saw that Jesse was still sitting in his plane the way Tom and Charlie Ward had left him. Snow covered his hair. Farmers or enemy soldiers had stripped his upper body of clothing, even Hudner's watch cap. The setting was now entirely peaceful, new whiteness glittering around the hulks.

While the six napalm-loaded Corsairs and Skyraiders climbed up almost a mile to begin their dives, the lone seventh continued on high above them, reaching toward heaven in the traditional tribute to their beloved now missing shipmate.

A radio voice began repeating, "Our father who art in heaven, hallowed be Thy name. . . ."

The napalm pods tumbled away and both aircraft and Jesse Leroy Brown vanished in sheets of fiery undulating red.

Epilogue

In the hours following December 4 the men of Squadron 32, officer and enlisted, as well as naval aviation personnel on the other carriers of Task Force 77, debated Hudner's decision to crash-land his aircraft, despite his good intentions. In hard fact, he could face a court-martial, and in extreme, prison, for the willful destruction of an aircraft. He had violated direct orders of his squadron commander; he had involved a helicopter and the life of its pilot.

He was to live under that shadow for days and weeks and while fellow pilots understood why and how it happened, the Navy was not—and never would be—administered under the precepts of "good intentions." The final disposition of his case would be in the hands of high-ranking officers in Washington, strangers to both Jesse Brown and Tom Hudner.

Although the Associated Press and United Press had carried a few scant lines about the death of the Navy's first Negro aviator, the nation's black press covered the story in as much detail as they could obtain. There were now twenty-some black newspapers serving their communities throughout the country. Shock and grief was expressed. They compared Jesse's breakthrough with that of Jackie Robinson, both occurring within three years. Robinson was still struggling for acceptance in the major leagues. But it seemed to the editors that for every inch of progress gained, there'd be a human loss of some kind. At the same time, they pointed to Brown's achievement.

To Bill Koenig fell the task of gathering together and legally logging the possessions of his former roommate to send home to Daisy. He'd seen Jesse reading the Bible on numerous occasions in the privacy of his bunk and now he had to place the well-worn pages in a carton along with Jesse's seldom-used architectural "tools" and photos of Daisy and baby Pam. Among his many books were *Five Great Dialogues, Love Poems, Old and New,* and *My Own Story* by Jackie Robinson.

Sometimes mail can arrive too quickly, and before Lee Nelson had a chance to inform his wife Lee of what had happened near Somong-ni, an envelope arrived at Newton Centre marked: THE ENCLOSED IS BEING RETURNED BECAUSE OF THE DEATH OF THE ADDRESSEE. The envelope had been opened and the postman voluntarily made a trip back to the post office and soon handed her the wedding pictures she'd sent to Jesse in early November. She fled to her bedroom in shock.

Much later, Daisy realized the similarity between her husband's final letter and the one written by Major Sullivan Ballou July 14, 1861, a week before the Battle of Manassas: My very dear Sarah—"Lest I should not be able to write again, I feel impelled to write a few lines that may fall under your eye when I shall be no more. . . ."

On April 13, 1951, President Truman awarded the Medal of Honor to Hudner, ending all speculation about the incident. Daisy attended the White House ceremony, as well as members of the Brown family. The city of Fall River presented a $1,000 check to Hudner, which he promptly endorsed to Daisy to further her education, adding to the $2,500 raised by the officers and men of the *Leyte* as a trust fund for Pamela's education.

Daisy and Pam were later sent the medals awarded to Jesse posthumously. The citation for the Distinguished Flying Cross said, in part:

> . . . pressing home numerous attacks on hostile troops moving to attack our forces, continuing his aggressive runs despite heavy opposition, his exceptional courage, airmanship, and devotion to duty in the face of great danger reflect the highest credit upon Ensign Brown and the United States Navy. He gallantly gave his life for his country.

He also received the Air Medal and the Purple Heart.

As Jesse had requested and made her promise, Daisy graduated from Alcorn State in May 1955 and began a lifetime career as a schoolteacher, at first in Westpoint, Mississippi, and then in schools in Texas, Germany, and finally in the Hattiesburg area. She achieved a master's degree at the University of Southern Mississippi in 1974. Pamela received her master's degree in social science at the same university in 1985. Jesse would have been so proud of both of them. Like his mother, he had always stressed education.

Daisy retired in 1990 and often goes down to the Gulf Coast with Snook Hardy to gamble: "Two little old black ladies pumpin' the slots. . . ." Snook had been Pamela's first- and sixth-grade teacher.

In 1973 during Black History Month, Daisy (now Mrs. Gilbert Thorne), Pamela Brown, and Captain Tom Hudner attended the launching of the USS *Jesse L. Brown,* a destroyer escort, first U.S. Navy vessel to be named after a black person. Surviving members of Jesse's family also attended. Both Papa John and Julia had died.

The past was present at the ceremony. The invocation was given by the Reverend Woullard, Jesse's pastor at the

Shady Grove Baptist Church, and Daisy was presented a key to the city of Hattiesburg, also becoming an honorary mayor. Professor Burger made the presentation. Hattiesburg had changed a lot in the last ten years.

Tom Hudner spoke briefly: "In the cold desolation of North Korea and through the years, I've always wondered why Jesse Brown was chosen to die. He had a tremendous future. He was in the van of those leading his people across the threshold of equal rights and acceptability. He was destined to spread his influence throughout society as he grew. He died in the wreckage of his airplane with courage and unfathomable dignity. He willingly gave his life to tear down barriers to freedom of others."

Hattiesburg named a street after Jesse and the local Elks Club also bears his name. A granite citation memorializes Ensign Jesse Leroy Brown. There has been a definite change in the city since the summer of 1949 when he and Daisy were pelted with eggs.

May 10, 1987, at the Tuskegee University Commencement and the dedication of the General Daniel "Chappie" James Center, named after the nation's first four-star African American general, President Ronald Reagan said, "I'd like to close with one story. Being from this campus, you know of Chappie and the Tuskegee pilots. I'd like to speak with you of a man whose name is not so well known as these, Ensign Jesse Brown, the first black naval aviator.

"On December 4, 1950, Ensign Brown's aircraft was hit while making a strafing run against the enemy. With tremendous skill, he managed to crash land on a rough, boulder-strewn slope. He survived the crash, waving to his friends as they circled overhead. They knew he was in trouble when he remained in the cockpit, even as smoke began to billow from the wreckage.

"Finally a fellow member of his squadron could stand it no more. As the others attacked and held off enemy troops, LTJG Thomas Hudner ignored the dangers of the mountain and enemy troops and made a wheels-up landing. He ran to Ensign Brown's plane, now erupting in flames, and found his friend alive, badly injured, trapped in his cockpit. Lieutenant Hudner shoveled snow to keep Jesse from the flames.

"Finally, over the battle-scarred terrain came a Marine helicopter. Lieutenant Hudner and the helicopter pilot struggled desperately to get Jesse out.

"Now, I would like to tell you that they both made it and that, over the years, they have been the best of friends, caring about one another. But that was not to be. Ensign Jesse Brown died on that slope in Korea. When he risked his life for those besieged Marines, Jesse didn't consider the race of those he sought to protect. And when his fellow pilots saw him in danger, they did not think of the color of his skin. They only knew that Americans were in trouble.

"Perhaps the most moving tribute was paid by Ensign Brown's shipmates. In a memorial printed in the ship's newspaper they wrote: 'We bid farewell to a Christian soldier, a gentleman, shipmate, and friend. He was a credit not alone to the Navy but to our country. His courage and faith in God Almighty shone like a beacon for all to see.'

"Today, you become part of the continuing saga, the history shaped by individuals like Dr. George Washington Carver, Chappie James, and Ensign Jesse Leroy Brown. What you do with your lives will keep America shining like a beacon of opportunity and freedom for all to see. Thank you for letting me be with you today. Good luck in the years ahead. And God bless you all."

Almost a half century later, the rust-encrusted hulks of the Corsairs flown by Brown and Hudner can be seen near the village of Somong-ni by the U.S.A. spy satellite that regularly passes over North Korea, reminders of a fierce war that has never officially ended.

The Flight of Jesse Leroy Brown is that larger story that had to be told.

Index

Y

Yates, Corley, 23, 24, 63, 231–
32

Z

Zastri, William (Lieutenant),
117, 118, 141–42, 150

In Appreciation

I wish to extend my deep gratitude to the following for their many contributions toward the writing of this book: Mrs. Daisy Pearl Brown Thorne; Mrs. Pamela Brown Knight; William, Lura, and Fletcher Brown; Issac "Ike" Heard; Dr. Martin Luther Beard; Vincent "Vic" Breddell; Capt. Charles "Curt" Carter, USN (Ret.), Cdr. Roland Christensen, USNR (Ret.); Capt. Lou Ives, USN (Ret.), Naval historian; Capt. Ort Rudd, USN (Ret.); Cdr. John W. Brannon, USN (Ret.); Capt. James McIntyre, USN (Ret.); Capt. Charles O'Reilly, USN (Ret.); Capt. Billie Spell, USN (Ret.); Cdr. Richard McKenzie, USNR (Ret.); Cdr. Herbert Sargent, USN (Ret.); Lt. Col. Don Tooker, USMC (Ret.); Cdr. Ken Snyder, USN (Ret.); Capt. Henry Frazer, USN (Ret.); Hill Goodspeed, Librarian, Emil Buehler Naval Aviation Museum; Janet Braswell, Reporter, *Hattiesburg American;* Dr. Robert Schneller, Naval Historical Research Center; Patricia Francis, Naval historian; John Weems, writing for the *Naval Institute Proceedings.*; Sandra Johnson, Pensacola Historical

Society. A special thanks to Lt. Cdr. Lee Nelson, USN (Ret.), for his voluminous notes and assistance at every turn; to Capt. Thomas Hudner, USN (Ret.), and Cdr. William Koenig, USN (Ret.), for their many contributions to the *Leyte*/ Korean period; to Capt. Eric Axel Jensen, USNR (Ret.), for his "carrier" guidance; to Sally Larrimer for her help with Ohio State; and to Anna Urband, former Head, Magazine and Book Section, Office of Public Information, Navy Department, the Pentagon, for her persistence in believing that the story of Jesse Leroy Brown should be told, and her help with flight records. An additional thanks to Bonnie Johnson, expert at keying a word processor, handling draft after draft without complaining.

—Theodore Taylor
Laguna Beach, California
January 1998